Praise for *The Price for Their Pound of Flesh*

"A brilliant resurrection of the forgotten people wh
country. Rigorously researched and powerfully told
price paid for the nation we now live in and restor
cans—their hopes, loves, and disregarded dreams—t<
Searching, revelatory, and vital to understanding our nation's inequities."

—Isabel Wilkerson, author of *The Warmth of Other Suns:*
The Epic Story of America's Great Migration

"Daina Ramey Berry's harrowing account of how slaveholders turned every aspect of a slave's life into a commodity to be sold on markets—from the reproductive possibilities of enslaved women to the corpses of deceased slaves—is a must-read for anyone interested in understanding American history or our contemporary dilemmas. Reading *The Price for Their Pound of Flesh* will leave you with an overwhelming sense of sadness but also with a great anger that we are still failing to fully overcome this history's legacy."

—Sven Beckert, author of *Empire of Cotton: A Global History*

"With remarkable detail, Daina Ramey Berry explores the exact amounts paid for slaves and how those prices were determined. But she isn't content to catalogue mere market values. She also takes great pains to document the value enslaved people placed on their own personhood, what she calls their 'soul values.' She does this by letting us hear the enslaved speak about their feelings, and when those records aren't available, she quotes observers. It is the voices of the enslaved that lift 'Pound of Flesh' beyond just an African American story to a profoundly human one."

—*Washington Post*

"Berry reveals the sorry history of scientific racism and medical experimentation on black bodies in American academia. To this story she adds the skinning and collection of the body parts of famous slave rebels such as Nat Turner and the disrespect and lack of burial rights accorded to John Brown's African American comrades. A macabre postscript reveals the apparent discovery of Turner's skull. Berry's book is sure to take its place as one of the foremost histories of American slavery that will instruct students of the subject and a lay audience alike."

—*Boston Globe*

"Slavery took many forms across the antebellum US, but all enslaved people experienced their reduction to the status of chattel, bought and sold at their owner's will. Yet surprisingly little scholarship has examined the monetary value of these individuals, whose worth increased from infancy through adolescence, peaking at the height of their productive and reproductive capacities and declining steadily to the point where the elderly were considered nearly valueless. Upon their deaths, they might regain some financial significance, as the bodies of many were sold to medical schools for purposes of dissection. Crucially, Berry also delves into the annals of slave communities to explore the emotional strategies by which the enslaved resisted their reduction to an 'exchangeable commodity,' centering their lives on spiritual beliefs that defined the soul, rather than the body, as the true location of their individuality. Berry's groundbreaking work in the historiography of American slavery deserves a wide readership beyond academia."

—*Publishers Weekly*, starred review

"Daina Berry has written the richest account of the many ways in which an enslaved African American's body was bought and sold throughout her or his lifetime. From the cradle to the grave and beyond, enslavers priced black bodies based on their imagined fitness for labor, sexual exploitation, use as collateral, and even their value after death as dissection cadavers. In horrific detail, Berry shows that there was a price tag placed on every pound of flesh. She also shows the efforts of enslaved people to assert that their lives had value beyond the money that could be rendered from their muscles and extracted from their bones. Out of the certainty that their souls were pearls beyond price, black people fought to make room for their own system of human values."

—Edward E. Baptist, author of *The Half Has Never Been Told:*
Slavery and the Making of American Capitalism

"This is an eye-opening look at what it felt like to be property and the extreme measures the owners would go to maximize profits and protect their investments. Where does one begin? Via Berry's ten-year search through life insurance policies, ledgers, slave trading records, cemetery notes and diaries, we understand how high the financial stakes were in owning Black bodies. . . . Berry is now seen as a breakthrough writer who completed the herculean task of filling in the blanks of one of the darkest episodes in American history."

—*Essence*

THE PRICE FOR THEIR POUND OF FLESH

THE PRICE FOR THEIR POUND OF FLESH

The Value of the Enslaved, from Womb to Grave, in the Building of a Nation

DAINA RAMEY BERRY

Beacon Press
Boston

Beacon Press
Boston, Massachusetts
www.beacon.org

Beacon Press books
are published under the auspices of
the Unitarian Universalist Association of Congregations.

24 23   8 7 6

This book is printed on acid-free paper that meets the uncoated paper
ANSI/NISO specifications for permanence as revised in 1992.

Text design and composition by Kim Arney

"Amen," by James Baldwin, is reprinted here by arrangement with
The James Baldwin Estate.

"The Ballad of Nat Turner," by Robert Hayden, is used by permission
of Liveright Publishing Corporation.

Library of Congress Cataloging-in-Publication Data

Names: Berry, Daina Ramey, author.
Title: The price for their pound of flesh : the value of the enslaved from womb
     to grave in the building of a nation / Daina Ramey Berry.
Description: Boston : Beacon Press, 2017. | Includes bibliographical
     references and index.
Identifiers: LCCN 2016014894 | ISBN 9780807067147 (paperback)
Subjects: LCSH: Slavery—Economic aspects—United States. | Slave-trade—
     United States—History. | Slaves—United States—Economic conditions. |
     Slaves—United States—Social conditions. | Child slaves—United States—
     Social conditions. | Women slaves—United States—Social conditions. | Older
     slaves—United States—Social conditions. | BISAC: SOCIAL SCIENCE /
     Slavery. | SOCIAL SCIENCE / Ethnic Studies / African American Studies.
Classification: LCC E443 .B446 2016 | DDC 306.3/620973—dc23
LC record available at https://lccn.loc.gov/2016014894

For my cousin Felicenne Houston,
who introduced me to the inner spirit
and allowed others to live beyond her death.

For my parents, Melvin and Felicenne Ramey,
who taught me the infinite value of my soul.

Contents

Author's Note

In a very real sense, I've been living with this book since childhood. I grew up in a small college town in California, in an area where most of my peers would say they didn't see race. However, much of my upbringing involved assessing the value of blackness. We lived in a pleasant community with close friends nearby. My father was the second African American scholar hired at the local university where my mother completed her law degree. After law school, she became a professor at a public institution in a neighboring city. Most of my friends' parents were professors as well. Although teaching came naturally to me, I initially pursued a career path outside the academy. But as I aged, I decided to become a professor in the hope that I could help others make sense of both the valuation and devaluation of blackness that shaped my upbringing.

Historically, black bodies in the United States have represented two competing values: one ascribed to the internal self and the other to the external body. White valuation of the black body under slavery is one of the most dramatic historical examples of the latter. An enslaved person had *individual* qualities that enslavers evaluated, appraised, and ultimately commodified through sale. Yet enslaved *people* had a different conception of their value, one that did not appear in historical scholarship until the late 1990s. My parents were the first to expose me to the history of slavery. They also taught me about internal values, which came from that legacy but were much different than the value of enslaved people. But in other settings, such as school, I noticed a different set of external principles that ascribed a negative association to my heritage.

Through each stage of our lives, my parents validated my brother and me, encouraging pride in our lineage and giving us a strong sense of who we were in the world. We celebrated and studied our genealogy by filling our house with art from the African diaspora. At a young age, I learned to value blackness in the form of imagery, history, and ancestry, understanding that we stood on the shoulders of many who gave their lives for us. However, as I grew and matured, I constantly experienced devaluation that contradicted the values presented at home. When I was in preschool, other children treated me like a pet: some boldly patted me on the head to feel my hair texture. In kindergarten, one classmate asked, "Why are your palms white and the rest or your body black?" A year later, when I was six, the neighborhood bully called me a "dirty n——r." And, in first grade, a classmate asked me what it was like to be a slave.

In school, I was reminded that something about me was different and not valued. I didn't see anyone who looked like me in the books we read or on my school's staff, or who represented me during career day. On Halloween in second grade, children snickered at the Afro-pumpkin that I had so carefully crafted to submit to the pumpkin contest. I loved my pumpkin and thought it would win a prize. Not only was it black and beautiful, sporting an Angela Davis hairstyle, but my mother was one of the judges! Every time I valued aspects of my black girlhood, my African American ancestry was ridiculed and devalued. In social studies, I could not understand why some of my classmates stared at me with pity and sorrow when teachers mentioned slavery and civil rights history. I was raised to be proud of this history, not ashamed. I come from a lineage of survivors.

My life has always been structured around the academic calendar because of my parents' careers and the community in which we lived. In each stage of schooling from elementary and middle to high school, we took summer tours around the United States. These long road trips from the west to the east, north, and south, exposed my brother and me to the diverse group of people who shaped this country, from the Mayan and Powhatan, to the Italian, Irish, and Polish immigrants who entered the United States through Ellis Island. We studied the Donner Party and the California Gold Rush as well as American slavery on Southern plantations. We hiked the Appalachian Mountains, backpacked in the Grand Canyon, chased bison at Yellowstone National Park, and learned about water technology at the Hoover Dam. During the long car rides in between destinations, we played games and took pictures every time we crossed a state line. My parents gave daily lessons on a range of topics, from creating a budget and managing money, to understanding anatomy and physiology. Those educational road trips meant a great deal to me, and I was filled with mixed emotions during the last one, when my parents drove me to college.

During my undergraduate education, my organic curiosity about values persisted, and I decided to major in economics. Things changed when I took a class on slavery from a female professor who looked like me. It was my first experience outside of the home in which I learned about African American history and my peers did not stare at me. This professor, Brenda E. Stevenson, supported my curiosity and encouraged me to become a historian. She was the second scholar to suggest that I study history, and later, she became my dissertation advisor. The first person to recommend I study history was a visiting scholar I confronted a year earlier for his excessive use of the N-word in an African American survey course. These experiences, one positive, the other negative, played an important part in my decision to pursue a graduate degree in history. I knew I wanted to write books about slavery without alienating my audience.

Remnants of my upbringing resurfaced in graduate school in a pendulum-like manner. I felt like a balance ball in Newton's cradle being pounded with racism on one side and academic success on the other. The ups and downs were difficult, but I found my way to a platform from which I could study and share the tremendously difficult balancing act enslaved people navigated as human property. This book is evidence of that journey.

How is black life valued and devalued at different points in American history? This is the fundamental question at the center of my life and my work. The seesaws and pendulums I experienced led me to look to history for answers. I found them, but also found many more questions in the voices and experiences of those who were enslaved. These questions inspired me to analyze value and personhood.

While I, and other scholars, contend that enslaved captives aboard slave ships in the Middle Passage had their personhood devalued, it is also true that their bodies, as commodities, increased in value over the course of their lives, reaching a peak in early adulthood. The tension between person and property merged in human chattel, and their awareness of their market value evolved as they matured.

Dave Harper and many other formerly enslaved people taught me about the valuation and devaluation that comes with blackness. "I was sold for $715," he shared in a postslavery interview in the late 1930s. "When freedom come," he said, "give me $715 and I'll go back."[1] Harper and others knew that they were more valued in slavery than in freedom. Henry Banner noted, "I was sold for $2,300—more than I'm worth now." Some scholars deliberately interpreted such reflections to mean that enslaved people preferred captivity to freedom. This bothered me. I couldn't fathom why anyone would prefer captivity unless they did not value themselves. The many voices I encountered in the archives, as I wrote articles, books, and encyclopedias about gender and slavery, spoke to me loudly and clearly. Enslaved people, of course, preferred freedom.

This book, which encompasses a decade of research, addresses the value of enslaved peoples' lives before birth, through the stages of growth, to death and beyond. By questioning and analyzing life cycles, it becomes clear that human chattel could never escape commodification. My study emerges on the 140th anniversary of the end of Reconstruction and in the early stages of contemporary social justice movements to value black lives. I hope that readers will understand the historical antecedents to the racial seesaw I experienced as a child in a community that did not intentionally devalue me. And I welcome each reader to take this journey through the stages of enslaved life as a person as well as a commodified good.

This is a coming-of-age story, a narrative of the valuation of black bodies. It is a lengthy tribute to my parents for teaching me to appreciate my life and the lives of others, whether they look like me or not. Finally, and most importantly, this book gives voice to enslaved people and their feelings about, and reactions to, being treated as property.

The Price for Their Pound of Flesh is a response to questions that have consumed me for most of my life. Only now, after many years of research and reflection, have I found the language to answer them.

Preface

This book is written in a historical moment that historians have not yet named—a moment when black persons are disproportionately being killed and their deaths recorded. We witness the destruction of their lives via cell phones and dash and body cameras. The current voyeuristic gaze contains a level of brutality grounded in slavery. I call this moment *the historic spectacle of black death*: a chronicling of racial violence, a foreshadowing of medical exploitation, a rehearsing of ritualized lynching that took place in the postslavery era. African Americans and their allies respond by rejecting the devaluation of their bodies with the phrase Black Lives Matter. This book, however, argues that the historical record is clear: Black *Bodies* Matter. They did 150 years ago, and they do today. This is not a "red record" like that catalogued by Ida B. Wells-Barnett in 1895, but rather a historical reckoning, a financial recapitulation of black bodies and souls. It traces the internal self-worth African Americans held on to when external forces literally and figuratively sought to strip them of humanity. Here you will see that African Americans created a protective mechanism to restore the soul by valuing it intrinsically, instinctively, innately . . . immortally. They deployed Paul Laurence Dunbar's mask, W. E. B. Du Bois's double consciousness, Maya Angelou's caged bird, James Baldwin's "Amen," Toni Morrison's *Beloved*, and Alice Walker's *The Color Purple*. I see the soul values, as do many others. Through the historical reckoning in the following pages, readers, too, will see the infinite value of African American souls.

AMEN

No, I don't feel death coming.
I feel death going:
having thrown up his hands,
for the moment.

I feel like I know him
better than I did.
Those arms held me,
for a while,
and, when we meet again,
there will be that secret knowledge
between us.

>   —James Baldwin,
>   *Jimmy's Blues and Other Poems*[1]

List of Images

The Value of Life and Death

Appraisal Price Range: $0–$5,771 [$169,504 in 2014][1]
Sale Price Range: $0.14–$3,228 [$4—$94,822 in 2014]

> *We are a race of beings who have long labored under the abuse and censure of the world, that we have long been looked upon with an eye of contempt and that we have long been considered rather as brutish than human and scarcely capable of mental endowments.*
>
> — Benjamin Banneker to Thomas Jefferson,
> August 19, 1791[2]

> *Just think of a people that hold four millions of their fellow-creatures in chains—four millions of human beings in chains!—and sell them by the pound.*
>
> —*The Christian Recorder*[3]

"Many a man, fifty years old, had not seen and felt what I had before my twentieth year."[4] These are the words of Jourden H. Banks, who was born into slavery, sold three times, escaped twice, and ultimately reached freedom. His early years were pleasant compared to those as he matured into adulthood. In his narrative, published in 1861, we learn many things about the value of the enslaved and the ways enslavers, traders, and medical doctors trafficked human chattel from birth to death and beyond.

Banks lived on a Virginia plantation with his parents and sixteen siblings. His mother served as the cook, his father was the headman; the family was intact. As a young child, he played with his enslaver's son, Alexander, who was just a year older. By age five, Banks realized that he and Alex were different when his playmate began beating him. Banks fought back, because his father warned him that he had to respond or suffer continued beatings. Embracing this spirit, Banks kept track of how many whippings he owed Alex and returned them, blow for blow. Even in childhood, Banks's actions showed a nascent understanding of his soul value, separate from his enslaver. As he processed the distinctions between himself and his nemesis, Banks experienced another epiphany: Alex attended school, while he was sent to "scare crows in the fields." In his words, "the dreary days of boyhood began in the fields."[5]

This moment, during enslaved childhood, served as a turning point in Banks's understanding of the reality of his condition. Historian Wilma King calls this "the quantum leap" into the world of work.[6] As they aged, enslaved youth and young adults learned and intimately understood their place in the world. Banks's maturation solidified his understanding of enslavement, especially during three pivotal events of youth and early adulthood: the sale of his two sisters, the nearly fatal beating of his mother, and the slow death of his enslaver. Of the latter, Banks remarked, "I saw him in life, and I saw him in death; but he left me in chains."[7]

Enslaved adults knew very well that the death of their enslavers often meant the breaking up of their families. Thus, when Banks was put on the auction block in the summer of 1857, he had a message for his potential buyers. He fought the traders and tried to liberate himself by running away: "I gave them evidence that they had a man to deal with and I determined now to see how they would treat me as a prisoner."[8] During interviews with potential buyers, Banks remained defiant by not revealing information about his health and skills, because he knew it would affect the monetary value placed on him. Despite these efforts, he recalled being purchased that day for $1,200.

Exploring the ways enslaved people like Banks recalled and responded to their monetary value throughout the course of their lives is the primary thrust of this book. In particular, I examine enslaved and, occasionally, free blacks' values, along with the individuals who had a vested interest in their fiscal vitality throughout their lives, upon their deaths, and even after death. The intimate relationship between enslavers, physicians, and human property shows just how commodification—the act of being treated as a commodity—touched every facet of enslaved people's births, lives, and afterlives. From the enslaved perspective, this knowledge came gradually as they matured. Importantly, this book is also an intellectual history of enslaved people's thoughts, expressions, feelings, and reactions to their own commodification.

Organized around the stages of life, each chapter represents a window into enslaved people's awareness of their monetary value and places them in conversation with enslavers' accounting of their bodies from birth to death. Rather than follow a chronological structure, the book is organized around the life cycle of an enslaved person's body. Many studies address the fiscal value of enslaved people's work; this book does that, yet it differs by examining the spiritual and financial value of human commodities before and at birth, and even after death. That they were treated as disposable property before they were born and after they died forces us to reconsider the life cycle of human property. What did it mean to have a projected or real price from preconception to postmortem? Even the unborn children of expectant mothers were marked with a monetary value. And, when an enslaved person died, who would receive money for his or her body? For a period of time, the financial value of the bodies of the enslaved was sometimes contested in court, depending on the cause of death. During this time, death became a monetized value that accrued interest until the case was settled.

Some dead bodies were cultivated as cadavers, trafficked and sold to medical schools for human anatomy courses at major institutions throughout the North and South. Untangling what I call the *domestic cadaver trade*, I also address some aspects of enslaved people's ideas about the afterlife and their preferences for specific burial rituals, even when doctors wanted to harvest their bodies for dissection.

Banks's narrative also describes his experience as a fugitive in a Kentucky prison and his thoughts about death. Jailed in Smithland, Kentucky, in October 1857, he remained incarcerated for seven months and two days. The jail was "more like a place of punishment than a place of detention," as authorities spent much time trying to extract answers from the prisoners. Banks found it ironic that the jailers believed that the "worse we were treated the more likely we should be to tell where we came from." He and his fellow captives shared a code of secrecy, vowing "not to tell their real names or place of abode." If they did, Banks reflected, "[w]e might just as well turn and go back home ourselves" and "save the masters expense." Just like slavery, prison life was "a trap."[9]

During his time in jail, physicians came to treat the sick, enslavers came in response to notices, and two whites came when convicted of murder and other crimes. While subjected to this dual captivity as an enslaved prisoner, Banks had an encounter with an emaciated man who was assigned to share his cell; the man was near death. Banks was interested in him and wanted to know his story. The doctor who treated his sick cellmate developed a rapport with him and discovered that he suffered from tuberculosis and needed care. The two talked often, and from Banks's perspective, the sick man made the mistake of trusting the physician. The doctor, described as "very kind," found out where the man came from, as well as the name of his enslaver. He promised the sick man that he would purchase and care for him. Shortly after, the enslaver came to the jail to claim his property. The doctor had informed him that the sick man would not survive the journey back to his homestead, "but his reply was that he did not care about the value of his life, he would rather take him dead, as a caution to his other slaves, than not get him at all."[10] Witnessing this exchange, Banks observed: "This was a case that shows with what a spirit of revenge the owners pursue the slaves who escape. Here is a man offered more than the poor skeleton of his slave is worth, but the malicious gratification of getting him home dead or alive was so sweet that he would not receive the price of his pound of flesh."[11] With that, the sick man and his enslaver left, leaving a deep impression on Banks's understanding of himself as human property.

The enslaver had refused to sell a nearly dead man to a physician who was willing to pay a "price for his pound of flesh" above market value, preferring to make an example of him, and asserting that dead or alive, he had use for his enslaved body. But what was the physician's interest in this man? Had he developed an affinity for him or did he have ulterior motives? Doctors, just like planters, found ways to use enslaved bodies at all stages of health. They, too, had a price tag for the dead.

Enslaved people represented an exchangeable commodity in the eyes of traders, enslavers, and doctors. By exploring the web of relations among these groups of people, we find that the financial value of human chattel touched every facet of their lives. Banks modified the Shakespearean phrase "the price for his pound of flesh," from *The Merchant of Venice*, further emphasizing the knowledge base of enslaved people. Their awareness and intellect have always been present in the historical record, but few scholars have asked, "What did the enslaved think?" Much of the existing literature is about what enslaved people *experienced*, but if we attempt to add their engaged understanding, this narrative changes. Enslaved people like Jourden Banks had very particular ideas about their value, ideas that differed greatly from their enslavers. Looking at their views of commodification shifts the way we interpret slavery and adds to our understanding of social and cultural systems that continue to (de)value black life (i.e., mass incarceration, elite athletes, and performers).

Part of a new economic history of American slavery, this book incorporates the voices of those traded on the auction block along with the valuations of their captivity. Enslaved people speak back, through their words and actions. They reach out from these pages and invite the reader to hear their stories, to see them as human beings, *and* to understand them as commodities, just as they did. Enslaved people of all ages recognized the multilayered values ascribed to their bodies, and, to borrow from the great philosopher Alain LeRoy Locke, their values were self-actualized.[12]

We begin this journey before conception because even enslaved people's *imagined* lives had a monetary value. The chapters follow the maturation process to and through adulthood and end at death and the postmortem travels of their bodies and spirits. This journey hinges upon capitalism and commodification, as well as human emotions and expressions of love, loss, and grief. It is an examination of a most unique product—a product that has the ability to emote, express, respond, reject, and liberate. This is the story of human chattel and the duality of their position in life and death.

When enslaved children entered the world, their birth announcements came in the form of federal records, such as ship manifests, or private papers, such as business ledgers, bills of sale, or plantation lists of births. Their parents were not showered with gifts to start them on their journey. Instead, announcements consisted of simple statements in public and private papers, with notations like "Molly's infant born today," or loud pronouncements at auctions, such as "Look at this fine specimen . . . will make a good hand." Today's birth announcements look quite different. Included in these formal introductions of a child to friends and loved ones are typically the name, age, date and time of birth, weight, footprints, and sometimes a picture. Just as contemporary parents look forward to the birth of their children or create a forever home for an adopted child, enslavers noted the birth of enslaved infants. However, rather than record details about the newborn, they appraised them with a monetary value that typically increased as they aged.

Like birth announcements, obituaries and death notices serve as public pronouncements of a person's passing. They contain brief overviews of the life of the deceased, often published in local newspapers. These notices signal the opening of probate, if there are outstanding debts on the deceased's estate. Being "carried away" or "passing on," as enslaved people referred to it, marked a transition into another world for those who viewed death in this way. Reflecting on the end of life, one enslaved person noted, "When I leave this world I am going to take the wings of the morning and go into the building where there is eternal joy."[13] The idea that there was a place of peace and a space for redemption gave enslaved people hope for a better world. Some saw it as a vision before their deaths and understood themselves as two bodies: one eternally free and the other navigating the space of a world with enslavement. On rare occasions, obituaries of some highly recognized or special enslaved people were published in local newspapers. From these public pronouncements, we learn about their lives, likely from their enslavers' perspective, but we know something about them that often sheds light on their personality, service, and legacy.

Enslaved people were valued in life and in death. But because they were people and property, multiple sets of values encompassed them and were placed on their bodies. *Value* is used here as a noun, a verb, and an adjective. It is active, passive, subjective, and reflexive. It is "rooted in modes or kinds of *valuing*" and requires an assessment of feelings. The first value signifies an internal quality. I call this their *spirit* or *soul value*. It was an intangible marker that often defied monetization yet spoke to the spirit and soul of who they were as human beings. It represented the self-worth of enslaved people. For some this meant that no monetary value could allow them to comply with slavery. Others, weakened by enslavement, negotiated certain levels of commodification to survive their experience. Still others were socially dead. While the value of the soul should not be located on a spectrum, this book addresses their living soul values, seeking to uncover "what the enslaved actually made of their situation." They considered conceptions of self in spaces that denied it. By centering their own thoughts and feelings as opposed to the "flesh and blood values" ascribed to their bodies, I demand recognition of the self-actualized values of their souls.[14]

The second form of valuation signifies external assessments rooted in appraisals, which were projected values that planters, doctors, traders, and others attributed to enslaved people based on their potential work output. The third value, also an external assessment, represents the market value in terms of a sale price for their human flesh, negotiated in a competitive market. It often marked the highest price paid for them as commodities. Exploring all three forms of valuation at once—soul, appraisal, and market—allows us to consider enslaved people as human beings and tradable goods, without divorcing one from the other. But enslaved people had a fourth external value, one constructed at and beyond death. *Ghost value* is my term for the price tag affixed to deceased enslaved bodies in postmortem legal contestations or as they circulated through the domestic cadaver trade.

Once an enslaved person died, whether buried or not, they were given a ghost value. Some were then sold or transported for sale to medical schools throughout the United States. Ghost values were also assigned for legal and insurance purposes, as indicated by state-sponsored executions, court disputes, and personal insurance policies. In other words, since enslaved people's values were calculated regularly, it was easy to determine the value of their bodies at death—ghost values. An individual enslaver could look at his or her most recent estate inventory, insurance policy, or bill of sale to find out how much one of his or her enslaved laborers was worth. Ghost values are also evident in the probate records of plantation owners who appraised the value of their laborers in their last will and testament. Legal disputes over hiring contracts that resulted in the loss of enslaved life gave courts the right to value deceased human chattel in order to settle cases.[15]

While not all dead enslaved people were sold, many were, as were free blacks and poor and marginalized whites. The enslaved body, although no longer enslaved, was still traded, sold, and used after death. In postmortem spaces, formerly enslaved and free black cadavers were used on the dissection table, in the halls of major medical schools, and by prominent physicians in the North and the South. Any unclaimed bodies, from blacks and whites, poor and marginalized citizens, as well as criminals of all races were subject to the cadaver trade. Several bodies were at the center of a legal process following a coroner's inquest to determine the cause of death. Anatomy professors justified this practice as being for the benefit of medical knowledge and confirmed that what they were doing was not sacrilege. The demand for hands-on medical research fueled the traffic in dead bodies and served as the lifeblood of the domestic cadaver trade.

When the enslaved died, few public notices marked the transition. Those buried were placed in coffins, mostly pine boxes, and lowered into shallow graves, often near the site of their enslavement or, for some, in public cemeteries. As noted, some of those more valued by their enslavers received obituaries, headstones, and elaborate funerals. Others entered the realm of death by way of execution, which was the beginning of an extended postmortem journey of their physical bodies. Life after death for enslaved people existed in a spiritual world. One remembered that "the Lord . . . carried me off in the spirit, and showed me this old body in the ground and my new body up in the air and me singing, 'Hark from the tune.'"[16] But from the enslaver's perspective, dead bodies of the enslaved also continued on in the earthly financial world. Enslaved bodies were appraised at the time of death, and some even accumulated interest, years after legal cases were settled. Such cases often involved financial recompense to the former enslaver for the death of their human property. It seems that few enslaved people rested in peace.

This book follows the trail and trafficking of the cadavers of the enslaved. Historian Ruth Richardson called our attention to the cadaver trade in the early 1980s, confirming that corpses were indeed commodities, but her focus was not the formerly enslaved. She discovered cadavers were "bought and sold, they were touted, priced, haggled over, negotiated for, discussed in terms of supply and demand, delivered, imported, exported, [and] transported."[17] The scholars Robert Blakely, Michael Sappol, and Harriet A. Washington have expanded our understanding of the underground disposal and traffic in dead bodies, of which African Americans occupied a disproportionate majority.[18] Their research provided a context for the discovery in the 1980s and 1990s of hundreds of improperly disposed African American remains in the basement of the Medical College of Georgia and in a well at Virginia Commonwealth University. Construction and later archival excavations led to physical evidence of the domestic cadaver trade that I describe in this study. I trace the contemporary connections to these remains and introduce readers to enslaved people who did not receive respectable burials. The question of what to do with their remains is still being debated.

Placing the history of this illicit trade against the backdrop of other forced migrations and the impetus of medical education allows for a new approach to slavery studies. My goal is to highlight the voices of the enslaved so that views of their life and death incorporate their spiritual, fiscal, and physical worlds. My hope is that the enslaved "body would not be disposed of like that of a dead animal but the book be closed with some dignity and solemnity."[19] I aim to counter the continued exploitation of the enslaved. Each chapter begins with an auction at a particular stage of life and ends with a burial. It is my hope that this pendulum swing between the body as property and death as liberation, between value and devaluation, will allow their souls to rest in peace.

CHAPTER 1

Preconception: Women and Future Increase

I surely would be a prophet, as the Lord had shewn me things that happened before my birth.

—Attributed to Nat Turner[1]

By American Law the child follows the condition of its mother. Mother free, children free; mother slave, slave children.

—James Redpath[2]

Adeline reluctantly stepped up on the block amid a crowd of unfamiliar onlookers. Arms crossed, head covered, she gripped her young son close to her chest to shield him from the spectacle of shame they were about to experience. The audience admired her dark olive skin and her evidence of fecundity. Her ten-week-old son was living proof that she was a child-bearing woman. Adeline had "a very fine forehead, pleasing countenance and mild, lustrous eyes," while her son was a "light-colored, blue eyed, curly-silked-haried [sic] child." Positioned on the Columbia, South Carolina, courthouse steps, the two awaited their fate. "Gentlemen, did you ever see such a face, and head, and form, as that?" the auctioneer inquired, taking off her hood. "She is only 18 years old, and already has a child . . . [who] will consequently make a valuable piece of property for someone." The bidder and Adeline struggled with her hood as he praised her skills. "She is a splendid housekeeper and seamstress," he continued. By this time, tears filled her eyes, "and at every licentious allusion she cast a look of pity and woe at the auctioneer, and at the crowd." As the sale continued, the auctioneer took Adeline's hood off three more times to show "her countenance," and every time, she quickly replaced it. When he was exposed, her son "cast a terrified look on the auctioneer and bidders," each time his face was revealed. Perhaps at his young age, he sensed his mother's terror. Within minutes, the sale was complete, and Adeline "descended the courthouse steps, looked at her new master, looked at the audience, looked fondly to her sweet child's face, and pressed it warmly to her bosom," while the auctioneer jeered, "*that* child wouldn't trouble her purchaser long."[3] The threat of separation followed enslaved people to the auction block.

This scene was a common one for childbearing enslaved women in the American South. They went to the market as real and potential mothers. One North Carolina enslaved person, Robert, recalled that his mother "was sold three times before I was born." She was sold "just like a pack of mules," but after Robert was born, and she was separated from her baby, she started having "fits." Her outbursts were so bad that the speculators took her back to the previous enslaver, and the money exchanged was returned. From then on, Robert's mother was able to remain with her children.[4] Enslaved women like her were valued for their potential and projected procreation, and they knew it. "I was worth a heap . . . kaze I had so many chillun," explained Tempe Herndon. "De more chillun a slave had de more dey was worth."[5] The law sanctioned valuing enslaved people before conception and adjusted women's market values accordingly.

Partus Sequitur Ventrem, the 1662 Virginia legislation that defined slavery based on the condition of the mother, guaranteed enslavement for enslaved women's progeny in all American colonies. Speaking in front of the Virginia legislature in January 1831, Mr. Gholson stated, "'Partus sequitur ventrem' is coeval with the existence of the right of property itself and is founded in wisdom and justice." He opposed statements made by Mr. Clay, who was not entirely comfortable with the notion of breeding for sale. In Gholson's estimation, planters were justified in doing so, because women missed work to care for their young and "the value of the property justifies the expense." Adamantly, he continued, "I do not hesitate to say that in its increase *consists much of our wealth*."[6] Women were valued for their fecundity, and traders made projections based on their "future increase." Their appraisals were linked to their ability to reproduce.

Aside from political debates over breeding, the memories of enslaved children are rife with their mother's and grandmother's experiences of being sold. "Grandma was a cook and a breeding woman," Josephine Howell of Arkansas explained, continuing, "She was so very valuable. They prized her high. She was the mother of twenty-one children."[7] Mollie Williams of Mississippi grew up in a household that divided enslaved children between two enslavers. Her parents had different enslavers, so every time her mother gave birth to a sibling, the enslavers would take turns for ownership of the newborn.[8]

The language and practices enslavers and traders deployed at auctions defined the boundaries of the commodification of women and children, particularly evident in comparisons made to cattle and other livestock. Viewed as "merchandise" rather than human beings, "when the children of slaves are spoken of prospectively, they are called their 'increase'; which is the same term used for flocks and herds." Enslaved mothers are called "breeders" past their child-bearing years. This systematic naming became part of people's vocabulary and daily references. Both enslaved people and livestock were "levied upon for debt in the same way . . . included in the same advertisements of public sales," "herded in droves like cattle," and literally driven in the fields by foremen who used whips to control the pace of their labor. Enslaved people were "bought and sold, and separated like cattle." At auction, they were "exposed" to highlight "their good qualities" and "described as jockeys show off the good points of their horses." For example, "their strength, activity, skill, power of endurance" were "lauded . . . and those who bid upon them examine[d] their persons, just as purchasers inspect horses and oxen." Countless descriptions show potential buyers opening enslaved people's "mouths to see if their teeth are sound; strip[ping] their backs to see if they are badly scarred, and handl[ing] their limbs and muscles to see if they are firmly knit." In short, "like horses, they are warranted to be 'sound,' or to be returned to the owner if 'unsound.'"[9]

The last four decades of the eighteenth century were crucial years for assessing enslaved women's monetary values, and they set the tone for the years that followed. Black women in early America filled the pages of Northern and Southern newspapers in slave-sale ads, became the subjects of legal proceedings in ownership disputes, served as collateral for loans among debtors and creditors, and commanded strong prices in an evolving domestic market for "sound" human property. Their monetary value was based on their age, skill, and reproductive status. Some enslavers rejected childbearing women; others preferred them. However, women's capacity to bear children, their labor skills, and, in some cases, their (perceived) physical attractiveness remained the primary factors in their inspections, valuations, and sales. But the choice to buy a childbearing, expectant, or current mother depended on the individual buyer's needs and desires. That choice also meant that potential buyers put a price tag on enslaved children before conception.

Who determined the cost of an unborn child? What was the fiscal value of enslaved people at preconception and how were childbearing women priced? The answers to these inquiries are linked to a mother's uterus, because the institution of slavery in the United States extended its reach into women's bodies. Enslaved women entered the market as objects and producers of goods; yet, they appeared as assets and as liabilities depending on the perspective of the seller or the needs of a potential buyer. So when K. G. Hall stated, "For Sale: A Young Negro Woman," to advertise an unnamed woman and her two children, he was not doing anything unusual. This woman was a "complete Washer and good ironer," but Hall did "not want a breeding wench."[10] Therefore, he placed the family up for sale. There was no mention of the father, nor any indication of the woman's age, except "young." The record only reveals her status as a "breeding wench" with young children in her care. Despite labor skills, her ability to procreate ultimately led to her sale.

On the eve of the American Revolution and the early nineteenth century, many American-born enslaved women shared this experience. They were sold because they gave birth and had young children to nurture. Because procreation and healthy children increased their monetary value, sellers like Hall capitalized by putting enslaved women and their children up for sale. The women's reproductive values were crucial to the expansion of the institution, particularly when the African supply source via transatlantic slave trading was abolished in 1808. This shifted the source to the natural, coerced, encouraged, and forced reproduction of enslaved women in America and other New World slave societies.

When the French and Spanish occupied Louisiana, eighteenth-century enslavers had relied on captives directly imported from Caribbean and West African countries. Georgia did the same, despite initially having a ban on slavery for nearly the first two decades of settlement (the ban was lifted in 1751). Across the South, slavery increased rapidly along with technological developments like the 1793 invention of the cotton gin. Responding to these impetuses, planters moved their enslaved people to the Southwest, enticed by lands included in the 1803 Louisiana Purchase.[11] As a result, Louisiana became the slave-trading center of the Deep South in the nineteenth century.[12]

Changes in the international slave trade and market innovations affected the domestic traffic in human beings. Given the markup for child-bearing women, it appears that the acquisition of land and technological inventions altered the face of slavery at the turn of the century. Women played an important role, as the shift to import more enslaved women assured enslavers that they could produce additional labor sources on their farms and plantations. They did not have to depend on the market to purchase human property. Instead, by making calculated choices about their enslaved population, they could, in fact, grow their own. Enslaved women's bodies were catalysts of nineteenth-century economic development, distinguishing US slavery from bondage in other parts of the world.

Incorporating late-eighteenth-century slave-valuation data into antebellum studies of enslaved prices provides an opportunity to untangle the web of trade relations and explore the fiscal strengths and weaknesses of female slavery. Most scholars interested in the monetary value of the enslaved examine the antebellum prices of prime male field hands, leaving discussions of women to brief summaries or passing footnotes.[13] But studying female price patterns offers another important perspective, particularly when we look at their fiscal values compared to other women. By examining a sample of 4,892 individual female appraisals from 1771 to 1820, one can speculate whether the monetary value of enslaved women during this crucial period of American history relied on their ability to give birth. U. B. Phillips, the first scholar to seriously analyze enslaved people's prices, argued early in the twentieth century that a "fertile woman usually commanded *no higher price* than a barren one." Further, he believed that "the prospective increment of picaninnies [sic] was offset by the loss of the woman's service during pregnancy and suckling and by the possible loss of either mother or infant during childbirth."[14] In his mind, pregnancy and the high infant mortality rate offset differences in women's prices, supporting his focus on male valuations.

If financial values for women did not fluctuate based on the capacity to bear children, then what made one woman more valuable than another? Maintaining women's centrality through comparisons *among* women enables gendered price studies to stand on their own. Such comparisons highlight the importance of women's role in populating the workforce (intentionally or unintentionally). In earlier studies of antebellum prices, childbearing women had higher monetary values than men. Yet, this trend is much more dynamic when including figures for the colonial and Revolutionary eras.[15] We cannot assume a static connection between childbearing and appraisals because shifts in natural increase, international laws concerning slave trading, and economic currents of supply and demand influenced a woman's value.

Childbearing women commanded competitive monetary values in the market under specific circumstances in the early National Era.[16] First, female values were dependent on ethnicity (in this case, African or American born), location (urban or rural), age (childbearing or not), and time period (pre- or post-Revolution), to name just a few factors.[17] Some of the variables included health, skill, and monetary values in five colonies and, later, states: Georgia, (French) Louisiana, Maryland, South Carolina, and Virginia. All figures throughout the book except those directly quoted are in US currency based on the consumer price index for 1860 dollars.[18] Given women's childbearing age range as fifteen to thirty-five, women across the South appear to have had higher financial values in all five regions than younger girls and older women, indicating that Phillips's assumption was incorrect. As we shall see in the coming pages and chapters, before 1800, the average age for women at first birth was nineteen. The age of first menarche in the nineteenth century was, in some cases, thirteen or fourteen years old. Yet, we have evidence of women in their thirties having children in the antebellum era as well. Many of these women were known as "breeding wenches."[19] Historian Kenneth Morgan noted that the traditional view that male slaves' market values exceeded those of female slaves on the auction block in colonial South Carolina has more "documentary support." He also explained that this male bias stems from "the low ratio of women to men."[20]

Not all the women I address in this chapter experienced sale through public auctions. Some were sold privately; others were mortgaged, transferred, exchanged, given away, used as collateral, or sold through a legal deed. Because colonial and Revolutionary records rarely contain black women's voices, we must rely on the narratives of their husbands, sons, brothers, uncles, and, most often, their enslavers to shed light on their experiences. Here we learn that not all women wanted to be mothers, and that some had greater attachments to their husbands than to their children.

The story of Tamar, an enslaved woman from Camden County, North Carolina, is representative of women's experience with pregnancy, childbirth, motherhood, and multiple sales.[21] Born sometime in the late 1770s or early 1780s, she encountered the auction block because her owner thought she was giving birth too often. In some instances, women who had "children too fast" were hired out with their progeny to someone willing to "maintain them for the least money," or "benefit [from] whatever work the woman can do."[22] However, Tamar's enslaver could not prevent her from living in the "woods" on a parcel of cleared land on which she cultivated corn and flax for sale. She also hired herself out and "obtained corn, herrings, or a piece of meat for a day's work." She raised her young children in this setting, but as soon as they "became big enough," five of her six children were sold away from her. Tamar's "husband" lived on a distant estate, twenty-five miles away, and could do little to prevent the breakup of their family. Tamar, however, responded boldly to her first sale.

After being forced to travel more than a hundred miles chained together on the way to an auction block in either Georgia or New Orleans, Tamar fled the coffle and escaped back home to the small plot of land in North Carolina on which she had been living. The risky nature of absconding forced her to leave behind her sixth child, an eighteen-month-old toddler. Apparently she was unable to "obtain" the child and therefore made the difficult decision to travel solo. According to her brother's narrative, Tamar "travelled by night, and hid herself in thick woods by day." During the journey, she experienced "great danger on the road, but in three weeks reached the woods near" her former residence.[23] Upon her arrival, she notified her brother, mother, and husband and remained in hiding. Sometimes she hid in "a hollow under the floor" of her mother's "hut," while other times she spent the night in the woods with her husband.[24] Here, in the woods, she and her husband gave birth to three additional children, of which two survived. After the birth of her ninth child, Tamar was discovered and "taken to the house of her old master," and her sale experience began all over again.

Tamar was subjected to multiple sales and several cruel enslavers. At one sale, she was sold along with her two remaining children. The whereabouts of her other offspring are unknown. In addition to being traded by various enslavers three times after her discovery, Tamar's sales brought her across state lines and through various transactions. Her first sale took her from North Carolina to an auction block in Norfolk, Virginia; next she was mortgaged to cover debts and transferred to Elizabeth City, North Carolina; finally she was "taken away in a cart" to an auction block in Georgia. Tamar represents larger trends in trafficking patterns of the enslaved. Excess enslaved people from Maryland and Virginia (Chesapeake region) were sold to markets in Louisiana and other parts of the Deep South. Such trade patterns were true of the domestic slave trade and of slave breeding.[25] As a result, the Low Country had fewer market particularities, except for the types of women placed on the auction block, because of the increased traffic in enslaved bodies in these markets.[26]

What can we learn about black women's experiences through Tamar's story? I argue that her nine pregnancies coupled with separations from all but two of her children explain the meaning of "home" and "marriage" under slavery. She ran away, only to return to her previous location, where she and her husband gave birth to more children. Discussions of self-liberated individuals emphasize a gender distinction among runaways, noting that women chose truancy—that is, temporary escape for one to two weeks— as opposed to complete flight, because of their children.[27] Yet, many women ran away in search of their partners who had been traded. Perhaps, like Tamar, they mourned the children lost to the auction block and hoped for more. It is also plausible that they desired intimacy. Pregnancy could have been an unintentional outcome of marital sex. Her story confirms that marital ties created bonds that warrant attention equal to the bonds of motherhood.

In the antebellum period, three classifications or groups of women—"breeders"; "fancies," who were high-priced enslaved women recognized for their "beauty" and sometimes exploited for sex; and skilled laborers—appear in the record, and as mentioned, some scholars contend that they often carried higher prices than their prime male counterparts.[28] Few historians explore the specific differences in monetary values based on gender and age. They only acknowledge gendered price patterns in statements such as "these women commanded high prices," but we are left with these questions: Higher prices than what? At what age? Than who? In the few instances when scholars identify the prices for which women were sold, they neglect to contextualize the significance of the financial values at that *particular* historical moment. Even if we know the prices—for example, $1,500 for a "fancie" and $600 for a "field hand"—the market values of individual women vary according to the buyer's desires, year of sale, and location of the market.[29] How typical were these values? Were classifications of enslaved people uniform or did they vary depending on the location? Finally, how did age, complexion, health, and perceived physical attractiveness influence a person's monetary value? Answers to these questions are considered in the chapters that follow.

Sale and appraisal data also suggest preferences for women with specific attributes, such as labor skills and evidence of having survived particular diseases. Some traders preferred American-born instead of African-born women, while others overlooked birth origin and/or women's ability to procreate. Enslavers who noted women's skills identified five types of female workers: house servants, field hands, cooks, laundresses, and seamstresses. Only 5 percent of the female laborers displayed evidence of work specialization, and for those who did, nonagricultural laborers such as house servants, cooks, laundresses, and seamstresses were the majority. A total of 214 women in the sample of 4,892 mentioned above have descriptors indicating labor specialization and/or skill. Of this group, 73 worked as house servants, 45 as cooks, 27 as washerwomen, and 18 as seamstresses. Field hands totaled 33, and 1 woman worked with livestock, 3 served as nurses, 7 worked in the market, 7 worked with farm equipment at the mill, and 1 worked in the shipyard.[30]

Late eighteenth-century and early nineteenth-century newspapers are rich with ads that specify women's various skills and health conditions. In 1798, for example, John Manson of South Carolina advertised two "Negro Wenches."[31] The first was a twenty-eight-year-old "regularly bred" cook described as a "good Washer and Ironer" who had been used for thirteen years for just about "every kind of House Work." According to Manson, the woman was "powerfully capable." He offered an extra incentive for the second woman. She was "about Nineteen years old, brought up in a family to [do] House Service" and child care. The younger woman was an attentive "Breeding Wench" with a "short stature." Because her height might have dismayed potential buyers, Manson offered her on a trial basis so that trustworthy buyers could make an informed decision. "She can be had on a trial for a short time," he offered, but only "to a person of respectability, who may have a wish to purchase her."[32] Both women had labor skills and experience. The latter was recognized as a "breeding wench" and offered for a probationary period, but in what capacity? How did potential buyers utilize breeding women before purchasing them during this time? Did breeding have the same connotations as it did in the antebellum era, when breeders were associated with animal husbandry?

Family separation became increasingly common by the late antebellum era, and some enslaved women blamed forced breeding. Fannie Moore explained that breeding women "nebber know how many chillun she hab."[33] Such casual references confirm that breeding was a commonplace practice during slavery. For potential buyers on the other hand, increase (natural or forced) became the focus, particularly in the nineteenth century.[34] Yet, newspaper advertisements that specified breeding women in the late eighteenth century alluded that the practice was not necessarily related to animal husbandry. Enslavers chose not to have "breeding" women, and their rationale is somewhat confusing. One way to untangle the choices planters made is to begin with clear definitions of breeding with respect to changes over time.

The terms *breeder* and *breeding wench* had broader, perhaps less offensive meanings in the late eighteenth and early nineteenth centuries than they did in the antebellum period. Nineteenth-century references often involved deliberate actions by enslavers who forced women to procreate in order to acquire additional sources of labor.[35] The use of "breed" or any derivative in the post-Revolutionary and early National Era should be considered a descriptive term applied to the birth of young animals and humans, and the notion of rearing or raising the young (as in teaching a person to have good breeding).[36] In most instances, these women were not described as breeders for profit, even though countless nameless women appeared in print *because* they were "breeding."

Upon the death of their enslavers, or because the women fit the description of breeders, women went to the auction block with and without their small children; some were pregnant.[37] One "Negro wench & child" were offered "For Sale or Exchange" in Virginia. This "young and Healthy" woman was advertised because "'tis not convenient to have a breeding Wench in the Family."[38] Why were this woman and child considered an inconvenience? Did the costs associated with providing for them outweigh the benefits of having them in the workforce? Or did the mother-child duo become burdensome because neither could perform the necessary labor due to their delicate health? Young mothers often had their field work disrupted by caring for their children and were seen running back and forth to nurse. That the seller was willing to exchange *or* sell the mother and child is telling. It suggests that he or she preferred not to care for them at this stage of life. The nature of *exchanging* enslaved people meant that this seller was open to the idea of getting them back, perhaps after the child reached a certain age and the mother was no longer breastfeeding. Nineteenth-century evidence also suggests that some enslavers felt that mothers of young children were a burden; therefore they hired them out to temporary owners until both could serve as contributing members of the enslaved workforce, if the child survived beyond age five or six.[39]

Enslaved women in the middle colonies as well as in the North were also advertised for sale or exchange due to breeding. For example, an ad for a twenty-three-year-old "Registered Negro Woman" appeared in a Pennsylvania newspaper in 1784. She was skilled in both "country or town work" and was up for sale because "she has a young Male Child, and a breeding woman does not suit the family she is in." Interested persons could exchange her for "another wench . . . of equal value."[40] Similar advertisements appeared in northern colonies. In New York, "A Likely breeding Negro Wench, who is now big with Child" no longer "suite[d] her Master" and was advertised for sale despite her "satisfactory" work.[41] Apparently her pregnancy *was* the reason for her sale. Likewise, Patrick Riley offered a "lusty able breeding Negro Wench, of 33 years old" for sale. He reported that she "is a good cook" and "can do any sort of House-Business."[42] In 1775, William Tongue, the broker for a deceased enslaver, placed a lengthy ad in the *New-York Gazette*. He divided the goods he was representing into four sections: human chattel, lands, houses, and goods. Ten enslaved people were listed. Half were women, some listed with their children. For example, "One Negro wench," aged thirty, was offered for sale "with or without her son, 5 years old."[43] Likewise, James Glentworth advertised "A Negro Wench, American born," along with her two children, a three-year-old girl and "a male child, at the mother's breast." He stipulated, "The mother and the children are to be sold together in the country." He also added that the woman "is a strong and laborious wench, and well understands the duties of a servant." Finally, and perhaps most importantly, "she is to be sold . . . on account of her breeding fast, which is disagreeable to the small family with which she lives."[44]

   Such ads speak volumes about the historical context in the North and South with respect to the market experiences of enslaved women. Northern communities had little need for surplus laborers. They did not have the plantation community to support them. However, the use of the term "breeding" in these advertisements indicates that enslavers were not involved in a profit-making venture in the post-Revolutionary and early years of the nineteenth century. Instead, some enslavers were not prepared or willing to handle multiple pregnancies. Ads such as these suggest that enslaved women in Northern communities experienced both separation from their children and sales with them, because they were breeding. Producing additional sources of labor outside plantation settings led to excess enslaved offspring. Selling the mother and children represented one solution to this labor problem, and by the nineteenth century, the domestic slave trade served as another. Thus, "breeding" in the late eighteenth and early nineteenth centuries defined pregnant or nursing women, unlike the reference in the mid- to late nineteenth century, which regarded breeding as reproduction for profit.

Some women dreaded having children. They knew that they might be separated and could not bear such grief. When asked if "she could turn out *a child a year*," one woman replied, "*No masa, I never have any more, and I sorry I got these.*"[45] This woman likely understood the connection between her body as a source of physical and reproductive labor. Her statement should not be read as a rejection of motherhood, but rather an assertion of her own (unfree) will. Hannah Jones of Missouri had vivid memories of breeding. "When dey want to raise certain kind of a breed of chillun or certain color," she explained, "dey just mixed us up to suit dat taste."[46] What these women felt about motherhood did not matter, because the power over and control of their "increase" was not theirs.

Antislavery literature from the antebellum era capitalized on the plight of enslaved mothers. Activists and artists published narratives, articles, images, and poems on the topic. Frances Ellen Watkins Harper, an African American poet, as well as John Collins, a Quaker artist and author, wrote about enslaved mothers. Harper and Collins both published poems entitled "The Slave Mother" in 1854 and 1855, respectively. In Harper's poem, reproduced here in its entirety, an enslaved mother calls out to God, looking for answers to cope with separation.

> Heard you that shriek? It rose
>   So wildly on the air,
> It seem'd as if a burden'd heart
>   Was breaking in despair.
>
> Saw you those hands so sadly clasped—
>   The bowed and feeble head—
> The shuddering of that fragile form—
>   That look of grief and dread?
>
> Saw you the sad, imploring eye?
>   Its every glance was pain,
> As if a storm of agony
>   Were sweeping through the brain.

She is a mother pale with fear,
    Her boy clings to her side,
And in her kyrtle vainly tries
    His trembling form to hide.

He is not hers, although she bore
    For him a mother's pains;
He is not hers, although her blood
    Is coursing through his veins!

He is not hers, for cruel hands
    May rudely tear apart
The only wreath of household
    That binds her breaking heart.

His love has been a joyous light
    That o'er her pathway smiled,
A fountain gushing ever new,
    Amid life's desert wild.

His lightest word has been a tone
    Of music round her heart,
Their lives a streamlet blent in one—
    Oh, Father! must they part?

They tear him from her circling arms,
    Her last and fond embrace.
Oh! never more may her sad eyes
    Gaze on his mournful face.

No marvel, then, these bitter shrieks
    Disturb the listening air:
She is a mother, and her heart
    Is breaking in despair.[47]

This image of a child being torn from his mother's arms is reminiscent of the auction experience of Adeline and her ten-week-old son.

On the other hand, in Collins's poem, excerpted here, the fugitive mother chooses to leave her child during part of her journey to freedom.

> With one long, sad, despairing cry,
> Her babe upon the ground she flung,
> And, as her heart were turned to stone,
> With madness flashing from her eye,
> Refused the helpless one to wone,
> Or listen to its moaning cry.[48]

In the end, the mother and child in Collins's poem are reunited and successfully escape to Canada. No matter how women responded to their enslavement, antislavery literature of the time clearly recognized the health and humanity of the enslaved.

Health also influenced some buyers' decisions in purchasing enslaved women. People lived in fear of widespread epidemics such as smallpox, cholera, yellow fever, and malaria, and wanted a healthy workforce. Three percent of the women in this sample had perceived disabilities and were listed as "crippled," "blind and deaf," "diseased," "superannuated," or mentally ill. In this group, 164 women had health information: 4 were listed with "disease" (nonspecific descriptor); 11 were blind or deaf; 15 had mental illness; 32 were crippled (nonspecific descriptor); 33 were superannuated; and 69 were sick, ill, or infirm.[49] One nameless woman, aged twenty-two, had already had smallpox and received the description "useful domestic" next to her age and skills. A similar ad appeared in a Virginia newspaper. "TO BE SOLD A HEALTHY strong young Negro Wench," according to the first lines of the ad. This unnamed woman was twenty-four years old and offered with her "male child, one year old." More important, "The Wench has had the smallpox and measles and can be recommended for her honesty and sobriety." She was a "plain cook." Any interested buyers were instructed to "apply to the Printer."[50] John Walters Gills advertised a twenty-one-year-old woman with "her two children, one about five years, and the other about seven months." However, he added, "she has a fine breast of milk and is good temper'd," indicating that the only reason for her sale was that she would make a better field hand. In addition, "her present owner dislikes breeding wenches about the house."[51] This evidence confirms preferences for breeding women or not, as well as detailed de-scriptions of their health condition.

As the supporters of the domestic slave trade strengthened their foun-dation, enslaved men and women experienced family separation quite of-ten. Isaac Griffin, born around the closing of the slave trade, witnessed the sale of a "yellow girl with child" on board a flatboat on the Mississippi River. "At Natchez, a man came on board who wanted to buy a yellow girl without children," he recalled. "Her master told her to say she had no one." Soon after, he said, "the man bought her, and the trader gave her child, six weeks old, to a white woman."[52] Griffin's story indicates that babies only a few weeks old were separated from their mothers (and fathers) and sold.

Brian Cape of Charleston, South Carolina, placed a "family of field Ne-groes" up for sale, indicating that they were sold for "no fault." The hus-band, described as "a stout negro man in the prime of life," appeared in the press, along with his wife, "a fine breeding wench, [and] her child, about 3 years old." The couple also had "a young girl, about 10 years old" that Cape promised would "be a useful servant" one day, who is "to be sold separate from the family."[53] Cape made a calculated decision to separate a young girl on the eve of puberty from her family. The ten-year-old daughter would soon be available for breeding.

Born around 1800, Gilbert Dickey witnessed mother and child separa-tions firsthand. He saw one woman who was "chained and handcuffed in the gangs, leaving a child only nine days old: the child raised by hand, and when a woman nearly grown, she was sold."[54] These recollections con-firm the deep pain that separation and sale caused enslaved people. Betty Cofer of North Carolina remembered seeing "some slaves sold away from the plantation." She saw "four men and two women, both of 'em with lit-tle babies."[55] Brothers witnessed their sisters being sold, along with their nieces and nephews. Bill Simms of Missouri remembered seeing his "old-est sister . . . sold on the block with her children." His sister "was sold for eleven hundred dollars, a baby in her arms sold for three hundred dollars. Another sold for six hundred dollars and the other for a little less than that."[56] Such recollections tell us a great deal about the monetary value of bodies.

Lydia Adams from Fairfax County, Virginia, provides additional insight into how black women were affected by separation and sale in the late eighteenth and early nineteenth centuries. Adams was born sometime between 1775 and 1785.[57] Like Tamar, she had a "husband," but Adams had a smaller family (four children). Reflecting on the separation from her children and her move to Missouri, she explained, "One by one they sent four of my children away from me, and sent them to the South: and four of my grandchildren all to the South but one."[58] When her daughter Esther was taken away, another enslaved woman offered the following words: "It's no use to cry about it . . . she's got to go."[59] Despite her reluctance, Adams understood that she had to comply. However, she had questioned her enslaved status since childhood, remarking, "I didn't believe God ever meant me to be a slave, if my skin was black—at any rate not all my lifetime."[60] Instead, she pondered the difference between slavery and indentured servitude, wishing that she could "have it as in old times" and work like "seven's years' servants."[61] Adams found some rationale for temporary enslavement but not slavery for life. Similar to Tamar, she lost all of her children to the domestic market at a time when the transatlantic supply had not been officially eliminated. Such evidence supports the quantitative record; women of childbearing age held financial value in the market and experienced separation and sale from their children.

Nearly two decades later, the case of an enslaved woman named Dinah from Prince George's County, Maryland, filled the pages of a lengthy trial proceeding in the Maryland Court of Appeals regarding ownership rights over her and her offspring after the death of Jane Fishwick, her alleged owner. Dinah appears in the historical record with seventeen others, listed as her children and grandchildren.[62] From 1812 until 1821, when the case was finally settled, legal officials in Maryland used state funds to depose seventeen individuals in order to determine Dinah's monetary value and that of her offspring. Local residents testified about her whereabouts, labor patterns, and progeny. All agreed that Dinah "was the mother or grand-mother of all the others claimed." In order to figure out her birth history, one deposition noted that Dinah "had seven children" and that the other ten were her grandchildren. Another believed that Dinah had poor labor skills, inferring "her work has not been equal to the charge of maintaining four small children."[63] Such testimony suggests that some believed childrearing prevented women from doing quality labor. Thus, in order to establish Dinah's fiscal value, the court requested the administrators of Fishwick's estate to provide the records from a Dr. Digges, the physician who attended the enslaved and free families in the county. According to notations in the account, Dr. Digges visited Fishwick's residence in 1775 to examine "one mulatto wench called Dinah, with a child at her breast."[64] Although it is difficult to determine Dinah's age in 1821, we know that she had a nursing infant forty-three years before appearing in court. Records indicate that in 1765 Dinah was worth $326, a considerably high monetary value for a Maryland enslaved woman at that time. Given that she had a nursing infant ten years later, Dinah was likely a "breeding" woman and, in this case, was valued for her fecundity or for her future increase well beyond the typical ages of childbearing women.[65] However, this case is even more revealing when we consider the following questions: Who has the legal right to capitalize on the birth of enslaved children after an enslaver dies? Who owns the unborn offspring of enslaved women?

When Fishwick died, she did not have a will. Creditors, family, and friends tried to claim the rights to Dinah and her descendants. In addition to Dinah, Fishwick's aunt had given Fishwick an enslaved woman named Dido in 1775. Included with this gift, Dido's unborn children "went with, be it boy or girl, to her and her heirs for ever." The long dispute over Dinah and Dido and nearly fifteen others makes it clear that slaveholding families and their descendants felt entitled to unborn enslaved progeny. This case alone suggests that it was common practice for enslaved progeny to be accounted for even before they were born.

Although Dinah, Dido, and Tamar experienced the constant threat of losing their children, they too were daughters. Moses Grandy, the narrator of one published account, shared the story of his and Tamar's mother. Their "mother" gave birth to eight children (four girls and four boys), and did all she could to avoid separation and sale.[66] For example, when she feared the auction block would become a reality, she relocated her family to the woods, as her daughter Tamar did years later, and remained in hiding. Living in harmony with the environment, Mother provided water for her thirsty children. Grandy shared that Mother looked for water "in any hold or puddle formed by falling trees or otherwise." Even if it was "full of tadpoles and insects: she strained it, and gave it round to each of us in the hollow of her hand."[67] They ate berries, potatoes, and raw corn. Once she believed separation and sale were no longer likely, she ventured back into slaveholding society. Upon her return, she quickly learned that family truancy did not circumvent family separation. On one occasion, they returned from the woods and discovered that the sale of one of her young boys had already been negotiated. Mother was so "frantic with grief" that she "fainted; and when she came to herself, her boy was gone."[68] She was distraught with the anguish and pain of losing another child; "the master tied her up to a peach tree in the yard, and flogged her" because of her dramatic "outcry."[69]

This enslaved woman spent her entire life fearing the separation, sale, beatings, and deaths of her children. Even though she tried to maintain family cohesiveness, her enslaved status did not protect her from temporary or permanent separations. For instance, her son Benjamin spent two years away from the family working on a vessel in the West Indies with his enslaver. Perhaps to her delight, Benjamin was scheduled to return to the community in which she, his wife, his brother (Moses Grandy), and his sister (Tamar) resided. Grandy "was very glad" and waited anxiously to see his brother. But just as it had happened with his brother, upon Grandy's return from the woods, Benjamin had already been sold. He struggled to relay the news to Mother, so he "got a boy to go and tell her." At this point, Mother "was blind and very old" and "she was unable to go" reunite with Benjamin "before he was taken away." Once again, Mother "grieved after him greatly." She was left to cope with yet another separation through sale.

At the end of their lives, some blacks found solace in the certainty of death. One mother who had birthed eleven children preferred death to sale. "When they're dead, it seems as if we knowed they wus gone. But when they're sold down South—ah!—ah! I don't know where they is," the sixty-two-year-old enslaved mother cried. She was brokenhearted by the separation, which was "far wuss" than death.

James Redpath, a Northern abolitionist who made trips to the South to speak with enslaved people, captured the grief associated with separation. He witnessed firsthand the suffering enslaved people experienced upon sale and death. After interviewing the previously mentioned mother of eleven children, he recalled a poem he read in the *Boston Saturday Express*, which reminded him "of another North Carolina slave-mother's reply":

THE SLAVE-MOTHER'S REPLY
All my noble boys are sold,
Bartered for the trader's gold;
Where the Rio Grande runs,
Toils the eldest of my sons;
In the swamps of Florida,
Hides my Rob, a runaway;
Georgia's rice-fields show the care
Of my boys who labor there;
Alabama claims the three
Last who nestled on my knee;
Children seven, seven masters hold
By their cursed power of gold;
Stronger here than mother's love—
Stronger here, but weak above;
Ask me not to hope to be
Free, or see my children free;
Rather teach me so to live,
That this boon the Lord may give—
First to clasp them by the hand,
As they enter in the Land.[70]

This story of separation describes the devastating impact of children being taken away from their mother in North Carolina and sold further south to Alabama, Georgia, and Texas. In the mother's imagination, at least one of her sons escaped to a swampland, possibly a maroon community—a remote landscape where enslaved people lived in isolation—or Indian territory in Florida. Her wish for them was to enter the land where "the Lord" can hold them close by His hand.

A Northern abolitionist who witnessed a large auction in Louisiana confirmed the experiences of mothers and their offspring at auction. He was appalled, as most antislavery supporters were, at "the babies in the arms of their poor distressed mothers!" He saw firsthand an experience similar to that of Adeline and her infant son. "Can the babies feel their misery?" he asked. "Yes, indeed, they can." He continued, "Every mother will endorse my words. I shall never forget those looks of deep sorrow, which I perceived in the faces of all those poor little children upon the auction-stand. I know that they participated in the distress of their mothers; I believe that they were conscious of their horrible fate in that awful hour—to be sold for money to the highest bidder!"[71]

Redpath witnessed "a woman, with a child at her breast, and a daughter, seven years old," put up for sale. He thought "the poor black mother . . . with her nearly white babe" displayed anxiety and fear about her "uncertain future," which he believed would include a life of hard labor for her and "involuntary prostitution" for her daughter.[72] After a brutal inspection, the mother and daughter were sold. In many cases, mothers believed that they would not see their children again on earth, but they remained steadfast in the belief that they would reunite in death.

Some mothers could not bear living without their children and turned to death as an alternative to living. An abolitionist song reflects this sentiment:

While the infant and the mother, loud shriek for each other,
In sorrow and woe.
At last came the part of mother and child,
Her brain reeled with madness, that mother was wild;

The lash could not smother the shrieks of that mother,
Of sorrow and woe,
The child was borne off to a far distant clime,
While the mother was left in anguish to pine;

But reason departed, and she stand broken hearted,
In sorrow and woe.
Oh! List ye kind mothers to the cries of the slave;
The parents and children implore you to save;
Go! Rescue the mothers, the sisters and brothers;
From sorrow and woe.[73]

Due to the high rates of mortality during slavery, death and burials remained central to enslaved mothers' experiences. The risks associated with childbirth made women acutely aware of their own mortality. Even if they survived childbirth, many women feared the death of their children or separation from them at any stage of their lives. Lina Hunter of Georgia recalled a "oman dat dropped down in de path and died when she was comin' in from de field to nuss her baby." This new mother received "de biggest buryin.'" A coffin was prepared "'til it looked right nice," and the enslaved were excused from work until after the burial. Bodies on this plantation were "fixed up ... nice" and "dey Made new clothes for 'em." A formal service with crowds from "jus' evvywhar" witnessed prayers and listened to hymns and a message from a preacher. On this estate, those who died were respectfully laid to rest.[74] Not all enslaved people were this fortunate. Postmortem journeys for others were far from peaceful, as the following chapters indicate.

·   ·   ·

Black women in the Revolutionary and early National periods spent their teens and early twenties procreating and protecting their offspring from separation and sale. At times, they ran off and lived in seclusion until they believed their unity would not be compromised. Moses Grandy had vivid memories of his mother and eight siblings; however, she "had more children, but they were dead or sold away."[75] Uncovering the stories of black women of childbearing age during this time is crucial to our understanding of how enslaved people were valued and how their families developed through each stage of life and across time.

American-born women experienced sales and auctions through internal trade, while African women arrived in the colonies as part of the international trade. A cultural or ethnic lens pitting the African-born women against American highlights the distinction between the closing of the transatlantic slave trade and the expansion of the domestic slave trade. It is too simplistic to assert that the latter began after the former ended. In fact, according to one scholar, "The domestic trade was well developed, especially in Maryland, Virginia and South Carolina, before the end of the eighteenth century."[76]

Planters and traders assessed monetary values of the enslaved based on sex, age, skill, health, beauty, temperament, and reproductive ability, among other criteria. However, how do changes over time and across regions affect enslaved people's valuation? How do commentaries and testimonies about breeding change from one century to the next? If historian Jennifer Morgan's assertion that planters imagined "a handful of fertile African women" could "turn modest holdings into a substantial legacy" is correct, then what legacy did their African American daughters bring to the fore?[77] Focusing on reproduction, encouraged or forced, and on the monetary value and sale experiences of childbearing women serves as a good entry point for understanding the worth of human property, from preconception to postmortem. Examining the domestic market at the turn of the eighteenth century suggests that traders and enslavers alike recognized women for their ability to procreate. Some valued women during their childbearing years, while others did not want "breeding women" in their homes. Regardless, women's bodies were catalysts of nineteenth-century economic development, distinguishing US slavery from bondage in other parts of the world. This story changes when considering infants sold separately, the subject of the next chapter.

CHAPTER 2

Infancy and Childhood

AVERAGE APPRAISED VALUES:
FEMALES: $190 [$5,571 IN 2014]
MALES: $212 [$6,241 IN 2014]

AVERAGE SALE PRICES:
FEMALES: $236 [$6,940 IN 2014]
MALES: $258 [$7,578 IN 2014]

> *He sold their children as they grew old enough to bring the desired prices in the Southern market.*
>
> —J. H. Banks[1]

> *I have often known them to take away the infant from its mother's breast and keep it while they sold her. Children, from one to eighteen months old, are now worth about one hundred dollars.*
>
> —"N." (anonymous trader) to Professor
> Ethan Allen Andrews, July 25, 1835[2]

In 1854, Rachel, an infant girl, was placed on the auction block. Although she was wrapped in a "coverlet" and she was asleep, her face was exposed. An enslaved man had delivered her to the auction on the instructions of his enslaver. Rachel was "about a year" old and was for sale.

As the enslaved man sat on the courthouse steps with Rachel, waiting for the noon hour, the time and place for many public auctions, one wonders how he felt. Was it excruciating for him to carry out his enslaver's demand and bring little Rachel to the market? Or was he unmoved? What kind of exchange had he had with her parents? Did he feel partially responsible for what was about to take place? Imagine trying to keep the baby calm after she was separated from her mother and then handing her over to the sheriff at the start of the auction.

While the enslaved man sat holding Rachel in his arms, the Reverend Nehemiah Adams, a visitor from Boston on a three-month tour of the South, approached him to ask a few questions. Adams was startled to see an enslaved man holding an infant. "Is the child sick?" Adams asked. Responding with deference, the man replied, "No, master, she is going to be sold." Puzzled, Adams inquired about the child's mother, to which the man answered that she was "at home." The minister's mind was filled with questions, but most importantly, he worried about Rachel's mother. How did she feel? How much did she miss her child? Was the infant taken openly, or secretly? Who did this? By now, Rachel was "weeping and refusing to be comforted."[3]

This was too much for Adams, who chose not to stay and witness the sale. Later, he learned that Rachel had been sold for $140. Imagine her confusion as she looked at the group of potential buyers gazing at her, evaluating her earning potential. How did Rachel even begin to process what occurred? Her inconsolable crying is one clue, but she was too young to express her feelings in any other way.

Southern men, likely Adams's peers, were concerned about his reaction to the infant's sale. They consoled *him* by saying, "We are very sorry that you happened to see it. Nothing of the kind ever took place before to our knowledge, and we all feared it would make an unhappy impression on you." Through conversation, Adams learned that the seller faced financial difficulties and had to sell Rachel's mother before she gave birth. As a result, he claimed rights to the then unborn child. After a legal dispute, it was decided that "the child should be levied upon, be sold at auction, and thus be removed from him." Thus, Rachel's monetary value and her status as fiscally separate from her mother were discussed even before she was born. Once born, the commodification continued, and she was sold. Luckily for Rachel, however, her mother's enslaver purchased her "at more than double the ratable price," and she went back to her mother.[4] In a strange twist of fate, involving legal and financial transactions, the mother and daughter were reunited. Separations such as the one between Rachel and her mother rarely ended in reunification. They were extremely fortunate that their separation was only temporary.

What did it mean to be sold at auction before one could walk, talk, or fully comprehend? Did enslaved infants, toddlers, and adolescents understand that they were property? How did young children process and make sense of auctions like Rachel's? Answering these questions is a difficult task for the historian because we have little evidence from enslaved children except their childhood memories as adults. Chaney Spell of North Carolina remembered that she "wus sold fust time in my mammy's arms." This memory was so vivid for her that decades later, she claimed that her sale to a Mr. McKee was "de fust thing dat I 'members." Studies suggest that early childhood memories are often associated with trauma.[5] Some of the most vivid recollections come from difficult experiences. Thus, forced separations like Chaney's made a significant impression. Such experiences were so painful that enslaved people speak of being "cried off" rather than carried off.[6] Harriett Hill, also from North Carolina, remembered her first sale as well. "I was sold away from my dear old mammy at three years old but I remember it," she shared in a mid- to late 1930s interview. Perhaps anticipating skepticism, she quickly followed up with, "I remembers it!" Such recollections confirm the likelihood that by age ten, children understood they were property. Even though they may not have grasped the totality of their status, they realized that they could be taken from their mothers and fathers, and that somebody besides their parents claimed ownership of them.[7]

This chapter examines the awareness and valuation of enslaved children from birth to age ten. The first decade of their lives oscillated between innocence and adolescent joy to the stark reality of their status as chattel—or human property. In their early years, children did not understand or know that they were enslaved. Their days involved playing with other children, both black and white. Gradually, they became aware of their status and the fact that their bodies could be bought, sold, transferred, deeded, gifted, raffled, compensated, insured, and executed. By age ten, their lives had fully shifted into labor and servitude, ushering in a host of other realities.

Drawing upon the testimonies of the formerly enslaved, travel literature, pricing data, insurance policies, and burial records, this chapter traces the evolution of the commodification of enslaved children as it took root during this tender decade. Their early childhood education included the awareness that they were living property, but a unique form of property that also had a soul. From them, we learn about the internal and external values placed upon their bodies.

CHILDHOOD REALIZATION OF ENSLAVEMENT

Enslaved children were rarely protected or spared the realities of slavery. However, they frequently had no understanding of themselves as property until they were sold for the first time or witnessed a sale. Countless narratives from formerly enslaved people like Frederick Douglass, Elizabeth Keckley, and Harriet Jacobs include a moment of shock when children first learn they are chattel. Until that point, they had spent their lives with other children and were cared for by elderly enslaved people, often grandparents. Some served as playmates to their white peers and had memories of playing hide-and-seek, hopscotch, and tag with them. Others, like Douglass, lived with biological family members, such as parents or grandparents. "Living here, with my dear old grandmother and grandfather," Douglass explained, "it was a long time before I knew myself to be a slave. I knew many other things before I knew that." He recalled that "for the most part of the first eight years of his life," he was "a spirited, joyous, uproarious, and happy boy." Annie Burton of Alabama also had fond childhood memories: "On the plantation there were ten white children and fourteen colored children." They spent their days "roaming about from plantation to plantation, not knowing or caring what things were going on in the great world outside [their] little realm." Likewise, Keckley vividly remembered the birth of her enslavers' child, whom she referred to as her "earliest and fondest pet," one she had to take care of even though she herself was only four years old. Her earliest memories were from that part of her life, which was preparing her for the inevitable. The peace of early childhood did not last long. It was just a matter of time before enslaved youth had their childhoods bound by the yoke of slavery.[8]

Henry Gladney of Virginia remembered being given to his enslavers' children. "I was give to his grandson" to "wait on him and play wid him," he shared in an interview. As he aged, he had a better sense of his role.

"Little Marse John treat me good sometime; and kick me round some-time," but he understood that "now dat I was just a little dog or monkey, in his heart and mind, dat it 'mused him to pet or kick me, as it pleased him." Rebecca Grant experienced multiple whippings for not referring to her enslaver as "Marse Henry." She found it difficult because he "was just a little boy 'bout three or four years old—come 'bout half way up to me," she recalled.[9]

As they aged, the realities of their oppression became clear and, for many, frightening. At age four, Keckley learned to "render assistance to others" and to be "self-reliant," qualities that would enable her to transition as she matured. Douglass lamented, "As I grew larger and older, I learned by degrees the sad fact" that the land on which his grandparents lived belonged to someone his grandmother referred to as "Old Master." He also discovered "the sadder fact, that . . . grandmother herself . . . and all of the little children around her, belonged to this mysterious personage."[10]

Mingo White of Alabama was separated from his parents at around age four or five. "I members dat I was took up on dat stan'," he relayed, "an' a lot of people came round an' felt my arms an' legs an' ast me a lot of questions." His enslaver coached his human property on how to respond to potential questions and asked them to lie about their health. Sadly, White recalled that he was quite young when he was taken from his parents, "jes' when I needed 'em most." His father had one last parting wish and that was for John the fiddler to look after his son. John did, and White remembered "many a night" waking up to find "myse'f 'sleep 'twix' his legs while he was playing for de white folks."[11] White was fortunate to have a fictive or pretend caretaker, assuming their relationship involved mutual respect. After all, White had just learned his first few lessons of enslavement: all whites had authority over him; his parents were separated and sold; and he needed a father figure to care for him. The physical closeness he describes, being in between John's legs, hints at other outcomes to their relationship that will be addressed in the next chapter.[12]

According to Douglass, childhood for the enslaved included "clouds and shadows [which began] to fall upon" their lives at an early age. Such realities were "grievous to my childish heart," he explained. He was to live with his grandmother only "for a limited time." As soon as children "were big enough," they "were promptly taken away" to live and serve their enslavers.[13]

The reflections of Burton, Douglass, and Keckley confirm children's early awareness of their enslaved status. As they aged, they became governed by the rhythm of agricultural and nonagricultural labor. They also noticed a stark contrast in the behavior of their white peers, many of whom would, or had recently, become their enslavers.

As enslavers in training, Southern white youth were raised much differently than the enslaved. They were protected from the exigencies of heavy labor, and their parents spent time educating and preparing them for adulthood. White parents taught their children about slavery and clearly explained the differences between enslaver and enslaved. Some learned about the institution from bedtime stories and books such as *The Child's Book on Slavery; or, Slavery Made Plain*, which sought to educate children about an institution that might seem incomprehensible to a young mind. The book opens with the following explanation: "The *design* of this little book is to show the truth in regard to Slavery, and to give important information concerning it to all readers who do not already know it well." The other objective of this literature "addressed to children and youth" is to introduce slavery to a wide readership. Geared to a Northern audience, the book explained the business of slavery to readers who knew little about it. In order to "understand it fully, you must take the reliable testimony of others, just as you take the testimony of those who write Geographies and other books." Rich with biblical language drawing upon the story of Moses, the book elucidates the concepts of liberty and freedom and even evokes the American Revolution. In the chapter "What Is A Slave," children learn that "to be a slave is to be held and treated as a piece of property." As property, they were sometimes kept by enslavers until they died or "sometimes [the enslaver] sells them or perhaps gives them away to his children." The book also makes clear that enslaved people "according to slavery can not own" themselves and "slave parents can not own their children."[14]

Through books and training, white children learned the difference between themselves and the enslaved. They also experienced a shift when they had to separate themselves from their enslaved peers with whom they played. By age ten, enslaved and free children recognized that their lives were on very different trajectories.

Visual cues, including coffles—enslaved men, women, and children chained together in an assembly line—heading to auctions, also captured these realities. Witnessing a coffle traversing the neighborhood would have made a significant impression on a young person's mind. The sounds of the clanking chains marked the rhythmic cadence of the enslaved on their way to a market. One can imagine the looks on young people's faces as the enslaved people headed to courthouses, town centers, and auction houses. "When I was about seven years old I witnessed, for the first time, the sale of a human being," recalled Elizabeth Keckley.

Like Rachel's owner, described earlier, Keckley's owner had experienced a financial challenge. Enslaved people were liquid forms of property, easily converted into cash. As Keckley quickly learned, selling Little Joe, the cook's son, was a solution to the family's financial embarrassment. Without knowing why, "his mother was ordered to dress him up in his Sunday clothes and send him to the house," but what happened next made a lasting impression on Keckley. Little Joe was "placed in the scales, and was sold, like the hogs, at so much per pound." His mother, still unaware of the transaction, had no idea that *the price of his pound of flesh* covered her enslavers' financial embarrassment. Apparently, the enslaver went to buy hogs for the winter, but had not had enough money to cover the cost. Little Joe was stolen from his family so that the enslaver's family could afford food during the cool months. The sale transpired while Little Joe's mother was laboring in the fields, worried about the whereabouts of her son. But the story does not end with Little Joe on the scales and his mother in the fields. Keckley vividly recalled that Little Joe's mother became suspicious when she saw her dressed-up son put on a wagon heading for town. When she inquired, the enslaver assured her that he would return the next day. However, each day that he did not return, Little Joe's mother mourned for her child and received whippings for not controlling her grief. Sadly, "the mother went down to the grave without ever seeing her child again."[15]

Enslaved siblings separated from each other and their mother during sale.

Little Joe's sale was an important milestone in Keckley's life. To her, it revealed the significance of an enslaved person's age and the duplicity involved in separating children from their mothers. Shortly after this episode, when Keckley was eight years old, she saw the separation of her own parents and was forced to part with her father forever. Watching her parents cry, hug one another, and say their final good-byes was an image that became a haunting memory. "My father cried out against the cruel separation" but still had to give "his last kiss" as he pulled "my mother to his bosom; the solemn prayer to Heaven; the tears and sobs—the fearful anguish of broken hearts." "The last kiss, the last good-by; and he, my father, was gone, gone forever," she lamented. It was all too much for the young Keckley, who was reminded that she, too, could be sold at any time and that her life and the lives of her family members were valued on the same scale as livestock. She learned that "love brought despair." Keckley realized early on that her family's humanity was ignored and that the capital investment in their bodies was all that mattered to members of the planter class and their allies. This lesson was an excruciating but significant one for enslaved children and anyone else witnessing or experiencing similar events.[16] Their lives were at the mercy of their enslavers.

Historians have commented on enslaved children's awareness. Eugene Genovese noted that "slave children had a childhood, however much misery awaited them."[17] Wilma King, author of the foremost study on enslaved youth, proclaimed, "Enslaved children had virtually no childhood because they entered the work place early and were more readily subjected to arbitrary plantation authority, punishments, and separations." As a result, enslaved children grew "old before their time."[18]

VALUATION OF ENSLAVED CHILDREN IN LIFE

Keckley, Douglass, and many other enslaved children learned that they were evaluated at every stage of their growth and development, and that separation typically involved sale. As they grew older, however, their appraised monetary value changed. Their fiscal values increased and decreased depending on their health, strength, and skill, the primary criterion for assessment being the amount of labor they could perform throughout the course of their lives. These figures were computed during annual appraisals that captured projected worth at particular ages or stages in their life cycle. On large plantations and small farms alike, enslavers conducted estate inventories to compile the net worth of their workforce. They also appraised them in wills, insurance records, personal letters, and broadsides when advertising upcoming sales. Enslaved people's appraisals were a measurement of financial values recorded for a host of purposes. They were done for tax assessments, probate settlements, legal depositions, medical examinations, and compensation for executions. These valuations should not be confused with market prices, which were for sales at auction or via private transactions.

Human commodification occurred at the moment of sale. The sale price was a different form of valuation than an appraisal. It reflected the market value of a person at a specific moment. Sale prices were often higher than appraisal prices due to the nature of competitive transactions, such as auction sales. However, auctions were only one type of public sale. Private sales also yielded monetary values that differed from appraisals. Taken together, appraisals and sale prices reflected the valuation of human beings in different contexts and could produce variations in the fiscal values settled upon.

Countless formerly enslaved people describe auctions; some discuss inspections and appraisals. When they refer to their valuation, their recollections usually reflect sale rather than appraisal values. Enslaved people likely had little awareness of their appraisal values because these assessments were not necessarily conducted in their presence. Enslavers recorded appraisals in accounting books like the *Cotton Plantation Record and Account Book*, by Thomas Affleck, produced in the nineteenth century. These books contained preprinted columns for enslaved people's births and deaths, crop production, and appraised values. When filing their taxes, enslavers accounted for their human chattel based on such methods as an informal head count or an official assessment done by other planters and, in some cases, tax assessors and physicians. Even if they were present during their appraisals, enslaved children were not always privy to their external values. In these settings, a bid caller was not yelling out purchase prices because appraisals often involved enslavers' personal documentation.

Some appraisals and most sales involved a public or private physical inspection, in which potential buyers asked enslaved people a series of questions, examined their bodies, and sometimes demanded physical exercise to assess strength and agility. For example, an enslaved boy in Richmond, Virginia, was placed on the auction block along with other "likely" men and children—meaning that the quality of the enslaved up for sale was good. The setting was described as a "long, damp, dirty-looking room with a low, rust-timbered ceiling." Men, many of whom came from surrounding areas, arrived an hour before the bidding began, as agents prepared for the event near the "counting room," which was partitioned off for that purpose. In this space, with walls covered in tobacco stains, "unweaned" children waited for their fate to be determined, along with men and women who were also for sale. Some were humiliated by the excessive touching and fondling involved in their inspections. This particular auction was organized by the firm Dickinson, Hill & Company, under the condition that all purchases had to be made in cash "on time." Enslaved people were "stripped naked, and carefully examined as horses are—every part of their body, from their crown to their feet, was rigorously scrutinized."[19]

Many enslaved children have vivid memories of the sale experience. Marlida Pethy of Missouri recalled that when she was "nine or ten years old," she was "put up on de block to be sold." Of the stand, she recalled, "It was just a piece cut out of a log and [it] stood on [one] end." Her recollection about her price is even more telling: "Dey was offered $600 but my mistress cried so much dat master did not sell me."[20] The mistress's attachment to her human property was so great in this case that the family decided not to sell Marlida. Such interventions were not always successful or helpful. Several enslaved people reported that their mistresses were as violent and sadistic as their husbands.[21] In this case, we do not know if Marlida preferred to remain with her mistress. All we know is that Marlida was not sold and that, decades later, she remembered the monetary value she carried at auction. It made a deep impression on her young mind.

The sounds, sights, and smells of slave auctions contributed to the horror of enslaved children's lives. Loud, rhythmic bid calls echoing from the mouths of auctioneers competed with chatter from potential buyers, the rattling of chains, and the everyday noises of a town center. Joining these audible oddities was another unpleasant sound that could be heard above all others at the end of a sale: the cries of wailing mothers, overcome with grief after being separated from their children.

At that moment, all children understood their status and experienced, for the first time and likely not the last, the overwhelming heaviness of loss. Some parents had protected their children from the realities of enslavement, allowing them the innocence of childhood. However, at auction, the point of separation, children witnessed the full intensity of their parents' distress. The breaking up of families was devastating for the enslaved and also for some others who witnessed it. For many abolitionists, particularly visitors to the Deep South, the sound of shrieking mothers and crying babies and the sight of confused and frightened children were too much to bear. During one Louisiana auction where 149 enslaved people were sold at once, a Northern abolitionist said that none of the enslaved people would "raise his or her head and eyes" to gaze out at the potential buyers in the audience. "Some poor girls," overcome with emotion, were "weeping audibly and are all looking sad—sad—sad!"[22]

Many enslaved adults recalled horrific experiences on the auction block. Charles Ball was four years old when separated from his mother. On the day of his sale, he "was naked" and never owned any clothes. His new owner dressed him, but Ball vividly recalled that his "poor mother," who knew it might be the last time she saw her son, "ran after" him. She took him "down from the horse" and held him tight, then "wept loudly and bitterly" over him. When it was time for him to leave, she "walked along the road beside the horse," pleading with the owner not to take her son. After being physically separated, his mother was whipped, and Ball remembered "the cries of my poor parent" as they became less audible the further he traveled. Despite the fading sounds of her cries, and as "young as I was," Ball explained, "the horrors of that day sank deeply into my heart, and even at this time though half a century has elapsed, the terrors of the scene return with painful vividness."[23]

In countless descriptions of auction scenes, auctioneers cannot be heard over the cries of enslaved parents. W. L. Bost of North Carolina vividly remembered that, when he "was a little boy, 'bout ten years" old, a coffle of enslaved people stayed on his "place" on their way to a market. He saw that they "nearly froze to death" because they came in December before sales on the "first day of January." The coffle included "four or five of them chained together." It was so cold that he saw "ice balls hangin' on to the bottom" of the women's dresses. "All through the night," Bost explained, "I could hear them mournin' and prayin.'" He remembered hearing the auctioneer "cry 'em off" as they stood on the block and saw weeping mothers calling for their children and husbands.[24]

Witnessing these scenes as a boy had a profound impact on Bost's young mind. He was thankful that his enslaver did not sell any of his human property. Seeing the yearly coffles was evidence that his family was fortunate. His memory of trading season included a critical analysis of the way enslaved people were treated like hogs and sheep. They were driven "jes like sheep in a pasture." The speculators "rode on horses," and when the enslaved were cold, "they make 'em run 'til they are warm again." All of those for sale were kept "in the quarters jes like droves of hogs," and during the night he heard them crying.[25]

Enslaved children learned to fear auctions, even if they were not initially separated from their parents. Anna Kentuck and her little boy, Armstead, three years old, were sold together for $1,950; however, the sale was later canceled, and the two approached the block a second time. One witness described "Armstead, the poor little boy" as "living proof" that "even little children can feel the atrocity of being thus sold." As the second sale commenced, Armstead began to cry "most pitifully" and hid his face "under the white apron of his weeping mother."[26] The two cried together because they knew that ultimately they could be separated.

Martha King also remembered being sold at five years old. She was placed on the auction block with her grandmother, mother, aunts, and uncles. "I can remember it well," she told interviewers in the 1930s. "A white man 'cried' me off just like I was an animal or varmint or something." King even recalled her monetary value: "Old man Davis give him $300.00 for me."[27] Their mothers' reactions intensified enslaved children's understanding of separation. They witnessed their mothers' devastation and helplessness. Fathers, if they were recognized and present, desperately tried to make deals for their families to stay together. These efforts were difficult, because, although many sales began with instructions that families would not be separated, market needs trumped conditions of sale and families were often separated.[28]

The "Great Auction" in Georgia held on the eve of the Civil War is an example of a sale in which enslaved families were to remain intact. A total of 436 enslaved people were sold on March 2 and 3, 1859, at a Savannah racetrack. Local and national newspapers advertised the sale and included the stipulation that "the Negroes will be sold in families, and can be seen on the premises . . . three days prior to the day of sale, when catalogues will be furnished."[29] Auction catalogues, similar to contemporary ones, listed the merchandise (in this case, human property) with detailed descriptions of physical attributes, skills, and sometimes notes about personalities. Even though the advertisement indicated that families would remain intact, the needs of the buyer often took precedence.[30]

As for W. L. Bost, we know that he was not sold, but he witnessed auctions and could recite bid calls decades later. "I remember when they put 'em on the block to sell 'em," he noted. "The ones 'tween 18 and 30," people considered prime, "always bring the most money." The auctioneer, who stood away from the human chattel, "cry 'em off as they stand on the block." Perhaps haunted by this scene, Bost said he could hear the auctioneer's voice "as long as I live."[31] Hardy Miller of Arkansas recalled that enslavers paid "one hundred dollars for every year you was old." Thus, she noted, "I was 10 years old so they sold me fore one thousand dollars."[32]

For enslaved children, the reality of their commodification was clear by age ten. But what did it mean to them to have a monetary value? How were enslaved children valued at this time? Was King's $300 value average, high, or low? Placing the fiscal values in context can enhance our understanding of slavery, capitalism, and the monetization of black bodies. The realization that these were human products, however, adds an essential dimension to this study that we cannot overlook.

Commodification Data for Enslaved Children

After analyzing 15,256 appraisal and sale values for male and female children between the ages of zero and ten, I found that the commodification of black bodies evolved as enslaved children aged. We know that when they were young, their monetary values were low, for several reasons. First, there was a high incidence of infant mortality as enslaved children had a low survival rate in the first few years of life. In addition, their diet, consisting of cornbread, pork, hominy, and vegetables, for those fortunate enough to have gardens, didn't support their grueling and labor-intensive lifestyles. Children, in particular, were especially challenged because they were rarely strong enough for heavy field labor, yet oftentimes were forced to work too young. Those who labored in nonagricultural or domestic settings were equally challenged by chores that kept them on their feet for large portions of the day. Given these factors, children under age ten had low monetary values, and appraisers rarely used gender to differentiate value for the first decade of children's lives. Instead, they waited until they could better assess strength and skill.

Appraisals and sale prices for children ten and under were relatively low compared to those older, as indicated in the following chapters. Yearly appraisals for females indicate an average value of $190, while males were $212. For those who entered the market and were sold, like Martha King, these figures increased, respectively, to $236 for girls and $258 for boys. It is not surprising to find a roughly $50 increase in market values over appraisal values, because sales by auction, transfer, gift, and other types of transactions involved negotiation and bargaining. Settling on an agreed price typically meant that the final cost was higher than the appraised value. King's $300 value seems to have been slightly higher than the average price paid for girls her age.

Price and appraisal patterns suggest that gender was not a significant factor in assigning monetary values to enslaved children. This gender neutrality is reflected in plantation records, on enslaved people's birth and death lists, and in the clothing allotments provided. Girls and boys wore smocks; however, gendered distinctions appeared as the children aged. Boys were given pants and girls received dresses and aprons made of Osnaburg, a rough, plain cloth, and occasionally material for head wraps.[33] Enslavers often listed newborns as a mother's infant, "Chloe's infant" or "Hannah's child," and, on some occasions, denoted sex, "Lucy's infant girl" or "Mira's boy." Some planters even identified the name of the newborn. Going through this evidence age by age, I found that gender did not matter until children *approached* the age of ten. This milestone in their development as property was important because it marked the moment that gender differences emerged. Some enslavers could determine that their investment in human property was, at age ten, beginning to materialize. They had a better understanding of the strength and skills of growing children at age ten and began valuing them accordingly.

Previously, scholars were quick to note that children were rarely separated from their families before age ten. Their assumption was partly based on the legislation at the time. For example, in Alabama, section 2056 of the statute entitled "Master and Slave" states that children under age ten should be kept with their mothers unless an execution of sale was levied against the owner's debt. Depending on the enslaver's fiscal circumstances, the mother and child could be separated. But, "no levy or sale shall be made, by which a child under five years of age shall be separated from its mother."[34] Likewise, in Louisiana, law prohibited the sale of children under fourteen. Linking laws to parental rights, one statute noted that "husbands and wives shall not be seized and sold separately when belonging to the same master." In addition, "their children, when under fourteen years of age, shall not be separated from their parents." In the case that separation occurred, "such seizures and sales shall be null and void."[35] One wonders how officials enforced this law, given that so few enslaved people knew their precise age. Likewise, even with evidence that enslaved families were placed on the auction block to be sold as one unit, we have no way to know if they were sold as such; there were many exceptions.

For example, children born to incarcerated enslaved women at the Louisiana State Penitentiary experienced their first sale at age ten. Until this age, if their mothers gave birth while serving life sentences, they were considered "legal property of the state."[36] Enslavers whose human property had been given life sentences received compensation based on the "market value" of the convicted. Essentially, this form of compensation functioned as a refund by the state for the loss of human property to the prison system, not because of death. Therefore, enslaved women's bodies were valued by the state, which in turn reimbursed enslavers for the loss of their property to another layer of enslavement, a life sentence.

Records indicate that in 1840, there were about seven enslaved women and two children in the penitentiary.[37] Nearly a decade later, the facility had thirteen women and six children, all of whom were born in the penitentiary. Legislation passed in 1848 stipulated the terms and conditions of selling children from their mothers at age ten. Required to advertise the sale in local papers thirty days before the sale, prison officials had a state mandate to turn over profits from the sale of these children to the state treasurer. The advertisements noted the name and age of the child as well as the mother's name. There is no information about the fathers of the children, suggesting that the women either arrived pregnant or became pregnant by male inmates or members of the prison staff.

What was the early childhood experience of incarcerated youth who had an inevitable sale date set before they were born? Did they know they would be separated from their mothers when they were ten years old? How did their dual incarceration shape their understanding of slavery? Tracing the experiences of incarcerated enslaved youth and their mothers is difficult because of the dearth of studies about enslaved women in prison, but new scholarship in the post-emancipation era provides some insights.[38]

Louisiana legislation aside, eyewitnesses to auctions were troubled by the separation of mothers and children. When Professor Andrews, a Boston religious leader, traveled south in the 1830s, his journey included a steamboat full of passengers, several of whom were enslaved "young mothers . . . with their children, many of them infants." He quickly learned that family separation was common, even for mothers and their young children. In a conversation with a trader of human souls, Andrews learned the rationale. The trader assured him that he, himself, "never separates families," but made a distinction between buying and selling. In *purchasing* them, "he is often compelled to do so," for his business was to buy whatever the market brought. The dialogue between the two men went as follows:

> ANDREWS: Do you often buy the wife without the husband?
> TRADER: Yes, very often; and frequently, too they sell me the mother while they keep her children. *I have often known them to take away the infant from its mother's breast and keep it while they sold her.* Children from one year to eighteen months old are now worth about one hundred dollars.[39]

From this dialogue, we learn that the external values of enslaved infants and youth were easily discernible and have further evidence that mothers and their children regularly experienced separation.

On a visit to an auction in New Orleans, a newspaper correspondent shared the story of seven- or eight-year-old Jimmie, his infant sibling, and his mother. Although they were put up on the block as a family, Jimmie's mother "was conscious that some great evil was about to befall her." She stepped up on the block with her infant in her arms, and Jimmie joined her, "clinging to her skirts." When no one bid on the family of three, "*the mother and the little boy were put up separately and sold to separate parties.*" Next, in the heart-wrenching account, the mother "begged and implored" that her new enslaver "buy little Jimmie too," but she found that "her appeals were in vain, [and] . . . burst forth into the most frantic wails that ever despair gave utterance to." The two were forcibly separated, one going to Mississippi, the other to Texas, and likely never laid eyes on each other again.[40]

Cane Brake Plantation Patterns of Valuation

Looking at the records of individual plantations clarifies the patterns of valuation even further. For instance, the children on the Cane Brake

Plantation in Mississippi had relatively stable lives, often with their parents for much of their childhood in a community where other children were present. For a three-year period spanning 1856 to 1858, between 154 and 162 enslaved people lived on the plantation. Children age ten and under consistently made up around 38 percent of the population.[41] Dr. James Green Carson, a physician, operated this cotton plantation in Adams County. He kept meticulous records of his large estate by appraising every enslaved person at the beginning *and* end of each year. Pregnant mothers had a special "x" mark next to their names, and if the pregnancy went to full term, babies (under one year) appeared on a different list. When infants reached age one, they were listed below their parents or other adult caretakers or fictive kin (similar to "play cousins, aunts, and uncles," individuals who are part of a family but not related by blood) in the plantation records.

Annual record of the enslaved people valued at the beginning and end of 1856 at Cane Brake Plantation, Mississippi.

Given the stability of this particular estate and the detailed records, price patterns reveal uniform values for those under age ten, regardless of gender. The pattern was as follows: all children under age one were appraised at $25. Once they turned one, their values increased to $75. From then until age ten, children's values increased $25 per year. Thus, by age ten, boys and girls alike were valued at $350. In 1856, the community had thirty-one males and eighteen females, along with eleven infants (six boys and five girls). Some boys were presumably named after their fathers or shared their names with adult males like Dave B[ig], age thirty-six, and Dave L[ittle], age nine; or Lockhart, age forty-nine, and Lockhart S[mall], age five. All of the infants under age one also had names and were identified in gender-specific groupings, but none had assessed values. Six boys— Hartell, Caesar, George, Jerome, Philip, and Jack—ranged in age from one month to four months. The infant girls included Kate, Betsy, Margaret, Josephine, and Jenny, who ranged from three days old to six months. If they survived to one year, which most did, they were given a $75 value and placed on the larger list of enslaved people. In 1857, there were four more infants in this population, suggesting that women had "successful" pregnancies. Likewise, in 1858, the number of infants rose to sixty-three, increasing the enslaved population by eighty-nine newborns over a course of three years.[42] Given that a physician owned these enslaved people, they likely received medical attention when necessary.

The relationship between physicians and enslaved people has been written about in the literature on slavery, but the emphasis is on medical care rather than physicians as enslavers. The dual role of medical professional and enslaver is worth noting because one might assume people owned by doctors received better care. Did physicians offer better day-to-day care than enslavers without medical training and knowledge? It is difficult to know. However, evidence of enslaved women healers has been well documented.[43] Carson's enslaved population included a steady stream of newborns at a time when infant death rates were extremely high.[44] He also seems to have maintained his population of infants who survived past one year. Cane Brake Plantation might be an outlier in terms of health care for those enslaved, because Carson hired a plantation physician, Dr. Benjamin S. Waller, whom he paid $250 per annum.

Perhaps his upbringing and attitude contributed to this decision and the desire to create a stable population.[45]

Carson had experienced several hardships as a young child. His father died when he was two, and his mother, when he turned fourteen. As a result, he lived with his uncle, who also died shortly after he became his guardian. Then, his uncle-in-law, a "wealthy Mississippi planter" named James Railey, became his guardian. Carson attended the University of Virginia and became dedicated to "Christian service." He married Catherine Waller of Kentucky, and the two eventually set up Cane Brake Plantation. He also attended the University of Pennsylvania Medical School to help solidify his training and provide a strong financial base for his growing family.

Mrs. Carson characterized her relationship to their enslaved property as supportive. In the evenings, some came to check on her, and she gave them "apples or some other little rarity which they consider a great 'treat.'" Over the years, the couple added to their bound workforce, purchasing forty-two enslaved people from the "swamps of Florida" in the winter of 1836. On average, each cost $672, meaning that the Carsons spent approximately $28,000 on human property that year. Carson believed they were "the best looking set of negroes" to date. He was particularly "impressed with the size of the men who were all over six feet tall." He protected his investment in his human chattel by hiring a physician to manage and attend to the health of his enslaved population. The Carsons' attitude about slavery was that the enslaver was "responsible for his slaves" in the same way a parent was responsible for his or her children.[46]

Whatever their feelings of benevolence, the Carsons kept enslaved people for more than twenty years. In 1839, the family hired an overseer to manage the Mississippi plantation and paid him $1,000 per annum. Thirty years later, in 1863, the plantation comprised an orchard, vegetable garden, melons, peaches, taro, fruits, poultry, and other natural products that enslaved people cultivated. The quarters where the enslaved lived had a "village for 200 negroes" and what were considered "neat cottages." This enslaved community received religious instruction and even had a paid minister on the property.[47]

Cane Brake provides a fascinating record of the valuation of life on a large plantation, with medical care, religious instruction, and families that remained intact. Enslavers, however, also considered their financial loss upon the death of their enslaved.

VALUATION IN CHILDHOOD DEATH

Whether alive or dead, enslaved bodies were commodified. On a plantation in South Carolina, Dr. Johnson paid Charlie Grant, an enslaved man on his estate, two dollars to exhume a deceased two-year-old enslaved infant. Johnson hoped to sell the child's body to physicians in Philadelphia through a clandestine traffic in dead enslaved people whose bodies were used in medical schools to advance anatomical research. The physicians paid for the deceased, "ones that cut up fresh," so they could use them for dissections. Medical professionals at universities such as the University of Virginia negotiated the value of these cadavers and paid $20 to $30 per "subject" as part of an underground traffic in dead bodies.

Understanding the ghost value of enslaved youth at death is as important as probing their fiscal values in life. Enslaved children died at high rates. Enslavers registered such deaths in plantation ledgers, cemetery records, diaries, and on lists. The enslaved also made note of their responses to the loss of life. Moses Grandy, a formerly enslaved man, recalled the death of his brother, who had been sold to an enslaver by the name of "Mr. Tyler." Grandy knew that his brother suffered because Tyler had a bad reputation for mistreating young boys. "One day he sent my brother out, naked and hungry," to find a pair of oxen, explained Grandy. But when he returned without them, "his master flogged him, and sent him out again." The young boy had no luck in finding the oxen, so "he piled up a heap of leaves, and laid himself down in them, and there died." Grandy learned that the "turkey buzzards" found him first and "pulled his eyes out." [48] After abolitionists heard this story, Elizabeth Poole wrote a poem entitled "The Slave Boy's Death" in response, which began with the following lines:

He sought the steers through brake and glen,
Through cheerless wood and plain,
Beside the homes of toil-worn men,
That spoke of want and pain;
He passed the slave in weary gang. . . .

She ended the poem with the boy entering a place of peace and glory:

> His senses died, his soul went forth
> On free and tireless wing;
> He left in peace this torturing earth,
> A spirit's joy to sing.
> And gladly closed his weary eyes.
> To be awakened in paradise. . . .
>
> And of the leafy grave,
> Where the low wind's bewailing sigh
> Sung the young wander's lullaby
> With nature and in peace he died.[49]

Grandy's brother created his own grave of leaves and died alone. Others received formal burials in such cemeteries such as Laurel Grove in Savannah, Georgia.

Many of the children under age ten buried at Laurel Grove were stillborn. Of approximately 3,024 records, 1,191 were children age ten and under. Approximately 15 percent (173 total) were dead at birth. The others died from illnesses and health complications such as cholera, congestive heart disease, fevers, measles, pneumonia, spasms, teething, tetanus, tuberculosis, and whooping cough. In several cases, enslavers paid local doctors to treat newborns and young children, hoping to increase the survival rates beyond age five. Those who did not survive were, at times, fortunate to receive a respectable burial in a segregated section of this cemetery.[50]

Enslaved children also died of mysterious causes. In Austin, Texas, on the eve of the Civil War, Louisa (age three) died of an "accidental poisoning," Jennette (age five) died of an "accidental burning," and a few others died of "unknown" causes.[51] Given cemetery records, we know that some enslaved youth were buried. Some, however, were exhumed and given to medical doctors for further study, such as the infant that Charlie Grant took to Dr. Johnson.

In addition to burying, selling, and transporting young children's bodies for medical research, enslavers took out life insurance policies on children age nine and ten to protect their investments.

Life Insurance

The Southern Mutual Life Insurance Company (SMLIC) established policies immediately before and during the Civil War. Information on the policies reveals the ways in which enslavers valued their laborers. Founded in 1848 in Athens, Georgia, as Southern Mutual Insurance, the company had offices in Columbia, South Carolina, and Baton Rouge, Louisiana, with agents who traveled throughout the South. Clearly well established, the company placed permanent ads in the Affleck plantation journals.[52] The Louisiana office, located on Camp Street in New Orleans, advertised an "extra Guarantee Fund of $50,000" and reported that it accumulated $500,000 in capital, assuring potential policyholders that it was the "only Company incorporated in the State" to insure "White Persons and Slaves."[53]

The SMLIC records are unique in the nature of detail for nearly four thousand enslaved people from ages nine to seventy-five, covering policies primarily in the Deep South. More than a thousand enslavers worked with hundreds of agents purchasing or renewing policies *throughout* the Civil War. This practice suggests that people protected their investments in human property not only during times of prosperity, but during periods of major economic risks, such as war.

Enslavers interested in policies for their enslaved had to apply to an agent of the company. Applications included a series of health-related questions; a medical examination of the enslaved person was also necessary to ensure she or he was in good health. The enslaved was then appraised to determine the premium, which was based on "year to year" death averages and the Carlisle table, an international mortality table used by insurance companies. The company used Southern regionalism to deter locals from buying insurance in the North: "We offer cheaper premiums; we take no discrimination as the northern offices do against southern risks."[54]

Forty-three children from age zero to ten were covered by policies through the SMLIC from 1856 to 1863. Of this group, twenty-three were girls, nineteen were boys, and one name was not listed. Laura, age ten, and the unnamed one-year-old served as the bookends of this short list; both had the highest price: $1,200. Both had a rate of 2.5 percent, but the unnamed infant had a thirty-dollar premium compared to Laura's premium of twenty-seven dollars. The policies for the other enslaved children ranged from six months to five years. The majority (65 percent of the sample) of those with policies from birth to ten years old were actually ten-year-olds, suggesting that enslavers began their valuation of enslaved youth before puberty. As with many other facets of their young lives, gender did not matter; this group of insured children had nearly perfect gender balance. That they survived the first decade of their lives was significant, because they were surrounded by loss.

Burial

Some of the most vivid memories of enslaved children were about the deaths of their parents. Bethany Veney remembered that both her mother and her enslaver died when she was around nine years old. These major life events caused a period of bereavement and fear because she knew the latter meant family separation.[55] While the loss of a parent was certainly traumatic for enslaved youth, so too was the death of their enslavers, because it often involved additional separation. Enslavers' wills were usually replete with instructions regarding their enslaved people. John Pikens of Greene County, Alabama, left unusual instructions for a deceased enslaved boy named Alfred. Pickens wanted Alfred's remains to be removed and relocated upon his death: "I do hereby desire that [Alfred's] remains be taken up and deposited at my feet whenever I may be buried." Apparently, during a long-term illness, Alfred had kept Pickens's feet warm with hot bricks, and Pickens believed that when he died, Alfred should be exhumed and reburied to "occupy the same position that he was allowed to do when we were living"—at his feet.[56] That Pickens made a provision in his own will to disturb Alfred's body confirms that enslavers saw their ownership extend beyond the grave.

◆   ◆   ◆

The first ten years of an enslaved person's life were transformative. Some experienced their first sale, while others died before reaching age five. In their first decade, enslaved children often witnessed the separation and sale of their parents and, at times, parted with them forever. In some cases, if they survived to age ten, their lives were covered by insurance policies. Those who were incarcerated with their mothers in the Louisiana State Penitentiary experienced their first sale at age ten. Little did they know at the time, their pubescent years would bring even more hardship.

CHAPTER 3

Adolescence, Young Adulthood, and Soul Values

AVERAGE APPRAISED VALUES:
FEMALES: $517 [$15,189 IN 2014]
MALES: $610 [$17,934 IN 2014]

AVERAGE SALE PRICES:
FEMALES: $515 [$15,131 IN 2014]
MALES: $662 [$19,447 IN 2014]

> *They abolished the external or African slave trade, in 1808, the effect of which gave an impetus to the infamous traffic of slave breeding and trading among themselves; and perhaps it was one of the main objects they had in view, the protection of their slave breeders and traders.*
>
> —Thomas Smallwood, 1851[1]

> *As was the custom, all the negroes were brought out and placed in a line, so that the buyers could examine their good points at leisure . . . once negotiated with the trader, paid the price agreed upon, and started for home to present his wife with this flesh and blood commodity, which money could so easily procure in our vaunted land of freedom.*
>
> —Lucy A. Delaney, 1891[2]

On the eve of the Civil War, an abolitionist attending the auction of 149 human souls in New Orleans, Louisiana, was intrigued by the bid caller's excitement over a seventeen-year-old field hand named Joseph who was on the auction block. "Gentlemen," the bid caller exclaimed, "there is a young blood, and a capital one! He is a great boy, a hand for almost every thing. Besides, he is the best dancer in the whole lot, and he knows also how to pray—oh! so beautifully, you would believe he was made to be a minister! How much will you bid for him?" The opening bid for Joseph was a thousand dollars, but according to the enthusiastic auctioneer, Joseph was worth more, considering his value over time. "One thousand dollars for a boy who will be worth in three years fully twenty-five hundred dollars cash down. Who is going to bid two thousand?" the caller asked his audience. As the price for Joseph increased to $1,400, each interested party eagerly made eye contact with the bid caller. Standing on the podium with a wand in hand, he tried to increase Joseph's price by assuring the audience that $1,400 was "too small an amount for" him. "Seventeen years only," he added, "a strong, healthy, fine-looking, intelligent boy. Fourteen hundred and fifty dollars! . . . One thousand, four hundred and fifty—going! going! going! and last—gone!"³ As the caller slapped his hand on the platform, just like that, in less than five minutes, Joseph was sold "to the highest bidder."

In the 1890s, Lucy Delaney described the enslaved experience on the auction block.

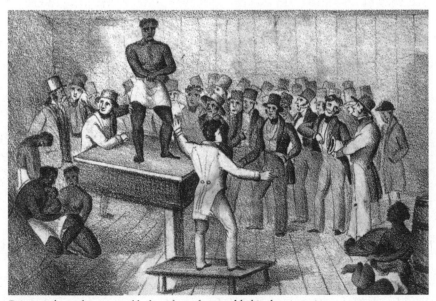

Prime male on the auction block with mothers and babies bearing witness.

We do not have direct testimony from Joseph about his response to this sale, in which he was sold with 148 others from the same Louisiana plantation. Joseph's enslaver, who provided religious instruction to his human chattel, decided to retire from planting in order to pursue a political career.[4] In two days, he sold an enslaved population consisting of field hands (like Joseph), carpenters, bricklayers, blacksmiths, coopers, drivers, and household servants. How did Joseph (enslaved person #2) *feel* about being the second person on the auction block that day? Did Joseph's experience differ at age seventeen, as he approached his "prime" working years, from the experiences of others who were younger or older than him? Had Joseph's adolescence and teen years prepared him for this moment? Was he conditioned to handle and/or witness auctions from previous exposure? Where were his parents? Did he have any siblings, given that there is no mention of his relatives? Yet witnesses said the enslaved stood "upon a platform, similar to a funeral pile erected for martyrs" holding on to their last embrace.[5] Joseph stepped on the block alone as the auctioneer described him with a host of complimentary adjectives. What was his mind-set? Did these descriptions comfort him, uplift him, or add to the trauma of being sold? Joseph and Isam (slave #21) were noted for their ability to preach, and they likely approached the block in silent prayer. Ultimately, their fate is unknown.

We have much to learn about the value of human property during each stage of life, not only the moment of sale. This chapter examines the experiences and valuation of the enslaved during the important years of puberty and young adulthood, from ages eleven to twenty-two. These years marked significant changes in the lives of girls and boys. Girls became women after the onset of their menstrual cycles—a defining moment of their maturation. As harbingers of additional sources of labor, fertile enslaved women commanded high prices in the market, and their enslavers appraised them accordingly. Young men also brought forth more laborers as breeders, and these years were equally important as they, too, matured. The men could be used for sexual reproduction even in their elder years. The institution of slavery, defined and extended by law through a woman's uterus and beyond, continued as long as enslaved women gave birth to healthy children. Women provided the vessel and seed, men provided the fertilizer, and between the two, additional enslaved laborers were born. But as with everything else in the lives of enslaved people, reproduction was fraught. Whatever value they held for themselves now worked in opposition to the devaluation they experienced through sexual interference and exploitation. As a result, many dreaded puberty.

ADOLESCENCE AND YOUNG ADULT AWARENESS OF ENSLAVEMENT AND SOUL VALUES

The pubescent years were terrifying. Not only were their bodies changing, but this was also a time when enslaved children experienced the separation they had feared all their lives. Daughters and sons were taken from their parents as the external value of their bodies increased. Market scenes from their childhood now made sense and haunted them for the rest of their lives. At this stage in their maturation, they knew full well that others claimed ownership of them and sexual assault came at any age.

However, their parents (if present), as well as other kin, reminded them of a value that enslavers and traders could not commodify—the spiritual value of their immortal selves. *Soul values*—my term for such valuation—often escaped calculation and developed during these years. Enriched through an inner spiritual centering that facilitated survival, soul values were reinforced by loved ones. Sometimes this internal value appeared as a spirit, a voice, a vision, a premonition, a sermon, an ancestor, (a) God. It came in public and private settings and was occasionally described as a personal message from a higher being, a heaviness in the core of their bodies. "My soul began singing," one enslaved person recalled, "and I was told that I was one of the elected children."[6] This telling, this uplifting, this singing of a "fearful trill, of things unknown, but longed for still" made the enslaved feel free during captivity.[7] Freedom of the soul matured in puberty.

Soul values, which came from deep within a person's heart, were often felt in childhood, yet not fully articulated until the early teens. Recreating the social and economic circumstances under which enslaved people suffered allows us to make educated conclusions regarding enslaved adolescents' internalized soul values. Unlike appraisal and sale values, these yearnings came from within; outsiders did not bargain for them. Such values shaped and defined enslaved people's characters. "From the time I was a little boy," Edward Walker related, "it always ground my feelings to know that I had to work for another man." These feelings were "not encouraged by my parents or the other slaves." Instead, they "came from within me and grew with the years." As he aged, Walker had the fortunate opportunity to learn to read and write and developed "a big taste for arithmetic." He "could add up numbers like a flash, could multiply and divide quickly, and correctly, and was good at fractions." These skills, his inherent yearning, and his belief in an incalculable soul value led to Walker's successful escape years later.[8] Enslaved people often expressed their soul values by running away.

The internal and spiritual lives of the enslaved varied. Some believed in a Christian or Muslim God, others relied on West African, Caribbean, and Brazilian religious philosophies such as Vodun, Santeria, and Candomblé.[9] Some enslaved people appeared to have no faith or did not comment on it. Historian Albert Raboteau reminds us that enslaved people's religion was an "invisible institution," which can be traced through enslaved testimony and behavior. For some, the idea of an afterlife was an extremely important part of their belief system. They held on to the notion that there was a place beyond the here and now where they would be redeemed and released from captivity. Some enslaved people dreamed that place was Africa, while others referred to it as heaven. In coastal Georgia, the large population of African-born enslaved people dreamed of flying home to Africa and anxiously waited for that to come to pass.[10]

In addition to an increasing spiritual awareness, puberty also represented the years "adolescents reached sexual maturity and [became] capable of reproduction."[11] The onset of menses for girls and the deepening voices of young boys served as physical manifestations of their transition into adulthood, as both sexes became physically stronger and more capable of heavy labor. Puberty also brought forth the importance of their increased commodification. These years generated outsiders' interest in their bodies, especially the interest of medical professionals and enslavers who actively sought ways to maximize their profits. For some, puberty simply meant more challenging health issues, and just as at other stages of life, enslaved people confronted death during these years. Some young women died giving birth; others within a few days or months of giving birth.

Young men, on the other hand, experienced complications such as shame or lack of arousal resulting from being forced to have sex on demand. As a result, they were physically assaulted by enslavers and spent much of their early teens and twenties on the auction block. Sometimes they took the stand with their parents, and on other occasions, their parents tried to purchase them.

One witness shared the following story of a young child and his father being auctioned: "I saw a beautiful boy of twelve years of age, put on the auction-block, and on one side of him stood an old gray-headed negro—it was plain he was his father—and he kept his eyes on the boy, and the boy kept his eyes upon the old gray-headed man, and the tears rolled in silence down the cheeks of each."[12] Imagine the gaze between the father and son. This was not the look of buyers and sellers inspecting property. It was a lingering stare that both knew might be their last. A paternal gaze with a son's eyes locked on his father's—a reverse gaze. The value between this father and son, immersed in tears and silence, was priceless. At twelve years old, this young boy knew it might be the last time he saw his father. They had likely lived together for all of the young boy's life and this would be the first time they were separated.

As with children under ten first learning about their captivity, for adolescents and young adults, separation and sale was a defining moment. This rare testimony describing a father and son on the auction block shows that paternal lineage was valuable to this duo and others. We know nothing about his mother or whether he had siblings, but we know the two held hands as they stood there together with an uncertain future on the horizon.

Some enslaved children remember their fathers fighting to keep their families together by raising funds to purchase them. Although it was extremely difficult for enslaved people to purchase themselves, Solomon Bayley, enslaved in Delaware and Virginia in the late eighteenth and early nineteenth centuries, spent much of his adult life purchasing yet, ironically, burying members of his family. He bought his family memebers with a clear understanding of American and British currency, both in circulation at the time. As a skilled tradesman, Bayley received small amounts of money for some of the labor he performed. After saving enough to purchase his wife,

Thamar, Bayley wanted to raise funds to purchase his only son, Spence. He knew that his son's enslaver had died and all of his property was to be sold. Bayley remembered when the two were first separated; Spence was only nine months old and too young to fully comprehend the transaction. Bayley, on the other hand, went into "a fit of distress" when his son was "sent away" from him.

Years later, in 1813, he learned that Spence was going to be sold again, and his friends and neighbors (both black and white) encouraged him to try to purchase the boy. When he arrived at the courthouse, Bayley heard the "crier" (auctioneer) shout "a likely young negro fellow for sale," and *he*, the father, laid the first bid. "I bid two hundred dollars," said Bayley, knowing full well that was only "half what he was appraised" for when his enslaver died. Bayley understood the difference in values and knew that an appraised value was not the same as a sale price. He waited anxiously to see if anyone else bid on his son. To his disappointment, a man bid $333 and one-third, "which was thirty-three dollars and a third more than" Bayley had. Discouraged by the thought of losing his son again, Bayley bid a second time. "A shilling," he interjected, and the trader responded with a bid of $20 more, increasing the price to $354. Sadly, Bayley "thought I must give him up, and let him go," but he decided to bid once more. In total desperation, he bid "a cent" and the "crier" rejected that bid, asking him to raise it to a shilling. The penny was the last of his money. Bayley's situation looked grim when the trader once again outbid him. As the price continued to rise, Bayley "cried, and turned off, and went and leaned against the court house." He exhausted all his cash and now pondered the loss of his son all over again. Luckily for him, through faith and prayer, bystanders (referred to as "three great men") came to his aid and gave him extra money to help purchase his son for $360 *and* a shilling. One of the men was a Methodist minister. Bayley signed the bond along with securities from the three men, who agreed to cover his costs so that he and Spence could be together.[13]

Imagine this scene from Spence's perspective. How might he have experienced this trade? What was it like to watch his father bid on him? Was he proud? Did he even remember his father? Did it matter? Here was someone who valued him in a different way. His father's actions show a man trying to live in freedom with those dear to him. Participating in an auction for his own child signals that some enslaved people faced their commodification in the very space in which they and their families were objectified. Spence witnessed his father actively trying to purchase him so their family could live in a place where people valued him beyond his market price. His father came prepared to buy him and play by the rules of an institution that defined his family as property. The institution of slavery did not always account for soul values. Such values disrupted appraisal and sale transactions daily. Spence witnessed his father's expression of love side by side with the cold calculation of market values necessary to purchase him. He also saw his father give up, cry, and almost accept defeat, that is, until three men stepped in and contributed funds to complete the sale. By age twelve, Spence knew that he had multiple values and interests on his body and his soul. Unfortunately, like his sisters, he too died "prematurely."[14]

Fathers were not alone in trying to purchase their families. Mothers, such as Charity Bowery, did the same. Bowery lived with her young daughter and twelve-year-old son Richard. She worried about Richard because she knew as he matured it would be "hard work for him to bring his mind to be a slave." Approaching the age of realization and a sense of their place in the world, Bowery brought all of her money to Mistress McKinley, hoping to purchase her son. But, according to Bowery, McKinley would not let her "have my boy." One day, after Bowery had been away, she returned to find her daughter crying in front of McKinley, who was counting a wad of money. At first, Bowery thought McKinley had hit her daughter, but when she asked the child what was wrong, her daughter "pointed to mistress's lap and said 'Broder's money! Broder's money!'" Richard was gone, and his sister understood that the only remaining part of him was the money in the lap of her mistress. Perhaps she could not fully process where Richard had gone or why he had left, but certainly she recognized that her brother's absence meant cash for McKinley. Bowery immediately understood that McKinley had sold her son. McKinley then looked Bowery in the face and said, "Yes, Charity; and I got a great price for him!"[15]

As young men and women grew up, they learned to distinguish between the multiple values placed on and within their bodies. Bowery's young daughter knew that money represented her "Broder" and that he was sold for "a great price" that day. She was probably beginning to understand what boys and girls Richard's age learned—their external market and appraisal values took them away from loved ones. Had Richard grasped the idea of an internal soul value? We do not know. There is evidence, however, that from a young age, some enslaved youth recognized that nobody could purchase their soul. It was the only place where they were truly free. For many, this freedom came at the moment of death, when the spirit left the body. Until they reached spiritual freedom, they still had to contend with external commodification.

VALUATION OF ENSLAVED ADOLESCENTS AND YOUNG ADULTS IN LIFE

No age was more important for the valuation of black bodies than these years (ages eleven to twenty-two), and the years of midlife and adulthood (ages twenty-three to thirty-nine), which will be covered in the next chapter. These were the prime fiscal and reproductive years of an enslaved person's life. Ages eleven to twenty-two represented a period of maturation and knowledge. We know from the writings of Walter Johnson, Wilma King, and others that enslaved youth learned they were both people and property. Johnson writes, "They were taught to see themselves as commodities." They viewed their own bodies through "two different lenses," which he describes as "the chattel principle," taking language from the formerly enslaved.[16] King underscores this point in terms of this age group, noting that "the majority of the slaves sold in the Upper South were teenagers and young adults."[17] I begin with a person's soul value to understand how enslaved youth and young adults worked against commodification. They clearly had another set of values for themselves in addition to the models that scholars suggest.[18]

"As soon as I came to the age of maturity and could think for myself," Thomas Likers explained, "I came to the conclusion that God never meant me for a slave, & that I should be a fool if I didn't take my liberty if I got the chance."[19] He and many others did so by making their way to Canada where they lived as free people. African American abolitionist William Still and Boston abolitionist Benjamin Drew collected the stories of individuals who successfully thwarted the institution of slavery and made their way north in the nineteenth century. Through these narratives, we learn how enslaved people valued themselves and how these internal values drove them to liberation.[20] Enslaved people rejected their status in many ways, including hiding out, feigning ignorance, destroying crops, murdering enslavers and overseers, suing for freedom, learning to read and write, and running away. In certain instances of that push for freedom and self-liberation, clear expressions of their soul values appear.

During youth, enslaved young women and men learned more about the internal value of their lives and did all they could to escape. At fifteen, George Johnson liberated himself because he always "felt" himself a free person "and wanted to be a freeman." Since the US government "didn't give me the liberty I wished, I concluded I would go where I could possess the same liberty as any other man."[21] Upon their arrival in free places, formerly enslaved young women and men worked for themselves, acquired land, and spent time with their families. The abolitionists Still and Drew shared the story of John Hill, who left slavery in Virginia because he "didn't like the condition of things there." He did not "like to be trod upon."[22] His ideas about liberty came from his family, including values taught to him by his parents, grandparents, and uncles. Through letters written to Still, we learn of his "remarkable intelligence," despite the fact that he had no formal training.

He proudly admits that "the whole family of us bought ourselves." Hill "came away" from slavery when he was eighteen years old. His uncles paid for theirs twice before being granted freedom. They "paid $1,500 apiece for themselves," Hill recalled. After his uncles purchased themselves, they purchased Hill and his mother. Witnessing this made a significant impression on him, particularly because he recognized the dishonesty of their enslavers. When they all settled in Canada, they leaned on values taught to them by Hill's grandfather, learned a trade, and created a firm that offered "pretty good wages." Hill took pride in paying his laborers good wages, something he was denied during slavery. Still remained impressed with Hill because it was clear "how much liberty was valued, how the taste of Freedom moved the pen of the slave; how the thought of fellow bondmen, under the heel of the slaveholder, aroused the spirit of indignation and wrath" in the letters he wrote to the abolitionist in Pennsylvania. These letters display Hill's intellect as he evokes phrases from Patrick Henry: "I had started from my Den that morning for 'liberty or for Death.'" He also bares his soul in longing for his wife to join him and enjoy the place where they would have the rights of human beings, not chattel. Impressed, Still published a series of Hill's letters because he wanted the larger, "ignorant" public to learn about the class of "brave intelligent fugitives" that Hill represented.[23]

George Johnson and Thomas Likers, self-liberated enslaved men (mentioned above) who were not as fortunate as Hill, experienced the hardships of public and private sales. Sellers prepared the enslaved for display, determined the condition of their health, and sometimes rated them on a five-point scale of 0 to 1 in increments of 0.25. Prime or full hands had a rating of 1 or A1 Prime, which represented a projection of the amount of work a person could perform in a given day. Prime "hands," typically between the ages of fifteen and thirty, were the strongest laborers on farms and plantations. Age was not the only factor in providing this rating. Other enslaved people had their rates set at three-fourth hand, one-half hand, or, for those unable to work or contribute to the plantation economy, zero.[24]

This rating system resembles US Department of Agriculture (USDA) meat grades, in which beef undergoes a "composite evaluation" to determine quality. For example, USDA Prime, the highest-quality meat, is typically younger, has better muscle quality, and is "firm, fine-textured, bright, cherry-red colored [and] lean." But as an animal matures, these characteristics are less refined and the "muscle color become[s] darker and muscle texture becomes coarser"; thus, the animal is downgraded to "Select" or "Choice." When agriculturists grade meat, they often do not know the age of the animal, so "the physiological age" takes precedence over the "chronological age"; they can determine the former through "bone characteristics, ossification of cartilage, color, and texture" of the meat. The link between meat grading and enslaved people might seem absurd, but the language used by today's USDA to rate meat uncomfortably mirrors the categories for rating enslaved bodies in the nineteenth century.[25] Abraham Lincoln established the USDA in 1860 when the meatpacking industry developed in conjunction with the growth of the railroad industry. In sale advertisements in nineteenth-century newspapers, these terms are peppered throughout the pages.[26]

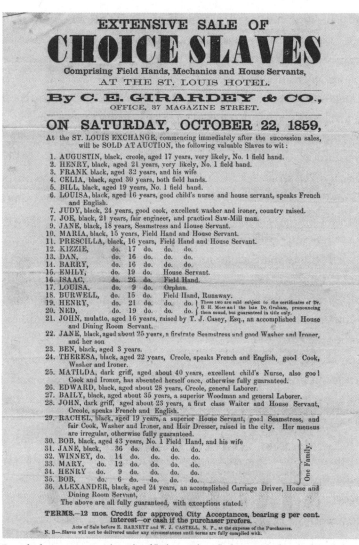

Broadside announcing the sale of "Choice Slaves" along with detail of Rachel,
#29, who has irregular "mensus [sic]." She is discussed on page 76.

Even at this heightened stage of external commodification, young
adults held on to their internal values. A. T. Jones, who understood his
fiscal value, did not have the means to purchase himself; however, he offered to pay $350 for his liberty, "which was a proportion to what others"
had paid for him. When his enslaver did not honor the sale and terms

negotiated, he wrote a pass for himself and had "no trouble getting to Canada."[27] He had tried to participate in the market process on enslavers' terms, but when it did not work out, he ultimately valued his soul more and chose self-liberation as opposed to self-purchase.

Bid callers or "criers" shouted out the values of enslaved people as "prime," "first-rate," or "A1," but enslaved people had different understandings of these terms. From freedom in Canada, Benjamin Miller explained what "first-rate" meant to the enslaved. Before his escape, his North Carolina enslaver had trusted him to travel to and from the market, run errands, or do favors. Sometimes his enslaver even gave him small amounts of money, but "I was still a slave," he explained. On one occasion, Miller said, he "bought myself for $450." Neighbors told his enslaver "he was a fool to sell me for $450, when he might have got $800." When his enslaver raised the price to $500, Miller was unwilling to pay it. Instead, he fled without paying and made his way to Canada. Reflecting on this pivotal event, Miller discussed what it meant to be "first-rate." "I have done first rate here," he explained. "I will tell you what *I* call first-rate . . . I say first rate, from the fact that we have to row against wind and tide when we get here, and being brought up illiterate, I consider that if we live and keep our families well fed and clad, *we have done first-rate.*"[28] Considering his deprivations during slavery, his journey to freedom, and the obstacles he encountered, Miller believed his actions and survival were first rate. This more expansive evaluation went beyond the simple calculations enslavers used to determine the work rates found in plantation ledgers, newspaper advertisements, and broadsides. It reflected Miller's sense of doing well for himself. George Ross, another self-liberated person, described his experience using the term another way: "I have been treated first-rate since I have been in Canada. I can't complain at all."[29]

In addition to the aforementioned rating system, another method to determine the monetary value of the enslaved was physicians' medical exams to evaluate whether individuals were "sound" or "unsound." Health, often measured by "soundness," played an integral role in the commodification of bodies. "Sound" simply meant healthy and able to work; "unsound" meant unhealthy, with a compromised work effort. Medical examiners aided enslavers, insurance companies, and traders to determine an enslaved person's health—including bodily integrity and perceived mental stability—which had a direct relationship to his or her appraised and market values. In some cases, various body parts or whole persons had warranties to confirm the quality of their health. Their dual commodity value confirms that people were being treated as property, particularly when their bodies were commodified and their humanity objectified in legal cases such as "warranty suits," or after death, through coroner's inquests. Legal historian Ariela Gross describes this process, noting that "sometimes the body of a slave was read for signs of character ... at other times ... as a piece of property."[30]

Healthy enslaved people were poked, prodded, and examined. At some sales, for privacy during a more physical exam, they were taken behind a curtain or into a "little room," but one wonders for whom this privacy was reserved. Northern abolitionist James Redpath said that, in these rooms, "the slaves were stripped naked, and carefully examined, as horses are—every part of their body, from their crown to their feet, was rigorously scrutinized by the gallant chivalry who intended to buy them."[31]

Redpath witnessed several slave auctions, including that of a young man in Petersburg, Virginia, whose "vest was removed and his breast and neck exposed." Next the enslaved man's "shoes and stockings" were "taken off and his legs beneath the knees examined." Even more vivid, "his other garment was then loosed, and his naked body from the upper part of the abdomen to the knees, was shamelessly exhibited to the view of the spectators." The auctioneer or "body-seller" as he was referred to, instructed the young man to "turn round," exposing his naked body from "the shoulders to the calves" to the crowd for inspection. To this, the auctioneer said, "You see, gentlemen, he's perfectly sound and a very finely formed n[——r]."[32]

Those interested in enslaved bodies were also concerned with "unsoundness." Medical professionals discussed definitions and conditions that qualified as "unsound," since this assessment compromised sale. Enslaved people recognized that their health and capabilities were under scrutiny, and some decided to intervene. One girl on a Richmond, Virginia, auction block had a right hand deemed entirely useless or "'dead,' as she aptly called it." Before the sale, she had a physician remove one finger, but an auctioneer "stated that she herself chopped off the other finger—her forefinger—because it hurt her, and she thought that to cut it off would cure it." When questioned about the finger, she said, "Now, you see it was a sort o' sore, and I thought it would be better to cut it off than be plagued with it."[33] Taking matters into their own hands was one way enslaved people responded to their oppression.

Some physicians wrote articles that classified all the conditions that qualified black bodies as unsound. Dr. Harris of the Savannah Medical College, for example, listed some of the common illnesses that would change the categorization of an enslaved body from sound to unsound, including strands of syphilis, varicose veins, aneurisms, bone disease, hernia, hemorrhoids, and rickets, if it disfigured women's reproductive organs.[34] The discussion of soundness and unsoundness was best articulated in specific values, particularly for enslaved women and their perceived capacity to reproduce.

Menstruation

Enslaved girls and young women were very private about their physical development. Older women taught them to protect themselves from abuse, because they understood the connection between their bodies and the institution of slavery.[35] Women and "their increase" populated and sustained slavery during the years after authorities banned the international trade in African captives. Given that the law sanctioned slavery through a woman's womb, it is no surprise that enslavers, traders, and medical doctors paid careful attention to gynecological health. The field of gynecology grew out of slavery and, in particular, enslaved women's bodies. There is a rich and well-documented history of US physicians, including the "father of gynecology," Dr. James Marion Simms, who conducted their research on enslaved women. Doctors in Europe and the Caribbean also examined black women's bodies.[36]

The most well-known European case involved French naturalist Georges Cuvier's exploitation of Saartjie Baartman, a Khoikhoi born in the 1770s in South Africa. She became the subject of scientists', physicians', and the general public's curiosity because parts of her curvy body—breasts, buttocks, and labia—were viewed as exceptionally large. Cuvier exhibited her in Europe for five years under the epithet "Hottentot Venus." People paid to see, touch, and study her body as she stood on a perpetual auction block, subject to the gaze of audiences worldwide. How did she grapple with the internal and external values placed on her? Did she remain composed? Treated with less decency than a mannequin, Baartman died in 1815. Her postmortem life and ghost value remained in circulation and on display until 2002. Cuvier made a plaster cast of her body and preserved her genitalia in a glass jar; both were displayed in Paris's Museum of Man until 1974. Nelson Mandela led an effort in 1994 to have her remains returned to South Africa, but the French government did not comply until 2002. Her remains were finally given a proper burial in South Africa in 2002.[37]

Caribbean enslavers also expressed interest in black women's bodies, as well as their reproductive organs. Dr. John Roberton of Manchester, England, for example, sought to determine whether women of African descent entered puberty earlier than European women. His theory was that climate had an impact of the onset of puberty, and he believed that warmer climates triggered women's menstrual cycles. He also thought that "the union of the sexes at an early age" led to early childbearing and was a result of "warm latitudes, where there is a low state of civilization."

To test his theories, he solicited statistics from people who attended and documented births. In June 1841, Roberton asked Moravian missionaries in Antigua and Jamaica for data on the age of first menarche among their "Negro populations." Slavery had been abolished in the British West Indies in 1833, but he longed to collect data, given the meticulous plantation and missionary records in both regions. Hoping to have between twenty and fifty cases, he wanted to know the "age of puberty in that race." A Mr. Elliott of Jamaica responded a few months later with a table that contained information on twenty-one "Negresses" ranging from eight to sixty years old. Most of the women between eight and eleven years old had "not yet" had their menses. But the age varied for those who had: "twelve cases in which the menses appeared, in one aged sixteen years, in three fifteen, in three fourteen, in three thirteen, and in two aged twelve years."

Other missionaries sent information to Roberton from church book registrations that listed whether girls had their menses at the time of baptism. "The idea of any (menstruating) younger than" twelve years, wrote a Mr. Zorn, "was ridiculed by nurses." Dr. Nicholson of Antigua reported in December 1841 from his own recollections that "menstruation before the twelfth year" was not common among black or white women, despite knowing of a few "rare" cases. In his experience, most girls became women during their fourteenth or fifteenth year.[38] This evidence supports the idea that enslaved women in the United States likely experienced puberty in their early teen years; however, evidence from American physicians tells a slightly different story, and one that includes health complications.

Enslaved women in the United States had reproductive health issues and complained about this to their enslavers, medical professionals, women healers, and just about anyone who would listen. Frances Anne Kemble, whose husband owned property in Georgia, encountered several enslaved women with health complications related to the female body.[39] However, according to Dr. Robert C. Carroll of Jackson Street Hospital in Augusta, Georgia, black women frequently suffered from "menstrual derangement." He was not alone in trying to determine the cause of such health challenges. Other Southern practitioners discussed these concerns in medical journals and with each other.[40] Many blamed "negro women" for their poor health, referring to it as "their proverbial carelessness" and their "reckless disregard" of their medical condition. Carroll's reports were derived from rare cases when black women were observed daily in a hospital setting "under the eye of the physician."

Mary, an enslaved "mulatto" woman, from Edgefield District, South Carolina, had irregular periods since age fourteen. The degree to which Carroll described her irregularity "both as to time and quantity" indicates the precise nature of her care. She gave birth to her first and only child at age eighteen, but the infant died three days later, marking the beginning of extended discomfort. Her condition does not appear to have been menstrual cramps, which some enslaved women cured by wearing a cotton string tied with nine knots around their waist, because her symptoms became more frequent and lasted for nearly a decade.[41] For eight or nine years after giving birth, Mary became very ill every month around the time of her menses. Described at first as occasional "hysterical symptoms," the frequency increased as Mary displayed "convulsive movements" daily, "generally about daylight," before being admitted to the hospital. Her enslaver removed her from the plantation, took her to an urban area, and admitted her to the hospital because she had "not been able to do work of any consequence for many months."

Think about this rationale for a moment. Mary apparently went to the hospital after years of physical pain and months of being unable to provide reproductive or productive labor to her enslaver. Clearly her symptoms became more disruptive, as her enslaver was not able to extract work from her. That he traveled an unknown number of miles to a local city suggests that it was important to him that she received medical care. But given contemporary knowledge, Mary could possibly have been suffering from a severe case of postpartum depression, which at that time was not entirely known. She may have been upset by the death of her child, or this may have been one of many losses. There is also the possibility that she did not want her child to grow up enslaved and that his or her death was a relief. We cannot uncover her mental state; we know much more about her physical condition.

After a thorough medical exam, Mary lay lifeless, pale, and "somewhat emaciated," with a "melancholy expression of countenance." She had diarrhea, back pains, gastrointestinal pain, and "tenderness on pressure over the region of the womb, extending up" to her belly button. The physician performed a "digital exam" and placed a finger in her vagina, "causing her to shrink from the pressure." Perhaps she pulled away because she did not want the doctor to examine her. She may have been uncomfortable with that level of scrutiny, as it may have been the first time a white male physician examined her. Most enslaved women were accustomed to black women healers tending to their health needs.[42] Possibly, she had some serious health issues. The attending physician found that the walls of Mary's "vagina are apparently healthy" and suspected she was feigning her illness. He therefore asked "another woman" to remain in the room to observe Mary's attacks. The very next day, at daylight, Mary experienced another one of her convulsive episodes that put her in "a state of apparent unconsciousness and lethargy." The physicians concluded that she was not faking and labeled her illness "hysterical catalepsy."

From April 25 through June 8, 1859, Mary remained in the hospital and received treatment. Her lengthy stay speaks volumes about how her enslaver must have valued her. Medical fees, including medication, testing, boarding, and other expenses, were not taken lightly by enslavers who sought to maximize the labor of their enslaved workforce. We know Mary's enslaver took her to the hospital because she had been unable to work. Perhaps Mary was worth the cost of this treatment because she was in her prime years. As time went on, Mary expressed that she was feeling better, while the doctors worked to restore her health. In addition to her "hysterical catalepsy," she had leucorrhea, a white or yellowish discharge of mucus in the vagina that caused an infection. Folk remedies to treat this condition included "tea made of poached egg shells or green coffee."[43] At the hospital, she received "a tincture of guaiacum," or evergreen tea, common in the Caribbean.

After one month of treatment, Mary felt stronger and had gone weeks without any pain. In June, she shared that she did not "remember any period when she has been entirely free from pain." She had her first normal menstrual period with no "nervous symptoms"; her enslaver was in the city, so doctors discharged her. About nine months later, her enslaver reported to the physicians that Mary rested for three weeks after being discharged (as instructed) and "she requested to be allowed to go into the field with the other hands, and has continued at work and [was doing] well ever since."[44] We have no way of knowing whether Mary felt violated during her medical care, but she was clearly relieved to be feeling better. Although her enslaver reported that she wanted to return to work, we must be careful not to assume that she enjoyed enslavement. She may have wanted to go back because she missed her community of family and friends while confined in the hospital.

Other women with irregular menstrual cycles were advertised for sale with added descriptors about their health. Nineteen-year-old Rachel of Louisiana was put up for sale along with a group of thirty-six "choice slaves" (see page 69 for illustration). All were described as valuable, and they ranged from age three to forty-three. Physical characteristics such as color, age, and labor skills followed their names listed on the public notice, but Rachel stood out from the rest. She had a "black" complexion and was "a superior House Servant, good Seamstress and a fair Cook, Washer, Ironer, and Hair Dresser." She had been raised in New Orleans, which partially explains her labor skills. However, one sentence marked her as different: "Her menses are irregular, otherwise fully guaranteed." Rachel's cycle was so important that the administrator of the sale made a special notation about it, perhaps for full disclosure or to avoid any future lawsuit. "The above are all fully guaranteed, with exceptions stated," and the conditions of the sale were reemphasized at the bottom of the broadside (poster).[45] Was Rachel sold that day? We do not know, but she was advertised with personal health information, facts that described her capacity (or not) to give birth—information made illegal today due to privacy laws. Rachel was not alone in having this private information made public.

In Natchez, Mississippi, in 1841, Bathsheba suffered from pregnancy complications. "After the most intense suffering," she "gave birth to an infant dead." Her enslaver had a physician examine her because "her suffering since then [the birth of the stillborn infant] has been great."[46] It is difficult to know whether Bathsheba tampered with her pregnancy or if her sadness was genuine, because some women did not want to bring children into the world.

Women described as "barren" were also discussed extensively and, in most cases, devalued for their perceived incapacity to give birth. However, given enslaved women's expressions of reproductive control, we cannot assume that all embraced motherhood. Some chose to terminate pregnancies, and others, like Margaret Garner, an enslaved mother of four children from Kentucky, participated in infanticide and took their children's lives.[47] Some enslaved women on a Tennessee plantation deliberately terminated their pregnancies, and physicians studied these cases to determine how they did so.[48]

Jamaican physicians were shocked to learn of an enslaved woman who performed a Cesarean section on herself. She had experienced labor pains that were too much to bear, so apparently "she took a very sharp knife and made a deep incision, and extracted the child and placenta herself." Her incision was so deep that it cut into the buttock of her child. Enslavers called for a "negro house doctor" after the mother "cried out for help," and he sewed her up "the same way we sew up dead bodies." The baby died of tetanus on the fifth day. The mother survived and years later gave birth to a healthy child.[49] Was this woman trying to terminate her pregnancy or was she simply trying to relieve herself of severe labor pains? Regardless of her motive, she asserted her right to care for her own body when others around her did not.

Rape and Forced Breeding

As external values took on new meaning during enslaved men's and women's teens and early twenties, these individuals came to understand another aspect of their worth—the price of their reproduction. Reflecting on her shift to adulthood, Harriet Jacobs described puberty as "a sad epoch in the life of a slave girl."[50] For her and many others, it marked the beginning of a period when all men could sexually assault them. Bethany Veney recalled being forced to entertain her enslaver and his friends by "singing and dancing." Later, she had to go to his room, where she performed more dancing and singing with "grotesque grimaces, gestures, and positions," as he informed her what "he wanted of me."[51]

But enslaved girls and women were not the only ones terrorized by sexual abuse; so, too, were boys and men. Historian Thomas Foster reminds us that "black manhood under slavery was also violated," yet most of the literature focuses on the sexual assault of women and girls.[52] Men recalled being treated like breeding animals. Their appraisers scrutinized their size, strength, and virility. John Cole, enslaved in Georgia, remembered that men were selected specifically for "raising up strong black bucks." They were sometimes taken on a "circuit" to visit other plantations and impregnate the women. After all, he noted, "this was thrifty and saved any actual purchase of new stock."[53] Laura Thornton, enslaved in Alabama, testified that enslavers "would work them to death and breed them too." In some cases, she added, "old massa kept one for hisself."[54]

As with girls, the exploitation of boys started at a young age. They were objectified on the auction block and made to run and jump, often with little or no clothing to cover their genitals. In New Orleans, brothel houses specialized in young boys, markets advertised them, and enslavers wanted to purchase them. Enslavers were both male and female. Historian Stephanie Jones-Rogers suggests that slaveholding women administered and sanctioned exploitation as readily as their husbands.[55] Some enslaved males learned about exploitation from their fathers. "I heard my father say," explained Oscar Felix Junell, "that in slavery time, they took the finest and

portlies' looking Negroes—the males—for breeding purposes."[56] Adrienne
D. Davis, a legal scholar, thus labels slavery as a "sexual economy" that began during these years, was reinforced predominately by elite white men,
and made enslaved women and men productive and reproductive laborers.[57]
Thus, enslaved women and men experienced exploitation at the hands of
men and women of every rank and class, from the enslaved to the free.

The meaning and practice of nineteenth-century breeding differed from
the eighteenth-century conceptions of the term outlined in chapter 1. Rape
and forced breeding became common experiences for the enslaved, particularly after the transatlantic slave trade was abolished in 1808. The values of
enslaved women's bodies, in particular, increased during the decades before
and after the law passed, and breeding in this century became associated
with animal husbandry.[58] Men too were valued for their ability to "make"
babies, and their experiences with breeding depended on location. Frederick Douglass explained it best: "I am from a breeding state—where slaves
are reared for the market as horses, sheep, and swine."[59] Southern newspapers confirmed such notions; so too did instructions among enslavers
and speeches among politicians.[60] Traders advertised breeding practices in
local newspapers. One North Carolina paper reported, "Since the discon-
tinuance of the African slave trade, some parts of America have become
great breeding districts, in which human cattle are raised for the Southern
market."[61] Clearly, by the nineteenth century, some enslavers used forced
reproduction, which often increased their enslaved populations. Some historians recognize these practices and describe them as the "fetishization"
of black bodies.[62] I have argued elsewhere that the exploitation of both
sexes occurred when enslavers forced enslaved people to copulate against
their will—which I labeled *third-party rape*.[63] We still have much more to
learn about this history, and the thoughts, comments, and feelings of the
enslaved on this subject are an important resource.

Many enslaved men recall being greased up and groomed for the auction block. One bystander in Louisiana referred to the preparations as
"dressing up the slaves to be sold." Some traders "kept a big, good-natured
buck to lead the parade" of enslaved people ready for sale.[64] Whether in
a yard, a private home, or a business, enslaved men were objectified on
the auction block, just as their female counterparts were. Potential buyers

tugged on their skin, opened their mouths, pressed against their muscles, and asked them a series of questions.[65]

Enslaved people testified about several forms of sexual coercion, but the stigma attached to nineteenth-century notions of breeding contribute to its scarcity in recent historical literature. We now identify broader categories of sexual abuse, including "physical penetrative assault, forced reproduction, sexual coercion and manipulation, and psychic abuse."[66] This spectrum of abuse was part of the slavery story. Sylvia Watkins, an enslaved woman from Tennessee, recalled that "white men went with colored gals and women bold[ly]." Continuing, she said that the white "women went with colored men too." In her estimation, the presence of single white women in some communities was a cover for them "goin' with one of their [male] slaves."[67] These "relationships" had a power dynamic that cannot be overlooked. With this in mind, it is no surprise that sexual abuse crossed racial and gender lines, even if we cannot always know the meaning behind such interactions.[68] But what happened to an enslaved man when he was forced to have sex with a woman he did not choose? How did he respond to the "sex on demand" nature of forced couplings? How did he become aroused enough to perform for his enslavers? What did he do when they wanted to watch? Likewise, how did women experience these shameful acts?

Sam and Louisa Everett of Virginia recalled orgies on their plantation where their enslaver "forced them to have sexual relations," even though they had other partners. Their enslaver made Sam expose his genitals and asked Louisa, "Do you think you can stand this big [n——r]?" When she hid her face from his "nakedness," her enslaver forced her to look at Sam. Next, "he told us that we must git busy and do it in his presence, and we had to do it."[69] Henry Bibb, who successfully escaped slavery, summarized such practices: "Every slaveholder, who is the keeper of a number of slaves of both sexes, is also the keeper of a house or houses of ill-fame." He viewed white men as "licentious" because they broke up "the bonds of affection" among enslaved families.[70]

When Robert Newsome, a small Missouri farmer, purchased Celia, age fourteen, he had no idea the transaction would end in his death. The middle-aged Newsome began raping her on their way home from the market. This was probably Celia's first sexual experience. Newsome repeatedly raped Celia for five years, resulting in the birth of two children. Despite her efforts to protect herself from him, Celia was pregnant a third time. She also had a relationship with an enslaved man named George that complicated her continued exploitation. By the time she turned nineteen, Celia had had enough of Newsome's abuse. In the summer of 1855, Newsome came to her cabin to have sex with her, but Celia refused, hitting him over the head twice with a large club and killing him. She understood the ramifications of her actions and was trying to "protect her principle," borrowing language from legal scholar Adrienne D. Davis and historian Brenda E. Stevenson.[71] She, and other enslaved men and women, understood that puberty meant their bodies would be valued for reproductive purposes. And, as young girls became women, they learned how to thwart abuse, whether it came from white or black men or white women. Celia likely felt justified in protecting herself from further exploitation because of her soul value, a value that Newsome could not commodify. He was interested in his own sexual gratification.

Next Celia covered up her actions. She dragged Newsome's body to the fireplace and burned him right there in her cabin. By daylight, she spread ashes throughout the yard with the help of his grandson, who had no idea he was burying his grandfather. Celia buried the larger bone fragments. A few days later, when Newsome's family could not find him, she confessed to the murder.

This story of an enslaved woman's rape is a familiar one. In their narratives, several enslaved women discuss their sexual exploitation. Given that the law sanctioned slavery through a woman's womb, black women faced widespread sexual abuse. For white enslavers, the more children their enslaved women bore, the more enslaved people they had in their labor force. Producing children was a cheap alternative to purchasing them at the market.

Some enslaved men spoke more readily about women's abuse than their own. Thomas Smallwood shared that enslaved women's "virtue is tampered with, trampled on, violated; and is entirely at the mercy and will of any and every debauchee who chooses to arm himself with the advantages he has over the poor coloured female." As a result, black women had a difficult time protecting themselves, and even if they had black male partners like Celia's George, their physical fidelity "is almost sure to be destroyed by some white man."[72] Based on his parents' recollections, Willie McCullough of North Carolina described breeding: "Some of the slave women were looked upon by the slave owners as a stock raiser looks upon his brood sows, that is from the standpoint of production." He understood the fiscal connection and added, "If a slave woman had children fast she was considered very valuable because slaves were valuable property."[73]

Some enslaved men and boys tried to defend their female relatives from sexual abuse. Bob, a Louisiana enslaved man tried to protect his sister Nancy from sexual abuse. One day when they were little, Nancy started to cry and told her brother that "I am very unhappy—I wish to die." Just as Bob asked her why, the overseer's son Peter came running across the yard with a whip in his hand, grabbed Nancy by the neck, and threw her on the grass. Bob jumped in between the two and yelled, "Peter don't hurt my sister. No! You shall not hurt my sister!" Peter struck Bob in the face with the whip and completely destroyed his eye.[74] Testimonies such as those of Thomas, Willie, and Bob are just a few stories about black women's sexual abuse told from the perspective of enslaved men. One father painfully noted that he was "TIRED on it" after seeing his daughter and other women being exploited.[75]

Returning to the story of Celia, how different would her narrative be if we could hear from George, her lover? As the community developed a case against Celia, George and others were interviewed. He denied involvement with the crime, even though some could not imagine how Celia could have committed it on her own. While she awaited trial, Celia gave birth to a stillborn child. When the court proceedings began, medical doctors testified about whether "a human body could be so completely destroyed in a simple fireplace in a span of only six or so hours." This case occurred before the use of cremation to dispose of bodies in the United States. The first American crematorium did not open until 1876. One could argue that Celia's actions represented one of the first makeshift cremations in US history. As this book unfolds, Celia's act will take on multiple meanings, some perhaps connected to the history of medicine.

In Celia's testimony, we learn that "she did not intend to kill him when she struck him, but only wanted to hurt him." Despite this, and the fact that she was guilty only of valuing herself enough to resist exploitation, Celia was "hanged by the neck until dead on the sixteenth day of November 1855."[76] Her children were given values and sold, but we do not know to whom or where. What happened to George also remains a mystery. We know that the state paid for her execution and valued her death over her life. We do not know if her body was ever laid to rest.

Some women were not as "successful" in ending their abuse. One woman, described as an "intelligent and conscientious" person, tried to refuse her enslaver's "criminal intercourse" on multiple occasions. Every time she did, he sent the overseer to flog her. After two severe whippings, she recognized that "her case was hopeless" and "gave herself up to be the victim of his brutal lusts."[77]

Some women like Madeline, described as "a beautiful quadroon," age sixteen, fought sexual abuse on the same night they were sold. Madeline's new enslaver was considered "a confirmed desolute [sic] rascal." After the $1,900 purchase, "her pitiful cries and groans of anguish, in the horrible night were heard for several houses from that of her inhuman new master." A Frenchman, Raimond Legrand, promised to purchase her and take her to France, but he did not have enough money to buy her. In response, Madeline, who valued herself more than the price tag on her body, tried to escape the next day. While being sought, she ran to the wharf and jumped in the river to her death. Her last words were, "Adieu, cher Raimond!"[78] Madeline preferred death to enslavement. She valued her soul enough to die.[79]

Commodification Data for Enslaved Adolescents and Young Adults

The external values of those in their teens and early twenties (between ages eleven and twenty-two) increased slightly from those in childhood, unless they were deemed unfit. Examining a sample of 19,041 appraisals and sales from eight Southern states between 1771 and 1865, we learn that the average appraised values for young women and young men were $517 and $610, respectively. Clearly, they were becoming more valuable as they approached puberty. As girls developed the capacity to have healthy children, their market values incorporated the ability to produce "future increase." Traders sold a twelve-year-old girl at the Richmond, Virginia, market for $550. She wore a "small checkered tartan frock, a white apron and white-colored handkerchief." When she stepped on the platform, the bid caller looked at his audience of "thirty to forty white persons present" and commenced the sale by saying, "Here's a girl . . . warranted, sound and strong." A few minutes later she was sold.[80] Market prices for young women and men sold in public and in private settings were, respectively, $515 and $662.[81]

There is a slight difference in women's appraisal and sale values. Many young women, such as the twelve-year-old girl in Virginia, had likely not experienced their transition into womanhood, usually signaled by the onset of menstruation. Buyers wanted to know that they would be good child bearers and were willing to pay increasingly higher prices for them. Boys became young men during these years, and enslavers measured their strength and skills so they could incorporate them into a variety of different tasks. For some, that meant learning a trade; for others, it meant that their enslavers could hire them out for modest payments.

Still, others were not valued as whole people; instead, their worth was partitioned for the benefit of enslavers. Fourteen-year-old Rachel, for example, had three-fourths of her value or time sold, rather than her whole person. She experienced a sheriff's sale where "the purchaser was to have the services of [Rachel] three fourths of the time," meaning that someone still claimed one-fourth "of her appraised value."[82] When the bidding began, Rachel began "to cry, and wiped her tears with the back of her hand." She made it a point to turn "her back to the people" who bid on a portion of her value. That enslaved people were divided while living should not come as a surprise to legal scholars. Consider the three-fifths clause of the US Constitution. First established in 1783, this rule counted enslaved people as three-fifths of a person when determining representation in congressional seats.[83] This parceling out was a financial vivisection of enslaved people, established first in our nation's constitution, and then maintained and continued by institutions invested in slavery.

Inspections and evaluations became even more obtrusive at this stage of life. Young men and women were fondled, poked, prodded, and made to walk, run, and jump; every open cavity was explored, from their mouths to their private parts. Some were stripped naked and, perhaps drawing upon biblical references, felt ashamed, as Adam and Eve did in the Garden of Eden. The humiliation experienced was difficult to express and something they preferred to forget. Lucy (age fourteen) endured the verbal taunting of her future enslaver as she approached the block in Louisiana. "Thou art mine, black little dove!" he claimed. An apologist who witnessed the scene described him as a "wolf" with a "lustful countenance." She stood there with a "sad, silent face," eyes cast down with tears falling onto the table below as he bid $1,025 to complete the sale.

A few minutes later, Rosa (age sixteen) stepped onto the same platform. Described as "a capital girl, well built, good natured and intelligent," she could not escape the molestation of the auctioneer as he touched her teeth and displayed them to an audience of several hundred men. Next he worked his way down her body to her "beating bosom," and the audience bid until her sale price reached $1,250.

In 1836, Tracy Edson of Louisiana witnessed the sale of a "good looking girl about eighteen." Some of the other enslaved merchandise "did not appear to be affected by their situation," while others "seemed deeply to feel their situation." The young woman "covered her face with her hands and sobbed aloud." Curious, Edson asked her why she was crying, and the young woman said that "she was afraid she should be brought away from her relatives." The young woman sold for $976, equivalent to $25,600 in 2014 dollars.[84] Why did she command such a high price? It is likely that she was in her fertility prime. Such scenes were common at large auctions in the Deep South, where the market values maintained the highest averages.

Cane Brake Plantation Patterns of Valuation

Young women appraised on Cane Brake Plantation in Mississippi displayed modest fluctuations in values based on their age. For example, the appraisals of twelve- to fourteen-year-olds increased each year by about $50 to $75. Dr. Carson valued Anna Eliza (age twelve) at $375 at the beginning of 1856 and increased her value to $450 by the end of the year. A year later, in 1857, she went from $450 to $600. Other young women had similar value assessments; by age nineteen, many of their projected values did not increase. From eighteen to twenty years old, Rachel L.'s appraised value at the beginning and end of the year remained $600. The values of men in this age range on this plantation increased by increments of $50 to $100. Male eleven-year-olds received values of around $400, and twenty-two-year-olds were valued at $800 to $900, with the exception of sixteen-year-old Thomas, who received a $1,200 value in 1858. Dr. Carson clearly valued Thomas over the other men, indicating either his field labor capacity or his artistry skill.[85]

VALUATION OF ADOLESCENTS AND YOUNG ADULTS IN DEATH

Enslavers used death as a mechanism of control. Although many tried to capitalize on market values upon the loss of life, others willingly killed their human chattel as a threat to the living. While such examples could be financially damaging to enslavers, they were psychologically instructive for enslaved people's soul values. Through funerals, postmortem autopsies, and insurance policies, enslavers manipulated the fiscal vitality of the institution, yet they were rarely able to commodify enslaved people's immortal souls.

Frank Bell, an enslaved man from Texas, witnessed and was forced to participate in the death or murder of his wife. He shared the following story: "When I's about seventeen I marries a gal while master on drunk spell. Master he run her off, and I slips off at night to see her, but he finds it out. He takes a big, long knife and cuts her head plumb off, and ties a great, heavy weight to her and makes *me* throw her in the river. Then he puts me in chains and every night he come give me a whippin', for long time."[86] Men like Bell were willing to risk their lives to see loved ones, but participating in their murder and its cover-up must have been devastating. What did he think when he witnessed the decapitation of his wife? More important, how did he feel about having to throw her head into the river? Unfortunately, we do not have testimony from Bell to learn how this experience sat with his soul. Studying enslaved concepts of death offers one way to see into experiences such as Bell's.

The loss of a parent became a vivid memory for those between the ages of eleven and twenty-two. They not only experienced death, but also witnessed it. "My ma died when I was about eleven years old," Janie recalled. She, like other women, suffered from overwork and died during pregnancy. "Old Marse was mean to her" and he whipped "her all the time." Even worse, Janie's mom worked in the fields "the very day she had a baby, and she borne the baby right out in the cotton patch and died."[87] Other enslaved teens and young adults remembered their parent's funerals. Catherine Cornelius said she "can still recollect my ma's funeral" because "they gave her a nice one." She was pleased "Brother Aaron" preached the funeral. Her mother was laid to rest in "their own burin' grounds" with planted willow trees as grave markers in place of headstones. "All of the coffins was made on the place, and they was plain wooden boxes"; they were "nicely made." A funeral procession "carried off" the bodies, and all the enslaved were allowed to attend. Whites and blacks alike cried and paid their respects to her dear mother.[88]

Some enslavers allowed similar elaborate services and showed respect for the dead, unlike Bell's owner who did not allow Bell's wife a proper burial. Willis Cofer of Georgia remembered very elaborate rituals to prepare the dead for burial. Someone washed the corpse with soap and hot water, then wrapped it in a "windin' sheet," and laid the body on a "coolin' board." Customized coffins to fit a person's body were common on Cofer's plantation, and men were laid to rest in "a suit of clothes," while women were buried "in de windin' sheets." The burial involved a short procession to a graveyard where the body was placed in the ground. Some more formal funerals had sermons, hymns, and a small service as late as two months *after* the body was laid to rest. The rationale for such a delay had to do with external values. Enslavers wanted to make sure the harvest period was complete and that enslaved people from neighboring plantations could attend.[89]

Octavia George, enslaved in Louisiana, remembered that "funerals were very simple for slaves." Her plantation did not allow a full service. Bodies were just taken to the graveyard and buried. The enslaved could not even sing at the cemetery. Instead, her mistress told ghost stories "after funerals and they would nearly scare me to death." One story involving the decapitated body of a man was a particularly vivid memory for her.[90]

On some occasions, the death of the enslaved involved an official postmortem examination. In these instances, the cause of death was the most important inquiry; the monetary value was the second. Legal historian Ariela Gross notes that postmortems occurred "to determine the monetary value of the slave's body at issue," and that "dissection after death was the final dishonor to a slave's body." In order to determine who made money off of the deceased, postmortems were "prerequisite[s] for any claimants' claim over a dead slave."[91] Evidence of postmortems is found in medical journals throughout the United States, Europe, and the Caribbean. Through these cases, we learn about the cause of death and the circumstances surrounding the valuation of dead bodies.[92] A spectrum of commodification continued in postmortem spaces.

Life Insurance

People or companies who insured young adults knew these were years of great physical and earning potential, but they were also risky years due to the myriad of health complications that came with pregnancy and rigorous labor. Such realities were reflected in the insurance premiums and corresponding appraisal values of individuals between the ages of eleven and twenty-two. Representative of the value of black bodies at death, insurance premiums are much higher than annual appraisal values discussed above. An examination of the records of 1,050 policies from the Southern Mutual Life Insurance Company reveals that enslaved people in this age range were of great concern to enslavers. The SMLIC functioned "to make a provision for the survivors in case of death." For their "slave policies," insurance agents helped patrons who depended on enslaved laborers for support and income. In the company's view, "paying a fifth or sixth of their annual hire" was sufficient to "replace the servants who may die" during the term.[93] Thus, individuals and companies insured their enslaved people, hoping to protect their investment in the event of death.

Jessup & Hatch, a leather goods and horse equipment company in Augusta, Georgia, insured two high-priced enslaved men, Andrew, age twenty-one, valued at $2,900, and Sam, age sixteen, valued at $2,700. These two men had the highest value of all those in this sample and were probably skilled tanners who worked in the company store making harnesses and saddles.[94] The firm paid a premium of $55 for Andrew's policy for the year (1864) with a 2.75 percent interest rate. Sam's policy had the same interest and term (one year,) but the premium was slightly higher at $74.25.

Ann, a seventeen-year-old enslaved woman, represented the most financially valuable woman insured, by her enslaver John Murray, through the SMLIC. Valued at $2,600, Murray paid $71.50 for the year at a 2.75 percent rate. "Twiggs," gender unknown, was only eleven years old, priced at \$2,300, with a one-year policy and a \$65.25 premium. Those a bit younger, such as twelve-year-old Lavinia and thirteen-year-old Laura were valued at \$1,800 with a premium of \$40.25 at the rate of 2.25 percent. One wonders if the terms of their policies had anything to do with their ability to give birth. The younger Lavinia had a five-year policy, while Laura's was for one year.

What do these policies teach us about enslaved people's monetary values? They tell us that enslavers capitalized on and thought about the deaths of their enslaved from the moment they were eligible to produce labor in industrial and plantation settings. They also tell us that valuable younger enslaved people had policies and premiums similar to those in their twenties, suggesting that the valuation of black bodies was a well-thought-out enterprise. Enslavers knew that the majority of their wealth was tied up in the lives of enslaved people and protected their wealth through insurance.[95]

Burial

In addition to separation by sale, some of the most memorable moments in enslaved people's lives were the deaths of their loved ones. Solomon Bayley, mentioned earlier, who went to his son's auction, was present at the deaths of his daughters Margaret and Leah. His two daughters died in 1821, just a few months apart—Margaret at age twenty-four in March, and Leah at age twenty-one in July. Bayley recalled that Margaret "bade us farewell, and looked as if she felt assurance and peace that destroyed the fear of death." In her last words, earnestly charged us to "meet her in heaven."[96] Leah, in her last moments, compared her suffering to that of Jesus and said, "I never shall say I suffer too much." Like her sister who had died a few months before, Leah "held out her hand, and with much composure of mind bade us farewell, as if she was only going for a short walk, and to return."[97] Just as today, the loss of a child is traumatic for any parent, yet Bayley shared these memories in an effort to celebrate their lives. We do not know how or where Margaret and Leah were laid to rest, and though the stories of their deaths end here, that was not the case for all enslaved people.

As mentioned earlier, some enslaved people received decent burials in plantation or city cemeteries. At Laurel Grove in Savannah, Georgia, 191 enslaved people between the ages of eleven and twenty-two received burials.

Most were laid to rest by their enslavers after suffering scarlet fever, typhoid fever, or yellow fever; a host of other illnesses such as consumption, pneumonia, syphilis, bronchitis, lockjaw, whooping cough, and pleurisy also claimed lives. Approximately fifteen different local physicians visited and treated some of them before their passing. This suggests that their lives had some value, as enslavers paid medical fees to white physicians for treating them. They also had to pay for burial expenses at the cemetery, further supporting the idea that these individuals were valued not only for their productive labor, but also perhaps for their humanness. Fourteen-year-old Mary Ann likely suffered breast cancer, as a Dr. Fish noted she had a tumor in her breast that could not be treated. A larger number of women, such as Maria (sixteen), Lavinia (seventeen), Maria Watts (eighteen), Julia (nineteen), Keziah (nineteen), Sue (twenty), Louisa (twenty-one), Katy (twenty-two), and Helena (twenty-two), died after giving birth. Many of their infants also died within days. For those who died under suspicion, like Cato (fifteen), a coroner's inquest took place to determine the events and perhaps the culprit.

•   •   •

If young enslaved people did not understand their commodification, those who experienced this humiliation knew very well that their bodies were treated as a movable form of property; by this age, they knew they were chattel. Between the ages of eleven and twenty-two, they experienced a deep understanding of soul value against the backdrop of market and appraised values. Some enslaved people knew in their core that they were not meant to be enslaved. They rejected the external devaluation experiences on the auction block and left slavery by escaping to Canada. Others, like the Bayley women, died enslaved yet expressed freedom of the soul as they looked toward the afterlife with grace and peace. Yet, as enslaved people aged and experienced more separation, they also acted out against their commodification through various forms of resistance. And when they did, many, like Celia, were executed. Upon their executions, their ghost values were assessed, and the financial transactions on their bodies continued. But what about their souls? The next chapter addresses the radical actions of some well-known enslaved people and the unlikely postmortem journeys of their bodies.

CHAPTER 4

Midlife and Older Adulthood

AVERAGE APPRAISED VALUES:
FEMALES: $528 [$15,515 IN 2014]
MALES: $747 [$21,950 IN 2014]

AVERAGE SALE VALUES:
FEMALES: $494 [$14,497 IN 2014]
MALES: $792 [$23,266 IN 2014]

> *I am here loaded with chains, and willing to suffer the fate that awaits me.*
>
> —Attributed to Nat Turner, 1831[1]

> *We shall meet in Heaven, where we shall not be parted by the demands of the cruel and unjust monster Slavery.*
>
> —John Copeland, 1859[2]

Sometime in the early 1830s, a middle-aged Virginia woman named Fannie reluctantly stepped up to the auction block. As she approached the platform, however, she refused to stand. Instead, she kneeled down in prayer. Melissa, her two-year-old daughter, was in her arms, and her young son, Gilbert, stood nearby suppressing his tears. Under her breath, she murmured, "Trust in the Lord, And you'll overcome, Somehow, Somewhere, Someday!" These had been the final words of Nat Turner, who some believe was her husband. He had shared this prayer with his congregation on the eve of the Southampton rebellion. Now, nearly two months after his execution, the auctioneer commenced the bidding process for Fannie and her daughter. Her son would be sold separately. Fannie had already endured the hanging and decapitation of her husband and several others involved in the rebellion, and afterward, she too was allegedly "tortured under the lash." Now, Fannie would be separated from her young son, knowing she was unlikely to see him again.[3]

"Hear ye, hear ye, hear ye! One healthy young N—— woman and baby for sale! Who'll give me fifty?" the auctioneer exclaimed. The younger child was to stay with Fannie, perhaps because she was too young for field and house labor. Mothers and their young children sometimes escaped separation, that is, until they reached a "workable" age like Gilbert and became more valuable on their own. Continuing in a rhythmic cadence, the auctioneer asked, "Who'll give me seventy-five? Who'll give me one hundred?" The distraught middle-aged mother and her children knew that their lives were on the brink of yet another devastating change. Because she was in her prime years, between the ages of twenty-three and thirty-nine, Fannie represented a valuable labor source that had the ability to procreate. Middle-aged enslaved people often held their highest monetary values during these years, and some appeared in documents as "prime hands," "A1 Prime," or a "full hand." We do not know which classification Fannie had, but we know that she was "SOLD to Planter Yarborough of Alabama for one hundred and twenty-five dollars!"[4] Within the span of just a few minutes, Fannie and Melissa were sold and separated from Gilbert.

Fannie, Melissa, and Gilbert had little control over their fate; this auction represented a pivotal moment in their lives. Fannie was in her midtwenties and had witnessed the harsh and inhumane treatment of many enslaved people over the years. Her children had too, and even though they were not old enough to fully process the recent events, they could tell by their mother's anguish that the outcome would not be good.

She tried to disrupt the sale by covering her baby girl, protecting her from the "biting cold," and the gaze of potential buyers. Remaining on her knees in prayer, Fannie expressed the value of her soul to her children. She kept her eyes on Gilbert, perhaps so that he could read her lips leaving an important message with him. She wanted him to trust the spirit of God to guide and direct him in her absence. Melissa valued her soul and taught her children to do the same. Historian Walter Johnson reminds us that many enslaved people did all they could to negotiate their sales. Their interference is evidence of their attempt to control their fate and an expression of their soul value.[5]

The Turner family had lived in and around Southampton County, Virginia, for their entire lives, until several members were sold in the aftermath of the Southampton rebellion. White people's fears were realized when Turner led one of the largest uprisings in US history, in 1831. During the two-day raid, approximately fifty-five to sixty whites were killed, including men, women, and children.

Turner's execution, for the purposes of this study, provides a context for examining the deaths and postmortem values, among other things, of middle-aged enslaved people and free blacks between ages twenty-three and thirty-nine. When an enslaved person died, some enslavers received compensation for their "loss" after they petitioned the state or by way of insurance policies. Direct descendants and family members of the deceased experienced loss, but did not receive financial support. I look to the aftermath of Turner rebellion as one of two case studies for exploring the ways in which enslaved bodies continued to hold economic value after death. The second case study examines enslaved and free blacks who were executed after participating in John Brown's raid at Harpers Ferry, Virginia (now West Virginia), in 1859. Like the descendants of Turner, those involved in this uprising were denied burial rights, and their loved ones were denied financial compensation. However, as we shall see, one fortunate soul was reinterred at the end of the nineteenth century.

This chapter examines the life and death of enslaved and free blacks in years that marked peak productivity in the fields, fertility, and the onset of aging—the ages of twenty-three to thirty-nine. In this stage of life, enslaved people had reached adulthood and often understood their financial value. They likely had already developed a sense of their own mortality and had experienced grief. But how did enslaved and free black families honor their deceased relatives when their bodies were not properly laid to rest? I argue that postmortem commodification disrupted the process of spiritual regeneration, renewal, and resurrection. Although we cannot fully know how or if the deceased communicate with us, we can study their postmortem journeys. The lives of Turner and others indicate that the value of black bodies in the mid-nineteenth century extended beyond the grave.

MIDLIFE AND OLDER ADULTS' UNDERSTANDINGS OF LIFE AND DEATH

Rather than ending discussions of their lives at the point of death, as most history books do, this study analyzes the monetary value placed on deceased leaders and other blacks by tracing the afterlives of their bodies. In afterlife, formerly enslaved people became cadavers commodified to extend their treatment as property beyond life. Using corpses of former human property for medical research caused families to be separated even in postmortem spaces. The denial and/or disruption of black burial rituals removed any hope of unity in an imagined afterlife, because the cadaver represented a human without a soul. Some enslaved people left testimonies about their conception of an afterlife.

The previous chapter indicated that some believed that when a person died, the soul left the body and served as an ancestor spirit until it was later reborn. Yet those with financial claims to the deceased body, such as enslavers and medical practitioners, maximized their investment in enslaved people while they were living and after they died. Enslavers literally found ways to profit from the institution of slavery years after those they held in bondage took their last breath. How do we make sense of such practices? A reconsideration of the enslaved life cycle and the meaning of life and death are good starting points. We must also consider the discourse on phrenology and the significance of an underground trade in bodies, body parts, and souvenirs from public executions.

What follows is a discussion of life and death, one mirroring the other. During their lives, enslaved people were separated, sold, and traded to new communities. In death, some of their cadavers were also separated as a result of mob violence following public executions. We have no way of knowing how common this was, but we can acknowledge that it happened. Some of their body parts were cut off, burned, and/or torn apart and kept as relics commemorating the event. These "souvenirs" traveled from one home to another and were passed down through many generations. The developing medical profession also fueled the traffic and shipment of cadavers to medical schools throughout the United States. Here, corpses were separated and torn apart through anatomical dissection. In life and in death, enslaved people were separated, traded, and forced to travel.

Relatives such as Fannie and her children were often denied the right to bury their loved ones, ensuring separation beyond death. Denying a person proper burial rites extended the exploitation of slavery to postmortem spaces that are difficult to excavate because we do not have direct testimony from the deceased beyond visions, dreams, and spiritual messages that those living believe come from the dead. This type of evidence cannot be qualified or quantified. But, if we start with the executions and explore the postmortem journeys of those bodies, the trajectories of commodification beyond the moment of death become quite clear.

VALUATION OF OLDER ADULTS IN LIFE

The monetary value of enslaved men and women in the midlife and adulthood years (defined here as ages twenty-three to thirty-nine) is far more complex than that of younger enslaved people. These years marked the beginning of a decline in value that started around age twenty-six for females and the early thirties for males. However, before their market decrease, enslaved men and women firmly understood their dual valuation as people and property; some likely knew they held economic value beyond death. Many fell victim to breeding, as enslavers tried to maximize the remaining years of their fertility. Others, like Fannie and her children, experienced separation and sale. Some enslaved people in this age range chose to reject the institution and participated in rebellions in the hope of gaining their freedom through death. They did not know that their enslavement would continue nonetheless. A few joined interracial movements, consisting of enslaved and free rebels, and planned attacks on white enslavers. No matter their choices, or the realities imposed upon them, midlife adults faced dehumanizing consequences for their actions and behaviors during life and after death.

By appraising the individual values of men and women, we learn that the fiscal value gap between the sexes began to widen during this stage of life. The divergence is likely due to the fact that women become less fertile as they mature and men reach a peak level of strength during these years. Enslaved people were considered "prime" in this age range, meaning their maximum earning potential hit its highest mark. According to historian U. B. Phillips, after the ages of thirty for field hands and thirty-five for skilled laborers, the monetary value of enslaved people declined.[6]

Commodification Data for Older Adults

Examining a sample of 17,652 enslaved values from nine Southern states between 1771 and 1865, we learn that the average appraised values for women
and men ages twenty-three to thirty-nine were, respectively, $528 and $747.
Looking specifically at these appraisals for what I consider middle-aged
people, it is clear from extant evidence that their enslavers assigned their
values as a projected value for the amount of work they would do over the
course of their lives. Such appraisals were customary, and enslaved people knew that their monetary values were constantly shifting, particularly
when they were sold at the market.

Andrew Boone from North Carolina "saw a lot of slaves sold on de
auction block." The process was demoralizing: "Dey would strip 'em stark
naked" and if they were "scarred up or whaled an' welted," they were considered a "bad n——r an' did not bring much." However, if they had no scars,
they brought "a good price."[7] Gender had a definite impact on the average
market value for enslaved people in this age range. Men sold for an average of $792 and women went for about $300 less, selling for $494. Men
with labor skills, such as artisans, blacksmiths, coopers, and engineers, for
example, commanded appraisal values over $1,100.[8] Enslaved people's rec-
ollections match these valuations. "Men or mechanics were worth from 12
to 1300 dollars," one formerly enslaved person recalled, "and boys 8 and 9
years old, 5 and 6 hundred dollars." In retrospect, "They had to be a mighty
heavy man to be worth that much."[9]

Cane Brake Plantation Patterns of Valuation

Enslavers constantly appraised their laborers' values and kept track of
changes resulting from life events, such as pregnancy and aging. On Cane
Brake Plantation, for example, Dr. James Carson evaluated his enslaved
workforce at the beginning and end of the year, as previously mentioned.
Tracing the lives of approximately 150 enslaved laborers from 1856 to 1858
provides further clarity to valuation in life.[10] In 1856, 15 percent of his enslaved laborers were between the ages of twenty-three and thirty-nine.
This group included ten females and fourteen males. Their appraised values at the beginning of the year ranged between $400 and upward of $800.
Most of their values remained the same at the end of the year, with the

exception of thirty-six-year-old Sarah, whose value increased from $400 to $450 in 1856. By 1858, her value increased again to $500 and continued to increase well into her late thirties. What did her increased value indicate? For the three years, we have records showing that Sarah was raising a young child named Lucy. By 1858, Sarah's daughter Lucy was four years old, meaning that she was almost at an age when she could work on small labor tasks. Given that she had an older toddler, Sarah's appraisal value probably increased when she stopped nursing and the chances of infant mortality diminished (around age five).

Carson's recordkeeping shows that he made clear distinctions between males and females. Sometimes he placed an "x" by the names of women who were pregnant, about to give birth, or nursing. Dorcas, Sarepta, and Annette gave birth to children between 1856 and 1858; Annette was thirty-two years old at the time, showing that the childbearing years for some women extended into their thirties. As with Sarah, Annette's appraisal value increased after she gave birth, from $500 in 1857 to $600 in 1858, when she appears in the plantation record book with a two-month-old infant below her name. Carson consistently valued males at approximately $200 more than females, which mirrors the market and appraisal patterns discussed earlier. Sam, however, was a man whose value decreased from $700 to $600. At age thirty, he would still have been considered prime, but, for some reason, at the end of 1856, his value dropped by $100. In 1857, he appears on the list with a $600 value that remains the same throughout that year, but in 1858, his value increased once again to $700. It is difficult to know why Sam's appraisal value shifted; he could have been injured, taken ill, or resisted enslavement; for some reason, Carson felt the need to document his fluctuating value.[11]

VALUATION OF OLDER ADULTS IN DEATH AND GHOST VALUES

No matter how the enslaved were valued in life, their postmortem values generated much attention and debate. Not all enslaved people experienced postmortem commodification, but from those who did, we can learn a great deal about their ghost values. As discussed, at every point and every stage of their lives, enslaved people had an appraised value, a suggested price tag for their bodies. They also had a value in death. The bodies of deceased adults were evaluated and appraised in an evolving market, one that was taking shape simultaneously with the professionalization of medicine. Medical students interested in human anatomy needed cadavers, and deceased enslaved people proved to be an invaluable resource for this clandestine market. One place where students knew they could acquire subjects for dissection was at the gallows of deceased blacks. Looking at public executions of enslaved people—and the swift actions of Northern *and* Southern medical students to exhume or snatch the bodies—we can see the domestic cadaver trade taking shape and the growing importance of ghost values.

Enslavers frequently profited from the death of their human property through legal measures and were often regarded as "the arbiter of life and death."[12] In 1705, the Virginia Court of Oyer and Terminer (a special court for slave felonies and other cases) set a precedent for compensation. By doing so, the justice system enabled enslavers to recover their human property loss, even if only for a fraction of their total value. This practice encouraged "owners not to cover up felonies in order to retain—or to sell away privately—a particularly valuable laborer."[13] In 1748, the Commonwealth of Virginia developed "An Act Directing the Trial of Slaves Committing Capital Crime," which stipulated that convicted enslaved people would be examined by the commissioners of the trial, who "put a valuation in money upon the slave" so that the enslaver would be able to "make suitable allowance" on the enslaved person's economic value. Thus, "the value of the slave executed shall be paid by the public."[14] Clearly, enslavers relied on the justice system to protect and reimburse them for their property loss. However, establishing monetary values for executed felons was not new to Atlantic world history. Enslavers in the seventeenth and eighteenth centuries in the British Caribbean also turned to the courts to recover partial or full value of executed enslaved people. Planters in the American South simply followed suit by adopting similar practices.[15]

What happened when enslaved and free black "criminals" died? Did the community also compensate black families? How did they exercise funerary rituals without possession of their relatives' bodies? These questions also apply to African Americans who were not "criminals." Such inquiries lead to a discussion of postmortem desecration *as a form of sale.* When the remains of deceased blacks (enslaved or free) were not returned to their families for proper burial, their bodies were still very much part of a viable market that continued to separate communities. Anatomical research disrupted many postmortem journeys and, like Fannie, Nat, and their children, even in death, these families would not be reunited and buried together. Their only hope was that they would meet again in heaven.

Modern anatomical research began in fifteenth-century Europe and arrived in the American colonies in the eighteenth century with physicians who trained in England, France, Germany, Italy, and Scotland. Before any legal justification for dissection, there was a connection between criminality and "extra punishment beyond death."[16] Dissection in many cases was perceived as desecration and punishment. Thus, by 1796, federal legislation supported the practice of dissecting those convicted of murder, regardless of race. When Nat Turner and his followers went to the gallows, Virginia medical students were nearby to claim the bodies for their research. As historian Todd Savitt explains, they "made great use of black patients both living and dead."[17] In the commencement address at a Northern medical school in 1824, students were encouraged to learn from "actual dissections" because "the most important discoveries and improvements in medicine" came from this practice.[18] Focusing on the "immense benefits . . . they brought to mankind," antebellum medical education included anatomy and dissection, which continue to be important today.[19]

Nineteenth-century physicians typically instructed their medical students to begin dissections within twenty-four to forty-eight hours postmortem, before rigor mortis or the stiffening of a decaying body. Students often worked with their faculty members, local coroners, graveyard attendants, jailers, magistrates, and most notably, grave robbers (also known as sack-em-up men, night doctors, or resurrectionists) to procure corpses for the dissecting table. I will address this practice in a later chapter, but it is important to note that the collection and distribution of cadavers has been institutionalized since the early twentieth century. The cases outlined here show the complexities of postmortem ownership rights and rites, particularly in the case of enslaved and free black bodies. Medical values of black bodies appear in court records as well as account books of medical schools, while the value of the body to families of the deceased was much different. Family members could not put a price tag on their loved ones, leaving their valuation infinite. Thus, the right to a corpse and the rite to bury clashed. Bodies used for medical dissection did not carry the same meaning as those bodies defiled for revenge in the aftermath of rebellions.

American residents, like those in many other slaveholding regions worldwide, lived in terror of enslaved unrest. They knew about rebellions in other parts of the world and worried that uprisings could happen in their backyards. These fears came to pass on several occasions and are well documented by historians. From them, we learn that some planned revolts were foiled before the enslaved and free rebels could execute them; scholars refer to these as "conspiracies." Others occurred, and black and white lives were lost as a result. In the aftermath of the Southampton rebellion and John Brown's raid on Harpers Ferry, captured ringleaders and their followers faced public punishment via hangings at the gallows. Even after they died, the punishments continued, as their bodies were subjected to castration, decapitation, and skinning, among many other forms of postmortem brutality.

Mobs customarily defiled the bodies of former rebels. Some did so to further punish the corpse and to relieve their frustrations about the events that took place; enslavers wanted to set an example so that others would think twice about revolting. Mob violence in the wake of a slave rebellion allowed those angered by the loss of life to exercise their rage. These individuals simply wanted revenge for the loss of loved ones. In some cases, they expressed rage by transforming bodies into commodities, as when flesh was used to make wallets, change purses, book covers, and lampshades. These "memorabilia" represented tangible symbols to commemorate the way individuals enacted retribution on others.[20] Some enslavers sought financial reprisal in the form of payment for the loss of their property upon execution and were given reparations, loosely defined as making amends to persons who have been wronged, either financially or through other forms of compensation. Others, whether they owned enslaved people or not, purchased or stole postmortem souvenirs from enslaved people's bodies. As we will see, there was a market for specific body parts, including skulls, ears, and teeth. Like vultures on a carcass, enslavers extracted wealth from every part of an enslaved person's body.

The historical record offers only partial answers to the question of "postmortem values," the term I use interchangeably with "ghost values" to describe the fluctuation over time of economic values assigned to corpses after death and pegged to the legal processes following an execution.[21] Studying the high-profile execution of Nat Turner, as well as those of John A. Copeland, Shields Green, and Dangerfield Newby (the African Americans convicted and/or killed for participating in the raid at Harpers Ferry), illuminates the dynamic nature of postmortem monetary values. These executions also provide direct and indirect testimony just moments before the rebels entered the afterlife, where their bodies or body parts were once again commodified.[22]

Postmortem History of Nat Turner

Immediately following his execution, witnesses note that Turner's body was given to medical students (possibly from the University of Virginia or Winchester Medical School in Virginia) for dissection. Turner was beheaded and skinned, and reports indicate that the students and other bystanders who sought retribution "made grease of the flesh."[23] One bystander apparently had a "money purse made of his hide," and Turner's skull was turned over to the coroner for study. A local doctor possessed his skeleton "for many years"; at some point, it was "misplaced."[24] William "Buck" Mallory boasted about being the person who skinned Nat Turner. Nearly thirty years after the rebellion, while traveling through Petersburg, Virginia, he admitted to tanning Turner's "hide" and that "portions of it are now extant in the 'curiosity shops' of many residents in and about Southampton." He later remarked that he "would have skinned old John Brown if he could only have had the opportunity." This information appeared in numerous newspapers and in Mallory's obituary.[25] Turner's body parts held value to some—ghost values—and they were commodified and traded as a result.

Aside from a handful of scholarly accounts, Turner's biography ends at the gallows. His legacy does not typically include the story of his dismemberment. Most popular interpretations of him focus on his leadership in a major US slave rebellion, not what happened to his body after he was hanged. How does our remembrance of him change, knowing that he was dissected and that some of his body parts became souvenirs? For some, this knowledge might confirm that the spectacle of black death during slavery maintains continuity with the lynching, bodily desecration, and digital dismemberment of people such as Robert Charles (1900), Laura and J. B. Nelson (1911), Jesse Washington (1916), Emmett Till (1955), Malissa Williams and Timothy Russell (2012), Micheal Brown (2014), and countless others. The practice of bodily dismemberment was quite typical for convicted criminals once the ropes were cut from the gallows. Postmortem desecration happened in the Caribbean and South America, and in the United States.[26]

Although it might seem unusual to twenty-first-century readers that Nat Turner's skull and skeleton became part of a clandestine market in bodily remains, journalists, medical historians, and anthropologists all note the frequency of such traffic and provide important context to this discussion.[27] We know from nineteenth-century anatomy that, for physicians, the study of skeletons represented "the most common anatomical display" and that bones were an important part of understanding human anatomy.[28] At the time of Turner's death, Virginia had two medical schools in operation: the University of Virginia (UVA) Medical Department (established in 1825; first graduating class in 1828) and Winchester Medical School in the Virginia Valley (established in 1826). Hampden-Sydney College, organized in 1775, did not fully establish a medical department until 1838; today, it is known as the Virginia Commonwealth University Medical Center. At UVA, Dr. Robley Dunglison served as founding member of the medical faculty and professor of anatomy and medicine. Incomplete medical catalogues suggest that a "Dr. Johnston" served as a professor of anatomy in 1833, and there was a vacancy for the professor of medicine.[29] The establishment of such teaching facilities meant that there were medical students and trained physicians nearby who would have an interest in cadavers. Also, given that Virginia did not establish legal parameters for dissection until 1884, bodies were often procured through an underground market. According to one historian, Virginia had an ample supply of cadavers, more than "the rest of the nation owing to the South's large slave population." In Missouri, a statute granted dissections of enslaved people "with the consent of the owner."[30]

So it is no surprise that people would want to study Turner's body; there was a significant mania about race and medicine and a desire for postmortem "justice." His body, in particular, represented all that whites feared about enslaved people. As locals tried to make sense of the events of late August 1831, some wanted closure, and apparently hangings were not enough. Others, including Midwestern medical and Southampton residents, wanted to know if there was a physiological or biological rationale for Turner's actions. They fed their curiosity by studying his remains. Medical professionals competed with grieving white Southerners who wanted revenge on Turner and his followers.

We know that Dr. Dunglison relied on enslaved people to assist him with his work at UVA. He hired a man named Nelson to work "in his garden and stable," and then "Fanny Gillette Hern and her youngest child, and later her husband David Hern," as well as others whom he borrowed from Thomas Jefferson's family. Throughout Dunglison's tenure, he hired and organized enslaved people to work at the college, serving both his personal and professional needs. Around the time of the Turner events, the faculty petitioned to establish an anatomical hall for the medical school, and the university purchased Lewis Commodore for $580 in December 1831 to work with the medical equipment and keep the anatomical hall clean. Some believe that he "handled the cadavers" and was affectionately known as "Anatomical Lewis." If any medical professionals affiliated with UVA had obtained Turner's skeleton or skull, it is certainly possible that Dunglison and even Lewis were involved.[31]

Information about African American skeletons and fully intact bodies appears in the historical records of medical schools, but not all have the notoriety of Nat Turner. At Thomas Jefferson Medical College in Philadelphia, for example, the faculty gave Dr. Robert Frame, the demonstrator of anatomy, a receipt for "1 Splendid silver wired Human skeleton, a Negro aged 40 years." Suggesting familiarity, perhaps while the subject was alive, the faculty noted that "when living [he] stood 6 feet 4 inches high, [with a] round chest." Did they know him or was this description based on post-mortem measurements before dissection? We don't know the answer, nor do we know how they came to possess the skeleton, but we know that the medical staff admired the bones, describing them as "extremely white and beautiful."[32] For them, whiteness symbolized beauty and was only found underneath black skin. The ability to peel back the outer layers of black-ness through dissection and/or maceration (soaking in a liquid) allowed doctors to study black bodies literally from their core. As a result, some nineteenth-century physicians generally found "the bones of the negro be-ing harder, whiter, and containing more phosphate of lime than those of the white man," which is one explanation for extraordinarily white bones among black cadavers.[33] Someone successfully administered the process of bone setting, which involved removing the skin and detaching any excess tissue. This highly skilled practice began with maceration to soften the skin for as long as it took to putrefy, loosen, and dissolve "all the ligaments and soft parts." Using a "macerating vessel," once the body seemed ready, the skeleton was removed, washed, and dried. After the skin was peeled away, the bones were cleaned and sometimes bleached; the skeleton was then set to wires and placed on a stand. Sometimes the bones were painted, "corresponding with the muscles." Only a skilled practitioner who knew the human body, likely someone with medical training, could prepare a body for skeletal ar-ticulation.[34] Was Turner's body prepared in this way? More importantly, did he imagine that his remains would be in circulation long after his death?

Given this type of evidence, how do we make sense of Turner's post-mortem life? Was he subjected to the skilled process of bone setting de-scribed above, or was his torso ravaged by angry bystanders who sought revenge? We know that while Turner was still at large, Governor John Floyd issued a proclamation setting a $500 reward for his apprehension. This record contains the only physical description we have of Turner while living: Nat was "between 30 & 35 years old, 5 feet 6 or 8 inches high, weighs between 150 and 160 lbs." Governor Floyd also noted that Turner had a "rather bright complexion . . . large flat nose—large eyes—broad flat feet—rather knock-kneed." His gait was brisk, and he had "a large knot on one of the bones of his right arm, near the wrist, produced by a blow."[35]

As for the "Negro" skeleton purchased by the Jefferson Medical College, it was clear that people knew the man before death, just as we also have a description of Turner after death. Expanding our conception of life cycles to postmortem spaces allows us to recover a *second* description of Turner, one that includes his decapitated skull. We also know a good deal about his geographic movement during the uprising, while he was in hiding, and ironically, after his execution. But most people do not think about bodies after death. We assume they are laid to rest or experience burial rituals satisfactory to the surviving family in accordance with the deceased's wishes. However, Turner's decapitated skull took on a new life after the execution; his head traveled in a different direction from the rest of his body or body parts.

Turner's skull became part of a postmortem traffic in crania that coincided with the development of the study of human anatomy in the United States. Egyptologist George Robbins Gliddon and craniologist Samuel Morton were two key figures in a skull trade that paid thousands of dollars during the nineteenth century to purchase and ship skulls from Egypt, where Gliddon collected them, to Philadelphia, where Morton studied them.[36] Similar to domestic traders like Isaac Franklin and John Armfield, who trafficked in human chattel from Alexandria, Virginia, to Natchez, Mississippi, Gliddon and Morton created a system of buying and selling skulls across the Atlantic.[37] Morton had a team that he sent out to collect the heads of executed criminals, at the gallows and in hospitals and jails. He used international contacts and negotiated the purchase price, often bartering to keep his costs low.[38] In one case in this elaborate trade network, Gliddon paid a wage of $7.50 to Egyptians who raided Nubian cemeteries. They worked under a makeshift insurance policy to cover the risks in the event they were detected. One of his hired gravediggers charged an extra twenty-five-dollar premium. After the police discovered some of Gliddon's workers, he paid fees amounting to $83.65. There were several people in his operation: doctors, merchants, customs agents, and ship captains. Morton and Gliddon's international trade in skulls stretched across more than three thousand miles and several continents. At the time of his death in 1851, Morton had in his possession nearly one thousand skulls divided by race.[39]

When Gliddon left Egypt in 1841, he had delivered more than a hundred skulls to his colleague in Pennsylvania. As a result, Morton developed the largest collection of human and animal skulls in the world. Morton used the skulls to study cranial capacity by taking measurements and making judgments about racial disparities. Along with a large cohort of physicians, he developed charts to map the skull shape and volume.[40] One widespread belief was that the larger the brain, the higher intellectual capability. Morton published his findings in the now famous *Crania Americana* (1839) so the world could see his collection, currently held at the University of Pennsylvania.[41] This was the context in which to justify the curiosity about skulls, including Nat Turner's. Morton likely never saw Turner, dead or alive. However, having Turner's measurements confirms that local doctors or mob vigilantes were probably curious about Turner's brain size and wanted to know how his skull compared to others.

Turner's skull was likely trafficked through a domestic trade that similarly brought his remains through multiple states and facilities, where it was either displayed or examined. Nearly seventy years after his execution, at the turn of the twentieth century, many people still alive claimed they had seen Turner's skull. They noted that it "was very peculiarly shaped, resembling the head of a sheep and at least three-quarters of an inch thick."[42] They seemed to want to find something different about Turner, something that would explain his behavior and justify their view of him as a monster. The fact that we have measurements suggests that someone, likely medical students, studied Turner's remains. A nineteenth-century physician noted that frontal views of "Negro skulls" appear "compressed" compared to European ones.[43] We also have evidence of skulls in transit, as the following 1838 advertisement placed in the Natchez, Mississippi, newspaper *Daily Free Trader*, suggests:

Found.—A NEGRO'S HEAD WAS PICKED UP ON THE RAIL-ROAD YESTERDAY, WHICH THE OWNER CAN HAVE BY CALLING AT THIS OFFICE AND PAYING FOR THE ADVERTISEMENT.[44]

That a newspaper advertised finding an African American skull "on the rail-road" confirms the notion that black body parts were in transit and that this was a regular occurrence. Racial science, a burgeoning discipline, piqued researchers' curiosities about the differences among various groups of people and provides a reason for Turner's skull to travel from Virginia to North Carolina, and then to the Midwest states of Ohio and Indiana.

Identifying medical doctors, schools, museum professionals, and anatomists who may have been in contact with Turner's skull is difficult. Dr. James Massenburg, one of the presiding justices at Turner's trial, had Turner's skeleton in his possession "for many years," while R. S. Barham's father claimed he "owned a money purse made of his hide." His skin was likely boiled off in Virginia, possibly by medical students and a local doctor who prepared his skeletal remains before they were sent to other physicians, including Dr. Leander Firestone of the College of Wooster, in Ohio.

Thirty-four years later in 1866, Firestone allegedly used Turner's skull in his anatomy classes. This college was almost six hundred miles away from the site of the rebellion, indicating that Turner's skull traveled over the Shenandoah Mountains, northwest across two or three state lines, depending on the trade route. Those who had the opportunity to study it recall the following engraving on Turner's skull: "This is the skull of Nat Turner, A Negro who led an unsuccessful revolt against his Owners in 1831."[45] This inscription infers that the Southampton rebellion was an act that involved one enslaved person (Turner) against his "owners," not the system. Deeming this act as "unsuccessful" reflects a narrative that the planter class supported. Was this an unsuccessful revolt? How does one define success? For some, thwarting the system of slavery, even if for one or two days, represented widespread success.

Despite differences in opinions and propaganda, evidence suggests that hundreds of black lives were taken in the aftermath of the Southampton rebellion. The *Liberator*, the antislavery newspaper published by white abolitionist William Lloyd Garrison, reported that "upwards of one hundred slaves [were] slaughtered by a mob." The writer described these violent acts: "noses and ears" were cut off, "the flesh of their cheeks cut out," and "their jaws broken." Some were even set up as shooting targets, while others were burned with "red hot irons." One man had his hamstrings and head cut off, and his head "spiked" to "the whipping post." Despite such graphic details, historians are still debating the number of dead and tortured. The reports also suggest that enslavers petitioned the legislature for compensation because their human property did not receive a fair trial, leaving them without specific enslaved laborers.[46]

The recent work of one scholar questions the loss of black life through the language of "atrocities," stating that only confirmed documentary evidence should be considered. Is there room for oral tradition? It certainly was accepted in the work of William Sidney Drewry, a white descendant who interviewed Southampton residents living at the time of the rebellion. This raises the questions: Can black descendants of Fannie, Melissa, and Gilbert weigh in on these numbers and experiences? What about formerly enslaved people from all over the United States and Canada who faced backlash in the aftermath? Harriet Jacobs had a lot to say about the impact of this uprising. Even though she lived sixty-seven miles away, she witnessed whites (enslavers and non-enslavers alike), whom she referred to as a "troop of deamons [sic]," muster up and raid the cabins of enslaved and free blacks. She described the terror and torture blacks experienced for weeks: "Every where men, women, and children were whipped till the blood stood in puddles at their feet." She recalled that "some received five hundred lashes; others were tied hands and feet, and tortured with a bucking paddle, which blisters the skin terribly." White men sexually assaulted some black women; their husbands were whipped for "telling lies" about it afterward. Jacobs believed that this went on for more than two weeks and only calmed down after Turner was captured.[47]

It is difficult to know how many innocent people lost their lives, and historians have not reached a consensus on the number. We know that census records often undercounted African Americans, so the number of black lives lost post-rebellion may have also been grossly underestimated. This is especially true if we only count those who made it to extant records in archives. If enslaved people received monetary values at death, and some of their enslavers were compensated for the loss of life, as this study suggests, then it is quite possible that free blacks killed in the aftermath might not be a part of the "documented atrocities." We cannot always provide "verifiable details" to historical memories passed down through generations, as is the case in any family's history, but we should not rely solely on the records of white descendants.[48]

In the aftermath of the Southampton rebellion, legislation in Virginia and beyond was enacted to control African Americans' movement. This alone is evidence supporting the disruption created by the uprising. To be sure, the individual white families whose relatives were killed in the events of August 1831 went on with their lives and continued to own enslaved people. Many of them prospered, "returning to stability in 1834 and 1835."[49] Yet, whites all over the South lived with the constant fear of rebellion, just as enslaved families lived in fear of separation. The enslaved and free, white and black, remained chained to an institution that damaged relations between these groups. This tension continues today and is evident in the movement #BlackLivesMatter. In the case of the enslaved, perhaps the hashtag should be #BlackBodiesMatter.

As for Turner, on the eve of his execution, he allegedly said, "I am here loaded with chains, and willing to suffer the fate that awaits me."[50] This is the only evidence of him speaking back, a voice from the soon-to-be deceased, ready to meet his maker. These words give us space to pause and think about how Turner's descendants would like him to be remembered. What inscription would they write on his tombstone? Perhaps it would incorporate the words spoken in his last sermon. Maybe the epitaph would describe him as a son, brother, husband, and father, someone more important to others than the demeaning inscription on his skull or the references historians suggest.

The act of inscribing something identifies and places an object or person in historical context. Just as we inscribe wedding rings, tombstones, and other important objects today, the field of medicine used inscriptions and engraving as a way to educate. Practical anatomy at the time encouraged students to make inscriptions on the bodies of those whom they dissected. At Jefferson Medical College, for example, students in the 1830s traditionally prepared an anatomical specimen and left it at the college museum "as a memorial to their connection to their Alma Mater." According to this tradition, a student would inscribe his "name and date . . . on the specimen" to physically and permanently link him to the university and deceased body.[51] It allowed him to leave his mark and display his work for future students. In the late nineteenth and early twentieth centuries, medical students also took photos with cadavers to commemorate dissection.[52]

We have no way to know how many medical students or others had the opportunity to study or handle Turner's remains. Oral histories of Turner's descendants, however, confirm that Turner believed enslaved people had to "purchase their freedom with their own blood."[53] The question remains then, did Turner feel free at the time of his death? Is his soul at rest now? The poet Robert Hayden allows us to imagine Turner's thoughts and feelings in "The Ballad of Nat Turner":

> And there were angels, their faces hidden
>   from me, angels at war
> with one another, angels in dazzling
>   combat. And oh the splendor,
>
> The fearful splendor of that warring.
>   Hide me, I cried to rock and bramble.
> Hide me, the rock, the bramble cried . . .
>   How tell you of that holy battle?

In the space of darkness, Hayden allows us to imagine Turner's thoughts as he encounters "a sleep heavy as death. And when I awoke at last free."[54]

For many, death is freedom. It relieves the soul from earthly suffering and gives way to an afterlife that they believe contains peace and freedom. Many enslaved people looked to an afterlife in heaven to survive the harsh realities of their mortal lives. In their religious reflections, some explained that God's mercy lifted them up. "My soul began singing," one formerly enslaved person recalled, "and I was told that I was one of the elected children and that I would live as long as God lives." This person took pride in knowing that "another home" exists, "a house not made with human hands." The home was a "building . . . way back in eternal glory," and because "I came from heaven . . . to heaven I am now returning."[55]

Turner also had visions and a strong belief in an afterlife. On several occasions, he made references to things told to him from the heavens or "figures I had seen before in the heavens." Turner believed that "divine inspiration" directed him before he was born, while fasting and praying kept his focus during life under the yoke of slavery. Yet, when the spirit spoke to him, he knew he was "ordained for some great purpose in the hands of the Almighty."[56] Thus, we should consider his words at the end of his earthly life to mean that he felt called for a special purpose, just as the unnamed enslaved person described earlier looked forward to returning to heaven. Even in his sentencing, Jeremiah Cobb Esq., one of the appointed justices of the peace, told Turner, "Your only hope must be in another world." Turner died on November 11, 1831. Perhaps his body parts are still in circulation. The most recent account of Turner's skull appeared ten years ago, suggesting that the labeled skull was an artifact ready for display at an unconfirmed museum, just as was customary in the nineteenth century.[57]

Aside from Turner's postmortem trafficking, we learn much about the commodification of enslaved bodies in life and death through the monetary values placed upon Turner's body. At his death, the court valued him at $375 (converted into 1860 dollars and controlled for inflation, his value was $360, which is equivalent to $10,200 in 2014), but the Commonwealth of Virginia paid the estate of Putnam Moore, Turner's enslaver, $375 upon Turner's execution.[58] This meant that *deceased* enslavers (killed in the rebellion) and their estates received compensation for the death of their human chattel. Turner's economic value makes clear, however, that his body had more financial value alive than dead.[59] Before his apprehension, rewards for him ranged from $500 to $1,100.[60] A typical prime hand between the ages of twenty-three and thirty-nine was worth close to $750. Why was Turner's value lower? First, no one likely wanted a rebel on their plantation, so his fiscal value while still at large was lower than his postmortem value. Second, the state may have put limitations on the total cost of executions and compensation.

Turner did not die alone. Many members of the black community lost their lives in the aftermath of the rebellion.[61] Writing nearly thirty years postrebellion, Thomas Wentworth Higginson commented on the reign of terror that swept through the South afterward. He noted that whites turned to the courts for retribution: "Petition after petition was subsequently presented to the legislature, asking compensation for slaves thus assassinated without trial." He relayed that "men were tortured to death, burned, maimed, and subjected to nameless atrocities."[62] Enslavers turned to the courts and filed petitions just as they would have done if their human property was executed or murdered. Such practices had been common prior to the Southampton rebellion.

Historical Precedents for Compensation

Southampton residents and Southerners in other states sought compensation for their human property in the aftermath of the Turner rebellion. For example, enslaver Robert Cunningham of Abbeville, South Carolina, sought reimbursement for the death of Ned, "who was unfortunately implicated in the late attempt to raise and insurrection." Thus, according to the "laws of the state," Cunningham believed that he would suffer without Ned's services and that his family would "experience considerable injury by the loss of the said negro at least to the amount of his value, which is not less than four hundred and fifty, or five hundred dollars."[63] Enslaver G. S. McLane of Charleston sought compensation for Glascow, who was charged with attempted poisoning, but he was willing to accept reimbursement that fluctuated by $50 dollars. The state executed Glascow for the crime and confirmed that "the facts in the foregoing petition are true," granting McLane "the value of the negro Glascow at two hundred pounds current money."[64] In Louisiana, abolitionist Theodore Dwight Weld found that if an enslaved person was *maimed and disabled*, and "rendered unable to work," the individual responsible for "maiming, shall pay the master the appraised value of the slave before the injury."[65]

Even the Creek Nation established legislation related to death and enslaved people's prices. In January 1825, the "Laws of the Muscogee Nation" stated, "If a negro kill an Indian the negro shall suffer death and if an Indian kill a negro he shall pay the owner the value. If person [is] not able to pay the value [he] shall suffer death."[66] The historical record reveals many instances of enslavers receiving compensation for the death of their human property. Such actions confirm the value by which human beings were appraised as property, and that appraisal was contested or confirmed, often through legal measures.

Despite the unrest in the aftermath of the Southampton rebellion, nine white males petitioned the court in nearby Buckingham County not to grant enslavers compensation for murdered enslaved people because they believed it would financially strain small enslavers or non-slaveholding whites. First, they worried that southwestern slave traders would not purchase from them, creating an excess of enslaved people that wealthy owners would purchase, leaving small enslavers or non-slaveholders at a financial loss. Next they feared that this would drain the white population, as large planters would move to other areas with their excess of enslaved people, and small or non-slaveholding whites would leave in order to avoid a black majority ultimately challenging their subsistence farming. Drawing upon statements made by President Thomas Jefferson, these petitioners did not support compensation, perhaps because they knew that they had to pay for it and that the system was designed to help enslavers. For them, colonization by sending freed or excess enslaved people to Liberia or Sierra Leone, West Africa, was a better solution. Given that the price of newborns was as low as $12.50, they felt that few enslavers would object to this plan.[67]

In most slave states, including Virginia, countless enslavers, large and small, filed petitions for recompense when their enslaved property died at the hand of the state, and sometimes for a host of other reasons like injury or disability.[68] Before executions, the enslaved were appraised for their value, so that the enslavers would receive compensation for their "loss." Such compensation was also common practice in the Caribbean.[69] After their human property was appraised, enslavers received payment to compensate for their property loss. Planters and farmers throughout the South filed petitions despite the particularities of colonial or state legislation. Even though few scholars have written on this topic, we know that in the late colonial period, all of the colonies, except those in New England, had some sort of compensation system. Likewise, for regions south of Delaware, compensation came from "public monies."[70] In colonial North Carolina, the law allowed compensation on three conditions: for enslaved people who were executed criminals, for enslaved people who died as a result of corporal punishment, or for enslaved people who died in the act of committing a crime. Once one of these conditions was met, the court "set the monetary value of the slave." If the enslaved person died in the process, "the county court evaluated the deceased slaves," and in all cases, the monetary values "had to be approved by the Committee of Claims [both houses of the legislature]."[71] The colony also set maximum figures on monies paid in order to avoid dishonest enslavers who gambled with the lives of their human property, seeking compensation so they could purchase a new, perhaps younger, enslaved person. In 1758, colonial officials also decided that castration could substitute for execution "in certain cases."[72] Thus, by the late eighteenth century, well before Turner faced the gallows, some colonies had set precedents for mutilation before and after death.

However, substituting castration for the gallows represented a gendered response that excluded women runaways and rebels. We know from the Southampton rebellion that women were beaten and raped; one woman named Lucy was hanged. But what does the historical record reveal about gendered rates of compensation?

Enslaved women participated in rebellions in both covert and overt ways. They were present at Southampton, testifying in court and aiding fugitives and even plantation mistresses.[73] The names of enslaved women also filled the pages of local newspapers, as bounties were placed on their lives to cover the cost to return them. The well-known story of North Carolina enslaved woman Harriet Jacobs, who published her narrative in the 1860s after a successful escape to the North, is an example of such a situation. Jacobs's enslaver made several trips to the North trying to find her, after placing a $300 bounty for her return.[74] She, too, made her escape during the middle years of her life and freed herself by age twenty-nine.[75] Newspaper advertisements, travel expenses, and bounties meant that enslavers valued the work of women, and they were willing to pay for their return. There is more evidence about runaway women in advertisements than in the extant compensation petitions.[76] Therefore, when legislation excluded their punishment, and castration increasingly became the punishment for men, what was substituted to punish enslaved women? Answering this question involves an examination of enslaved women's executions, as well as a discussion of life insurance policies.

Bodies of Enslaved Women

Like Turner and his followers, enslaved women resisted their enslavement and were also sent to the gallows. For example, Jane Elkins, an enslaved woman from Dallas County, Texas, the first woman executed in the state, went to the gallows for murder on May 27, 1853. Her enslaver had hired her out to care for the children of a widower named Andrew C. Wisdom. At some point, Wisdom raped Elkins, and in her own defense, she took the law into her own hands. One night while Wisdom was asleep, she hit his head with an ax and killed him instantly. She spared his children. After her arrest and subsequent trial, the court valued her at $700 and found her guilty of murder. Judge John H. Reagan presided over the case and accepted the guilty verdict from D. R. Cameron, the jury's foreman. The statement read as follows, "We the jury find the defendant guilty of murder in the first degree. We further find that the defendant is a slave of the value of seven hundred dollars and that the owner . . . has done nothing to evade or defeat the execution of the law." When asked if she had anything to say, Elkins did not speak and was sent back to the jail to await her execution.[77] She had no legal defense team and was convicted by an all-white male jury.[78]

What were her last days like? Did she have a family who pled for her release and proper burial? Did she have a partner before being hired out and raped by Wisdom? Did she have children, like Fannie Turner? We do not have the answers to these questions, but we know that she was hanged and, as with other "criminals," her body was exhumed and dissected.

On the day Elkins was executed, "several hundred people" traveled to Dallas "to see her die." The public spectacle of hangings was common at the time, but also suggests the desire of whites to witness what they believed was justice. Just as it is generally believed that there was a crowd for Turner's execution, so too was there a crowd for Elkins's hanging.

Medical practice in Dallas at the time was in its infancy; the city was founded around 1841, and the first medical schools did not appear until the early twentieth century. There were approximately five practicing doctors in the area, enough to form a medical fraternity. In 1853, the Texas Medical Association was established. After Elkins's body was placed in a shallow grave near the execution site, members of a medical fraternity resurrected her. Jane's corpse became a "medical cadaver" and was likely used for research.[79] The Elkins case is another confirmation that formerly enslaved people's corpses were tampered with after death. Unfortunately, we do not know who owned Elkins and whether or not he or she received the $700 her body was worth, but evidence from enslavers who had insurance policies on their human property adds to our understanding of ghost values.

In the aftermath of the Southampton rebellion, Southern planters sought to protect their financial investments in human property. The enslaved understood this process. For example, Moses Roper of North Carolina recalled that "if a man kills a slave belonging to another master, he is compelled to pay the worth of the slave" to the other enslaver. He also noted that these cases were not limited to the death of males, as there were "many instances . . . in respect to females" that he could share, but the circumstances around the death or murder of females were "too disgusting to appear in this narrative."[80] One wonders if Roper understood that women held different financial value because they were the harbingers of additional sources of labor. Their ability to give birth meant that enslavers did not have to purchase human property. Instead, they hoped that enslaved children would survive to a profitable age. In this regard, enslaved women were valued for their fecundity, as discussed in earlier chapters. But fertility did not protect women from abuse.

We can infer from Roper's testimony that women experienced some form of disrespect or assault, perhaps in place of castration. Mrs. Colman Freeman, an enslaved woman who self-liberated by fleeing the United States for Canada in the aftermath of the Southampton rebellion, remembered being threatened after the "rebellion among the slaves in Virginia, under Nat Turner." "The white people that had no slaves would have killed the colored," she recalled, "but their masters put them in jail to protect them from the white people." When people investigating the rebellion arrived at her mother's place, she and her mother were threatened and searched. Apparently, the white authorities were looking for guns and ammunition. It "was the first time I was ever silenced by a white man," Mrs. Freeman explained. "One of them put his pistol to my breast, and said 'If you open your head, I'll kill you in a minute!'" Fearing the outcome, she remained quiet and tried desperately to silence her mother, who "was inquiring" about their conduct. Unfortunately, according to

Mrs. Freeman, they "were as ignorant of the rebellion as they had been," and after surviving this incident, she and her mother made their successful escape to Canada.[81]

Life Insurance

Looking at a small sample from the Southern Mutual Life Insurance Company of 1,778 enslaved people between twenty-three and thirty-nine years old, it is clear that valuations had less to do with age and more to do with an individual's health, strength, and/or anticipated death. For example, as enslaved people aged through midlife, their appraisal values remained strong, with some worth as much as $3,000 on the high end and $150 on the low end. Gender marked variances in their values and policies. For example, an enslaved woman named Ellen (twenty-five) had the highest value ($2,000) among women in this age range. Likewise, Jim (twenty-eight) was the highest-valued male ($3,000). But if we trace other individuals, we learn that enslavers and their agents insured enslaved people during the Civil War; many of those insured held value well into their thirties, and these values are higher than average sale and appraisal data described earlier. An enslaved woman named Diamond had policies on her life while she was in her mid-thirties. At that time, she consistently received appraisal values ranging from $700 to $1,200, at rates from 1.25 to 5.25 percent, with premiums from $13.75 to $66.50. Many of the term lengths covered one to two months, renewable on the tenth of each month, from 1857 to 1862.[82] Unlike in market settings, her value did not decrease in her thirties, as it did for most women beyond their childbearing years, suggesting that sales and life insurance policies involved different levels of evaluation. Such findings confirm that the context of the valuation matters and that an enslaved individual might carry a value in one stage of life, in a specific geographic region, that would be different for another in similar circumstances.

We can understand the monetary value of enslaved people by tracing the individual policies of specific enslaved people. Take, for example, Diamond, mentioned above. Over the course of five years, Diamond had two different enslavers, John A. Moore and J. M. Newby, indicating that her living conditions changed when she switched households. Her experience with slavery under Moore may have been different than with Newby, depending on the location of their homes, the enslaved population, and the nature of labor. Both men lived in Augusta, Georgia, and Newby owned forty-five enslaved people, including some who worked at the Georgia Relief Hospital for the Confederate Army during the Civil War.[83] However, both enslavers used the same agent, Charles Hall, to maintain life insurance policies on Diamond. Newby's policies were for one-year terms, while Moore insured her by the month. Moore likely hired her out to work for other people, hence, the short duration of her policy, or he was trying to sell her and she may have been in transit, increasing the risk of loss. Regardless of his rationale, Moore renewed the policy more than ten times and maintained her economic value at $1,000. By contrast, Newby valued her for $200 more, at $1,200, and with higher rates and premiums.[84] This additional money involved amortized payments to cover for unpredictable loss. Such policies made investing in human property financially feasible for some enslavers, or at least those who took out policies in the decades leading up to the Civil War. In addition to individual interest in slave insurance, state governments also supported the practice and offered a measure of regulation for insurance agencies. Shifting from an enslaved individual's policy to state-regulated ones offers additional insights into the fiscal value of enslaved life.

The state of Maryland passed legislation in 1860 supporting slave insurance policies. In Chapter 390, the Senate issued "An Act to Incorporate the Southern Slaveholders Insurance Company of Maryland"; the primary function was to aid in recovering the costs of runaways. Such policies placed the burden on the enslaver, who was expected to take an active role in searching for fugitives. Yet, it also stipulated that after "a reasonable time," the enslaved person's monetary value would remain fixed, based on the insurance policy, "unless . . . disease or injury [changed] the value of such slave." When disease or illness was confirmed, "the value of the slave shall be ascertained by arbitrament and appraisement of two disinterested cogent persons." At least one of them would be selected by the company, and the other, selected by the enslaver.[85]

The John Brown raid at Harpers Ferry offers additional evidence on postmortem values and is the second case study of middle-aged enslaved people that confirms postmortem discrimination based on race and status in the aftermath of executions.

Postmortem Burial After Harpers Ferry

Despite the measure of protection available through compensation petitions and insurance policies, the institution of slavery experienced another blow in 1859 when white abolitionist John Brown and an interracial group of followers attempted to lead a slave rebellion. Like Turner nearly thirty years earlier, Brown had a group of followers who were middle-aged, both free and enslaved, and willing to die for freedom. At trial, Brown was charged with treason and sentenced to execution. On December 2, 1859, at approximately 11 a.m., Brown rode on his coffin, which was on a horse-drawn cart, to the site of his execution in Charles Town, Virginia (now West Virginia), which was well attended by military officers and civilians alike. White women and children were excluded from the execution, including Brown's wife.[86] An eyewitness described Brown as "feebler and feebler at each abortive attempt to breathe."[87] Continuing, he shared that "the criminal hung upon the gallows for nearly forty minutes, and after being examined by a whole staff of surgeons, was deposited in a neat coffin to be delivered to his friends, and transported to Harpers Ferry, where his wife awaited it."[88]

Even though Brown had been convicted of treason, his family had permission to carry out his wishes; most likely certain loving family members who were white and wanted to give their relative a proper burial were able to do so. In Brown's case, we see that his execution, although well attended, was not a scavenger hunt for body parts as souvenirs. Instead, Brown's family received his body and buried it according to his wishes. However, before his corpse was placed on the train for a family funeral and burial in North Elba, New York, "Eight members of the Medical College of Virginia . . . *Asked* for Brown's body for dissection purposes, and a professor of anatomy, Dr. Arthur Edward Peticolas" wanted the skulls of Brown and his followers for "the collection in our museum." Dr. Peticolas was willing

John Brown and two of his followers were hanged upon this scaffold in 1859 in Charles Town, Virginia (now West Virginia).

to pay five dollars per head, but the governor rejected the request and returned Brown to his widow.[89]

Fannie Turner and other blacks did not have this experience when their relatives were executed by the state. Nor were relatives given their loved ones' bodies for proper burial. The fate of two African Americans, one enslaved and one free, highlights this disparity. John A. Copeland, a free black from Oberlin, Ohio, and Shields Green, a fugitive from South Carolina, were part of the small group who had accompanied Brown in the two-day battle in mid-October. Green had been introduced to the legendary abolitionist Frederick Douglass in a secret meeting before the raid. During the conversation, Douglass shared that he did not want to join Brown on what he believed was a suicide mission that would "rivet the fetters more firmly than ever on the limbs of the enslaved." Even though Green was "a man of few words," Douglass admired his "courage and self-respect." When asked whether he'd join Brown, he responded, "I b'leve I'll go wid de ole man."[90] In the end, Copeland and Green did go with the "ole man," but these men did not receive the same postmortem treatment as their elder white comrade.

Copeland and Green died on December 16 on the same platform where Brown had died two weeks earlier, but they did not die in the same way. Their families were not given choices about what to do with their bodies. We know from their time in jail that both men were at peace with their fate. Copeland wrote letters to his family, offering a window into his thoughts on the eve of his death. He asked his brothers, sisters, and parents not to mourn for him because he could not die for "a more noble cause" and was prepared to meet his "Maker."[91] He repeated the phrase "meet me in

Heaven" throughout the letters, and like Turner, he was "ready." "We shall meet in Heaven, where we shall not be parted by the demands of the cruel and unjust monster Slavery," he stated on the eve of his execution.[92] Green, by contrast, leaves us with few words, only that he wanted to spend time in prayer and prepare for another world.[93] I can find no evidence that any enslaver received compensation for Green's death.

Immediately following their execution, and after the obligatory thirty-minute hanging time, Copeland and Green were cut down from the gallows and pronounced dead. For these men, however, the gallows marked the beginning of their postmortem journeys. There was a fight among medical students for Copeland's and Green's cadavers. Students from nearby Winchester Medical School dug up Copeland and Green, who had been put in shallow graves.[94] Medical students from three different institutions fought for the "rights" to Copeland's and Green's bodies. Those from Charlottesville (UVA) and Charleston (Medical College of South Carolina) were equally determined to acquire these new subjects for dissection and had traveled 115 and 524 miles, respectively, to do so.

Copeland's father had pleaded with Governor Wise before the execution for his son's body to be returned to the family, and received a telegraph stating, "You may send a man, but he must be a white man."[95] James Monroe, who represented the family of John Copeland, is our source of information about the struggle for the postmortem bodies. Monroe received permission from the governor of Virginia to "act as [Copeland's] agent in receiving the body."[96] It was agreed that after the execution, a local mortician would prepare Copeland's body for the journey back to Ohio so that he could be buried by his family. Monroe traveled 350 miles from Oberlin, Ohio, to Charles Town, Virginia, to bring Copeland home. But events unfolded differently, and, as stated earlier, medical students had taken the bodies.

Postmortem treatment clearly differed based on race and status. Copeland's free black family had avenues to procure their deceased loved one, but the family of an enslaved person like Green did not. The historical record does not have information on whether anyone came or wrote on behalf of Green, the fugitive insurgent affectionately known as "Emperor." However, when we calculate the money raised for Monroe's journey, the postmortem price tag placed on Copeland begins to emerge.

Monroe raised approximately one hundred dollars for travel via train; in addition, he had hotel and food expenses. Pondering the purchasing power of his money, he had to make sure his bills were not counterfeit. He also incurred mortuary fees to pay the mortician to prepare Copeland's body for transport, given he had received approval as the family representative. Before Monroe could collect the executed body, Winchester medical students visited him with a plea. A student from Georgia served as their spokesman and clearly displayed their sense of ownership of the bodies:

> Sah . . . you don't understand the facts in the case. Sah, this [n____r] that you are trying to get don't belong to the Faculty. He isn't theirs to give away. They had no right to promise him to you. He belongs to us students, sah. Me and my chums nearly had to fight to get him. . . . I stood over the grave with a revolver in my hand while my chums dug him up.[97]

Despite the approval of the faculty and the governor, the medical students believed Copeland's body belonged to them, not his family, because state legislation authorized the dissection of criminals; thus, the students felt entitled to take the cadavers. The faculty did their best to stay out of the situation and watched passively as the students took charge of getting the corpses. Copeland's body was likely at the university when Monroe arrived, but the medical students had different plans for it. They claimed that the governor "has no authority over the affairs of our college" and, to ensure that Monroe left without the body, informed him that they had broken into the dissecting rooms and removed Copeland's body to an undisclosed hiding place. The bold nature of their actions to remove Copeland suggests that the faculty secretly supported it, but in order to avoid any professional embarrassment, Monroe was given a tour of the facility the following day. He was not prepared for what he saw:

> We visited the dissecting rooms. The body of Copeland was not there, but I was startled to find the body of . . . a colored man named Shields Green. I had indeed known that he also had been executed at Charlestown, as one of John Brown's associates, but my warm interest in another object had banished the thought of him from my mind.

It had not occurred to Monroe that he would have trouble procuring Copeland's body, and he completely overlooked Green. He continued:

> It was a sad sight. I was sorry I had come to the building; and yet who was I, that I should be spared a view of what my fellow-creatures had to suffer? A fine, athletic figure, he was lying on his back—the unclosed, wistful eyes staring wildly upward, as if seeking, in a better world, for some solution of the dark problems of horror and oppression so hard to be explained in this.[98]

In his eloquent yet shocking description, Monroe acknowledged the disrespect of Green's body and his nonexistent burial rights/rites. The fact that no one closed Green's eyes was a sign of great disrespect. Monroe returned to Ohio alone. He had to pay the college undertaker for the prep work done on Copeland, a deceased son whose parents mourned an empty casket. He viewed his trip as a "failure" but was comforted by Copeland's parents, who graciously appreciated his efforts. On Christmas, two weeks after the execution, three thousand members of the Oberlin community held a memorial service for Copeland and Green. A small monument remains in place today in their honor.[99]

Little attention has been given to Dangerfield Newby. Just as Crispus Attucks was the first to die in the American Revolution, Dangerfield Newby, a mulatto from Virginia, was the first Brown follower slain in the raid. Newby was born into slavery and later freed by his white father before he joined Brown in his efforts. Although he had been granted freedom, his wife, Harriet, and their seven children remained enslaved. Harriet and Dangerfield had an "abroad marriage," which meant that they did not reside on the same estate; instead, the two lived fifty-eight miles from one

A rare photo of Shields Green, who escaped slavery in South Carolina, died in the 1859 Harpers Ferry raid, and later was seen on the dissecting table at Winchester Medical School.

another (he near Harpers Ferry, she and the children in Warrenton, Virginia). Newby enters the historical record through his participation in the Brown raid and through letters written by his wife. On August 16, 1859, just two months before the rebellion, she pleaded that her husband purchase her: "Master is in want of money if so I know not what time he may sell me an then all my bright hops of the futer are blasted for there has ben one bright hope to cheer me in all my troubles that is to be with you."[100] Scholars have analyzed the letters and determined that Newby's role in the rebellion was likely a last attempt at freedom in the hopes of unifying his family. However, analyzing his postmortem journey reveals another story, one of tragedy and redemption.

People who knew and interacted with Newby described him as a "quiet, sensitive, and very unobtrusive" man.[101] He stood about six feet two inches tall and was regarded by his comrades as "a brave fellow."[102] Newby was literate and sent letters to his wife, who was also literate, and to his children. Their literacy allowed them to communicate, even though they lived apart, and granted them a modicum of freedom because they could write passes for themselves, notes allegedly written by their enslavers that granted travel. With added mobility, they could learn about contemporary political events and stay in close contact despite the day's journey that separated the two. In addition to his wife and seven children, Dangerfield had ten siblings, of which he was the oldest.[103]

Reports about the details of Newby's death scarcely pepper the pages of history, and when they do, they give little consideration to his postmortem journey. He likely joined Brown after he tried to purchase Harriet and one of their children from her owner, Jesse Jennings of Warrenton, Virginia. Jennings promised to sell Harriet and one child for $1,000, but when Newby raised the money and the sale was refused, he had to consider another option. He joined Brown and his followers in the raid at Harpers Ferry. According to an eyewitness and the only black survivor of the raid, Osborne Anderson, Newby was one of the first to die after being "shot through the head by a person who took aim of him from a brick store window." Anderson considered Newby one of his "comrades at the Arsenal," someone who "fell at my side." Perhaps it was some comfort to Anderson that "his death was promptly avenged by Shields Green," whom he described as the "Zouave of the band" and the man who "met his fate calmly on the gallows with John Copeland."[104]

Apparently, Newby died after the gunshot wound. However, some suggest that he was also "slain with a six-inch spike." After he died, "angry citizens fired [more shots] into his body repeatedly," and those who did not have guns "beat" his corpse "with clubs." As with other historical insurgents, his body was dismembered and displayed. Newby's "ears were cut off as souvenirs," but perhaps nothing was more disrespectful than allowing the hogs to have their way with his remains. An eyewitness said one hog "scampered away" after putting its snout in the "dead man's face." Other

Dangerfield Newby was the first to die fighting in the Harpers Ferry raid in 1859. Although he was allegedly mutilated, his remains were reinterred in 1899 near the grave of John Brown in North Elba, New York.

hogs are said to have "rooted and tugged at the torn body, consuming its parts." Despite the gruesome details of his postmortem mutilation—that his ears were taken as souvenirs, his flesh eaten by hogs, and his corpse "left on the street where he fell for more than 24 hours"—he was later given a proper burial near the grave of John Brown.[105] This area of Harpers Ferry is often referred to as "Hog Alley," the site of Newby's postmortem destruction.[106] While Nat Turner and his comrades roasted a pig on the eve of the Southampton rebellion, pigs devoured Newby in the aftermath of the Brown raid. Despite these chilling references, the hogs were given more homage and respect than Newby.

Along with Newby, at least nine others lost their lives in supporting Brown. According to one account, "One body was taken away by some physicians for dissection," and "the skeleton is now in some doctor's closet."[107] Such evidence and frank language confirms the practice of using slain rebels for anatomical dissection. Watson Brown (one of John Brown's sons) and Jeremiah Anderson, white insurgents in the group, were considered criminals and "fine physical specimens" and were perhaps "donated" "to some physicians from the medical school at Winchester, Virginia." They, like their African American counterparts, "were packed into barrels" and "utilized for anatomical purposes."[108] Physicians and students at Winchester Medical School were some of the key figures in the afterlife of Turner's body as well, meaning that the need for medical specimens still existed nearly forty years later. However, in the Brown uprising, there is also evidence of burials that, for some, served as redemptive postmortem events.

We know that at least seven or eight bodies from the Brown raid were taken and reinterred in North Elba, New York, near Brown's final resting place, on July 29, 1899. This effort, led by Thomas Featherstonhaugh, Captain E. P. Hall, and Professor O. G. Libby (University of Wisconsin) involved exhuming the graves, transporting the remains to New York, and reinterring them next to the body of Brown. For nearly forty years, this small group of rebels had been buried "upon the banks of the Shenandoah River." Terence Byrne, "one of the hostages taken by Brown," said he knew where four of the men were buried. He led Featherstonhaugh and others to the site in the summer of 1899, and "they dug about three feet below" and found the "dry-goods box" and the remains of at least four bodies.[109] Because many of the corpses were wrapped in wool shawls, "a great deal of the clothing had been marvelously preserved," including three bone buttons that are now owned by the Avery Research Center at the College of Charleston.[110] Newby's body, among those "buried in a shallow grave at Harpers Ferry," was reinterred in New York. His wife, Harriet, who had written that she could not wait until the "bless hour when I shall see you once more," had been sold to an enslaver in Louisiana.[111] One wonders if she or their children ever learned about his stately burial forty years after the raid. He would be the only African American laid to rest with John Brown's followers.[112]

The funeral arrangements made by Katharine E. McClellan included a "handsome casket with silver handles." It is not entirely clear who led the effort for the reinterment, but photos of the ceremony show a large crowd. The Reverend Joshua Young performed the last rites as he had done for Brown years earlier; Bishop H. C. Potter of New York and a Mr. Whitelaw Reid made brief remarks to the crowd. The service also included the singing of hymns by four African Americans who had participated in Brown's service. Finally, "a detachment of the Twenty-sixth United States Infantry . . . fired a volley over the open grave" and the crowd of fifteen hundred departed after the benediction.[113]

.   .   .

Nat Turner, Shields Green, and John Copeland faced death by hanging. What did they think about in their last moments? Did they know that their bodies would be in circulation, reinterred, eaten, and dissected? They likely had no idea that their body parts would become commodities, souvenirs, or collectors' items. Nor that their actions would remain a topic of interest nearly two hundred years postmortem. There are probably countless other enslaved and free black people who experienced death and postmortem desecrations like those discussed here, and their stories are equally important. The afterlife of these middle-aged male and female bodies speaks volumes about the multilayered legacy of slavery. We must consider the life of the body, even after death, and the myriad ways in which black bodies lived beyond their shallow graves.

We do not know where Turner's remains rest or whether his skull was ever reunited with his frame, but we know that the Turner descendants found ways to honor him. Through oral tradition, they drew upon the strength of their beloved Nat, honored his words, and recalled his prayers, just as Fannie did before her sale as she was being separated from her son, Gilbert. Perhaps Gilbert's fate allowed some peace for the Turner descendants. We know little about Melissa.

Gilbert grew up away from his sister, Melissa, and his mother. Ironically, the auction block kept him close to the site of the Southampton rebellion. He was purchased as a wedding present by a woman he called "Miss Mary"; she paid $500 for him, the equivalent of $14,700 in 2014.[114] He knew her because she had given his father a Bible. Gilbert remained enslaved by this family until emancipation; later, he married and moved his family to Ohio, "the free state that seemed so near, yet so far from Virginia." With his wife, Sarah, and two daughters, Fannie and Lucy, the Turners kept the teachings of their slain relative close to their hearts. Perhaps unbeknownst to them, they followed a route similar to the postmortem journey of Turner's decapitated skull and settled less than a hundred miles from the anatomy class that displayed it in 1866.

Juxtaposing the afterlife of personal effects with that of the bodies brings us to the circulation of slavery relics in modern-day museums. Can descendants find peace knowing that Turner's Bible has been recovered and is on display in the National Museum of African American History and Culture in Washington, DC? Is it the same Bible that Turner preached from on the eve of the rebellion and Gilbert learned from when living with Miss Mary? Kept as a relic and passed down through one of the white families victimized in the rebellion (the Porter-Francis family), in 2012, they realized that the Bible did not have "the home it deserved" and that it needed to be seen. Although many members of the Porter-Francis families lost their lives as a result of the rebellion, they believed that "Nat Turner would have wanted his Bible to rest in Washington."[115] Henry Highland Garnet reminds us that the name "Nathaniel Turner . . . has been recorded on the list of infamy . . . [and] future generations will number him among the noble and the brave."[116]

Placing the deaths of Turner and other enslaved and free people in a historical context tells us a great deal about their postmortem commodification and travel. It also tells us how their families coped with loss. We learn that monies paid to whites for the death of their human property indicate that enslavers received reparations during slavery. They understood the value of their laborers and filed claims to cover financial losses. This is relevant given contemporary debates about reparations in the British Caribbean and aligns well with ongoing debates in the United States.[117] Each of the men studied in the Turner and Brown executions was middle-aged, with the exception of Brown, who was in his late fifties. Those enslaved at this age had different experiences with commodification and death than their free and older counterparts, who are the focus of the next chapter.

CHAPTER 5

Elderly and Superannuated

APPRAISAL VALUES
FEMALES: $268 [$7,868 IN 2014]
MALES: $433 [$12,716 IN 2014]

SALE VALUES
FEMALES: $301 [$8,842 IN 2014]
MALES: $546 [$16,023 IN 2014]

> *But old people are like old trees, uproot them, and transplant to other scenes, they droop and die, no matter how bright the sunshine, or how balmy the breezes.*
>
> —Lucy A. Delaney[1]

> *Be men and die like men.*
>
> —Isaac at the gallows[2]

Sometime in the mid-1830s, an enslaved man named Ponto and more than one hundred other enslaved people were placed on the auction block in Richmond, Virginia. "Come Ponto, stand up here, and tell the gentleman what you can do," shouted the auctioneer. Ponto mumbled something under his breath, to the dismay of the auctioneer, but he continued, "Gentlemen, what will you give me for Ponto? A good field hand, 32 years of age, and . . ." At this point, Ponto interrupted him and yelled out, "Gentleman, I is a rising 40." Disturbed, the auctioneer remarked, "He is described in the bill of sale, gentleman, as 32 years of age, which I presume is correct." To this, Ponto looked at the audience and said, "Why, gentleman, I has lived with Mr. Gordon rising 21 years, and when he bought me I was a heap better than I is now." The auctioneer, now visibly irritated responded, "Well, well, gentleman, you see the [n____r] before you; he is described as being 32 years of age; he says he is 40; it is for you to judge which of the two is correct." In an effort to move forward with the bidding process, he said that Ponto was "a first-rate plantation hand, strong and able-bodied," but Ponto interrupted him again, addressing the crowd. "Gentleman, I is not able-bodied; for, in the first place, I is troubled with sickness; and in the next place, I has got a wen on my right shoulder, as big as an Irish potatoe!" This last remark silenced the bidders, and the auctioneer quickly rushed Ponto off the stand, saying, "Gentleman, you see this fellow does not want to be sold; however, I shall find a master for him."[3] We have no way to know whether he found a master for Ponto, and we cannot confirm his age, because enslaved people had unusual birth certificates.

Ponto's interference with his sale may have been more common than we realize. Mr. M. W. Phillips, writing about enslaved people over age forty noted the confusion: "Lands and negroes are less productive at forty than at forty-two, we see a heavy loss. Is this not so? I am told of negroes not over thirty-five to forty-five, who look older than others at forty-five to fifty-five. I know a man not short of sixty, who might readily be taken for forty-five; another on the same place full fifty . . . who could be sold for thirty-five, and these negroes are very leniently dealt with."[4] In addition to not knowing true ages, enslaved people like Ponto used the sale to challenge and question their own soundness, casting doubt in the minds of potential buyers.

This chapter examines the values of enslaved people age forty and older. During enslavement, those who reached age forty were considered elderly, unlike today, when seniors are those sixty-five or older.[5] By forty, enslaved people fully understood their condition, as evidenced by Ponto's defiance. Those who experienced a social death or soul murder may have welcomed the opportunity to depart this world.[6] Others were extremely clear about their status and held on to their soul values. At fifty-eight, George Ramsey noted that even though he was not born free, he "didn't feel that anybody had a right" to him. He recalled that as he aged, it became clearer that he was not treated fairly. He had worked hard "and got nothing for it," and that did not settle well with his soul. This distressful realization, "cause[d] me to come away as quick as I did." Ramsey liberated himself by running away, just after he and his wife were separated via sale.[7]

The life cycle for those forty and older was coming to an end. In the nineteenth century, the average life expectancy of the enslaved (based on rather thin data) was twenty-five years. By contrast, the white population, on average, lived to age thirty-nine. To a contemporary reader, these are extremely low averages, yet they speak volumes about issues of health and aging in the past.[8] As with those under ten, care was important; health and survival were primary concerns for those who loved them. However, as the enslaved aged, their monetary values decreased and they became worthless in the market. Despite low external values, their soul values excelled. They carried great wisdom and stability for the community and were respected by younger enslaved family and friends.

Relationships with enslaved elders were not only important, but also primary to black and white families.[9] From the enslaved perspective, we know that some enslaved children and young adults knew their grandparents better than their parents. Slave narratives often discuss elders, as well as the wisdom and advice they shared. Enslavers also valued what they called "superannuated" enslaved people and placed the word "supra" beside their names in lists of the enslaved. Some enslavers found ways to work elders into their labor communities, while others tried to sell them. Historian Eugene Genovese summed up their experiences best: "The behavior of the slaveholders toward the superannuated ranged widely from full and kind concern through minimum attention to paternalist responsibilities to indifference and sheer barbarism."[10] Despite how they were treated, enslaved seniors represented an important part of the enslaved community.

Scholars have not been very interested in the financial value of the elderly because of the assumption that they did not contribute substantially to the plantation economy. Many did not consider soul values in their research. Yet, we have much to learn about the strength and meaning of soul values for those approaching death. Studies of market prices for the enslaved rarely consider people beyond ages thirty to thirty-five, yet some had relatively high monetary values during their senior years, confirming that enslavers capitalized on their bodies at all ages and stages of life.

Through narratives and obituaries, insurance policies, and plantation records, we learn about the role of the superannuated in the enslaved community and the early history of elder care. Why did enslavers sell elderly enslaved people? Who wanted to buy them? How did older en-slaved people experience appraisals, given their declining health? When they died, how were they laid to rest? Examining sale and end-of-life issues for the elderly is just as important as examining them at other stages of life, because, in this age range, the external—appraisal and mar-ket values—converged with the internal—soul values; one did not out-weigh the other. In other words, because their financial value was so low, enslaved people did not have to compete against the price tag on their bodies. In this space, they could exercise their soul values more freely. In exploring "the bell curve of life," a curve familiar to those who have studied enslaved prices, it is clear that the monetary value of the elderly paralleled that of children ten and under. This curve also represents life cycles coming full circle.

ELDERS' RECOGNITION OF MORTALITY AND SOUL VALUES

Polly and Davy, aged fifty and fifty-eight, respectively, joined nearly 150 other enslaved people at an auction in Louisiana. These two humble "grey heads" both sold for $500, after having spent their entire lives in bondage. A witness from the North explained the bell curve of life this way: "for *forty years* [Polly and Davy] have devoted their strength" to their enslaver. "They gathered forty harvests for him" and likely "brought him ten times as much as he is now getting for their worn-out bodies." Note that their enslaver did not count the first ten years of their lives, when they were groomed for enslavement.[11]

There are generally two approaches to understanding elderly enslaved people's place in the history of slavery. At one end of the spectrum, they were revered and treated with respect; at the other, they were isolated and disregarded. Enslaved voices that have been central throughout this study can help make sense of these opposing positions.

Enslaved people were pained to see their parents and grandparents marginalized. Moses Grandy found that elderly enslaved people had poor care and were isolated, depressed, and left to die. "When my mother became old, she was sent to live in a little lonely log-hut in the woods," he explained. To his disgust, "aged and worn out slaves, whether men or women" received little care. Enslavers treated elderly enslaved people like livestock—in Grandy's words, turning them out like "an old horse," not caring if they lived, suffered, or died.

Fortunately, he and his sister Tamar lived close enough to their mother's place in the woods that they could visit her quite frequently. On one of his "night-visits," he recalled hearing "her grieving and crying" as he approached the residence. "She was old and blind," he lamented, "and so unable to help herself." Grandy indicted enslavers for the "general practice" of mistreating elderly enslaved people, as he believed it was commonplace.[12]

When neglect occurred, literate enslaved people sent letters to their enslavers seeking support. Cyfax Brown sent a letter to his enslaver, St. George Tucker, asking for help to "support my self as I am old and infirme." In "his old age," Brown asked for "something if you please," hoping that the years he'd served would be returned with kindness. Phillis, an aged woman, wrote to the same enslaver and his wife two years later stating that "old age And infirmity Begains to follow me which Cause me to think that my Business in Life are nearly to an End." Her only request was to be able to live with the enslaver who owned her children because she was "going down very fast to my grave."[13] These requests exemplify the desire to live their last days in some comfort and care, peacefully and, if possible, with family. The desire to spend time with family at the end of their lives was common, especially since they spent most of their years laboring in the dwellings and fields of their enslavers. And they, like others, reflected on their lives and harbored dreams of an afterlife that involved a reunion with their deceased relatives.

Able-bodied enslaved people forty and older performed a host of tasks, including serving as cooks, nurses, midwives, seamstresses, body servants, gardeners, and caretakers of enslaved children. As for those under ten, labor assignments were rarely gendered at this age. Men and women also functioned in the spiritual and supernatural realm, serving as healers and diviners. They were "transmitters of Africanisms" and extremely significant to the enslaved community.[14] Slaveholding families even recognized those known for these skills. Margaret Hall Hicks remembered that the "negroes" on their plantation "all believed in being hoodooed . . . And were always . . . finding a rabbit's foot, or a green lizard, or a stuffed snake's skin under their doorstep." But, she explained, "there was always an old negro man or woman who could break the hoodoo." These individuals "were held in great respect and reverence, and reaped many nickels and dimes, and even larger amounts of money for their services."[15] In addition to such gifts, some women with special skills assisted in birthing babies and were affectionately known as "grannie midwives."[16] Elders also supervised and nursed both black and white infants and toddlers.

Enslaved people over forty understood that they had different values placed on their bodies, because they had experienced commodification for many years. They also understood that, by aging, their monetary values declined to the point that they could not be sold. One "old Baptist" man at sixty-two dreamed of life as a free man and longed for liberty: "I shold like bery much to spend de very few years I's got to live in freedom . . . [and] I would give any man $20 to $30 down, if he could get me free." He shared this with a traveler from the North who asked him about his worth; to this, he responded that his enslaver would likely sell him for $200.[17] Not only did the man know his market value, but he also understood the terms of sale, which sometimes involved a certain amount of cash down.

VALUATION OF ELDERLY ADULTS IN LIFE

Determining how many enslaved people aged forty and older were sound and commanded high prices is almost impossible. But we do know that their internal values were elevated and celebrated within their communities. By the time enslaved people reached forty, they had exceeded the life expectancy for those in bondage. Not surprisingly, even those who reached forty longed for freedom. One forty-five-year-old interviewed by a Northern abolitionist shared his desire for liberty when asked, "Do you know of any slaves around here, who are contented with being in bondage?" His response: "No, mass'r . . . Not one of dem."[18] Mortality schedules, which differed from the life-expectancy figure discussed above, suggest that, in 1850, blacks lived an average of 21.4 years, compared to whites, who lived about 25.5 years.[19] These figures are extremely low by today's standards. Thus, if enslaved people made it to forty and beyond, they held a special place within the enslaved community, whether they wanted to live or die.

At age forty, Hannibal preferred death to life and sometimes blamed God for his enslaved status. "I have often cursed God for my fate," he explained. "Death, to me, would always have been a welcome relief! I prefer it *now* to the prospect of living longer in my present condition." As a result, he did all he could to escape to a free state. However, in addition to his black skin, which identified his enslaved status, he was a big man, over six feet tall, weighing about three hundred pounds. When thinking about escape, he knew that he was "so much larger than most slaves," that "every one who sees me would demand a pass." More important, "the hounds, and half the devils who own them, would chase me." The thought of running away was too risky, and he knew that he'd either "be taken, or *killed*." In a conversation with a Northern ally who offered to purchase his freedom, Hannibal said, "The man would be shot who should come here, with any sum of money, proposing to buy me *and carry me North*." He also fully understood that freedom via purchase from a Northern ally was next to impossible, because as a free man, his testimony would compromise Southern enslavers. He would bear witness to his experiences. Thus, "the slaveholders here know that I know all about slavery, and that I could tell what I know."[20]

Enslaved grandparents like Old Maria were not spared from family separation, and sometimes this trauma was unbearable. Three generations of her family consisting of "old grand parents," their six children, and eighteen grandchildren experienced separation because of a gambling debt. Rather than put money on the betting table, their enslaver "staked six slaves . . . on a game of billiards, and they were won by a New Orleans gambler." When the moment of separation came and the six were placed on a train, it was too much for the elderly couple. The grandmother sat on a pine log in "her emaciated form, curved spine, and snow white hair." Her body contoured into a crouched position as she swayed back and forth in anguish. "Neither words nor tears" showed until the train left the station. In shock, she could not engage in a conversation with her daughter when she bid her farewell because she was "beyond tears . . . or mute in despair!" Her husband, "the grandfather," equally aged and "bent down with toil," stood with "a long staff that ran above his head," while he placed his right arm on the shoulder of one of his sons. A witness described the scene as "a vivid, life-like picture of an aged father, standing by the death bed of an *only, idol* son, on whom he had leaned for support and comfort in his old age." Ironically, in accordance with the bell curve of life, the grandparents' grandchildren were not taken away and they played nearby, not fully aware of the magnitude of the event. Their "doomed fathers and mothers" embraced one another as well as their parents, for what they considered might be their last touch. In addition to parents and their adult offspring being separated, the husbands and wives went to different enslavers as well. Bystanders recalled the sounds of a shrieking daughter and wife as she forgot to give her husband a parting gift. The train left, and she burst into "the most frantic wails" one could imagine.[21] Her elderly parents were left to care for their grandchildren in the absence of their parents, who were sold to cover a bet.

Commodification Data for Elderly Adults

Using a sample of 12,244 appraisal and sale values for enslaved people aged forty and older, I found that the elderly and superannuated had low economic values. On average, women were appraised at $268 and men at $433. Their enslavers knew that many in this age range had health challenges deeming them risky financial investments. Thus, appraisals at this age involved more extensive health examinations and sometimes warranties for soundness before they were sold. Enslaved people like Ponto preyed upon these uncertainties by openly speaking about their health issues to raise doubt among planters interested in purchasing them. As a result, market values for the elderly were also low. Mean sale prices for men and women were, respectively, $546 and $301. Some enslaved people, especially those considered sickly or near death, even had negative values or were literally given away in a group sale because they could not be sold on their own. As investments, those individuals were viewed as economic liabilities.[22] One "kind-looking" "mulatto" man, aged forty-five, went to the auction block in Richmond, Virginia, but "no bids were made for him," according to a witness. A twelve-year-old girl who had received heavy scrutiny from the crowd preceded the enslaved man on the auction block, and this contrast, in addition to his age, likely influenced potential buyers.[23]

Propaganda, including newspaper advertisements and posters or broadsides, often preceded sales. These documents itemized the merchandise that was to be auctioned and outlined payment terms. More detailed ads listed appraisal values or starting bids so potential buyers were often well educated before the sale. In January 1860, a husband and wife, Jake and Clarissa, appeared in an ad along with sixty-three other souls scheduled for auction in

Charleston, South Carolina. Jake, age fifty, was a "first-rate plowman and axeman." Clarissa, also fifty, was lauded as a "first-rate" midwife and nurse who could "mix and administer medicine." Despite their advanced age, they had noteworthy skills. Other elderly men and women were also for sale that day, making up 16 percent of the group that was being auctioned. Flora and Jupiter (both age fifty) had gardening skills indicated by the term "Gardiner" next to their names on the auction materials. Harry (age forty-five) was a "first-rate house servant," while Hammond (age fifty) had "a good eye for laying out ditches, etc." In order to purchase these elders, many who appeared with their children listed beneath them, buyers had to put "one third cash" down with the "balance payable in one, two, or three years," depending on securing the terms with "bonds bearing interest from the day of sale, payable annually." Potential buyers also knew that the "mortgage of negroes sold" had been secured and approved.[24] Although we do not know why these individuals went to auction, the enslavers clearly found a use for the elderly enslaved, particularly given that some were considered "first-rate."

Enslaved men like Isam (age forty) received less complimentary descriptions in market settings. He was "not able to bring more than $700, because his youth has gone." Allrick, described as a field hand, witnessed his monetary value decrease by 50 percent by the time he reached age forty-five. A witness to his sale noted that "he looks very good-natured," yet "twenty years ago, he was worth $2100, but is sold now for $1025." Another woman, also referred to as Old Maria, a sixty-year-old grandmother sold at the same auction, was described as having "gray hairs" by a Northern witness who noted that she "raised children, nursed grand-children," but they were "never her own"; they were the progeny of her enslaver. On the day she appeared on the auction block, this "meek, quiet, good-natured soul" could not contain herself as she was separated from her four children. The enslaver who purchased her children sneered that he only wanted "young hands." He paid three thousand dollars for Old Maria's children, and a separate buyer purchased her for two hundred dollars.[25]

Cane Brake Plantation Patterns of Elders' Valuation

At Cane Brake Plantation, Dr. Carson had nearly forty enslaved people over age forty. In 1856, he had twenty men and sixteen women ranging in age from forty to seventy-six years old. Some, like Thomas, age forty-four, had a high appraisal value of $1,200, which remained the same throughout the year. Most of his peers, however, were valued between $300 and $800. None of the elderly women received such high appraisals. Jane, age forty, had the highest monetary value, $600, at the beginning and end of the year. Isaac (forty-eight) and Edmond (sixty-five) died during the year, and Carson recorded this along with appraised values. Carson lost $650 upon the death of Isaac and got nothing for Edmund because he had no value before and after death. Eight different men and women had a value of zero dollars at the beginning and end of the year, and they remained on the plantation from 1856 to 1858. These individuals included women like Mima (seventy-six), Sophy (sixty-five), and Sue D. (fifty-five), as well as men like Hercules (seventy-six), Spencer (seventy-four), Sawney (sixty-five), and Hartwell (forty-eight). Given that this plantation community was relatively stable, the same "valueless" elders remained, indicating that Carson chose to keep them on the plantation even though they were not contributing to the economy.

One wonders about the soul values of these seven elders. They represented nearly one-quarter of the total Cane Brake population.[26] What did their presence mean? Certainly their longevity would bring a level of stability to the community, as older enslaved people had wisdom and experience to share with younger generations. They also were likely the grand- and perhaps great-grandparents of the younger enslaved on the plantation. We know they received health care because, as mentioned previously, their owner was a physician who had hired a doctor to care for his enslaved people. Did women like Mima, Sophy, and Sue serve as grannie midwives to the pregnant mothers at Cane Brake? The population could certainly support and sustain such ties.

In 1858, Carson's plantation contained a completely balanced gender ratio of seventeen men and seventeen women aged forty or older. Their appraisal values ranged from $0 to $800, with men's market prices averaging $100 more than women's. Three women, Appaline (forty), Jane (forty-two), and Sue T. (forty-three), had the highest values at $600. Senior men with high values included Adam (forty-one), Lockart (fifty-one), and Frederick (fifty-four), who all had a value of $700. Jim B. (forty-two) was valued at

$800.[27] As they aged, the cost of medical care became an issue, sometimes resulting in the sale or manumission of elderly enslaved people. This was not the case at Cane Brake.

Health and [Dis]ability

Although at times enslavers seemed obsessed with the health of their enslaved, not only did elderly enslaved people suffer from some of the illnesses that affected those in other age ranges, but their superannuated status magnified the impact. Their illnesses can be summarized in the following broad categories: internal, mental, physical, respiratory, and sensory impairments. Tom (forty-eight) and his wife Betsy (fifty-one) were placed on the auction block with issues of soundness. Tom had a hernia and Betsy was "old" and only good as a nurse and caretaker for small children. She sold for $100, and he for $250. Their market values align with the prices for children age ten and younger. Tom kept his head down the entire time, causing one bystander to surmise, "He feels dreadfully ashamed to be put up at auction, like a mule or a dog."[28] How did it feel to be sold after more than forty years of enslavement? What did the future look like for the elderly? How were they cared for in the remaining years of their lives? Answers to these questions vary depending on a host of circumstances, especially the enslaver's attitude toward emancipation.

Some planters, including Dr. Carson of Cane Brake, made provisions in their last will and testament to care for or free aged women and men. According to family lore, in 1837, Carson wanted to emancipate his enslaved, even though he had purchased forty-three the year before."[19] The family reported that he felt burdened by managing the enslaved and believed strongly in religious instruction, so he and his wife decided to postpone emancipation until after he completed medical school at the University of Pennsylvania. When he graduated in 1839, Mississippi law stipulated that manumitted enslaved people had to leave the state, so according to the family memory, Carson decided not to free his enslaved laborers until he could provide care for all two hundred of them in freedom. Carson had already paid $5,000 to send his driver Ned Morris to Liberia and could not afford to do the same for the rest of his enslaved population. Although he struggled to provide medical care during yellow fever and cholera outbreaks, he lost at least twelve enslaved people in 1849 to the latter, just after they moved to Airlie Plantation in East Carroll Parish, Louisiana. We know that he paid Dr. Benjamin Waller to serve as the plantation physician, but even that could not protect the enslaved from certain illnesses. Dr. Carson died on August 11, 1863, not too long after he had moved from Louisiana to Texas during the Civil War. In his last will and testament, he bequeathed his enslaved people to his children, but family memory suggests that he sent a letter before his death in 1857, asking his children to free the enslaved upon his death. Regardless of his actions, intentions, and motives, he clearly held the paternalistic view that he could take care of the enslaved and had been accustomed to certain comforts that he wanted his family to enjoy during his life.[30]

Just like the enslaved people who died from cholera on Carson's estate, hundreds of enslaved people, age forty and older, died in Savannah and were laid to rest at Laurel Grove Cemetery South. From 1852 to 1861, enslavers buried 712 elderly enslaved people at Laurel Grove. Many had lived well past their forties, including centenarians Betty Broughten (111), Sandy (106), Phebe (103), John Williams (100 and 10 months), and Die (100). Molly, owned by a T. M. Turner, was also 100 years old, but rather than dying of old age like her counterparts, she was "burnt by accident." In addition to paying burial fees, some enslavers hired physicians to visit and care for about 27 percent, or 192, of them. These individuals suffered from a host of illnesses including dropsy, rheumatism, cancer, apoplexy, pneumonia, and consumption. Twenty percent, or 152, died of "old age." They lived their entire long lives in bondage and were laid to rest in a cemetery around other enslaved and free black people.

Those who survived past the abolition of slavery in 1865 had to be cared for as well. Nearly fifty years after slavery, concerned citizens in Austin and Nacogdoches, Texas, sought to establish a home for formerly enslaved elders. In 1913, Austin mayor Alexander Penn Wooldridge held a meeting to discuss city support for the many "old darkies" who lived "solitary lives in miserable hovels." (Despite what seems to be offensive language to a contemporary reader, calling blacks "old darkies" was common practice, so much so that it was printed in the local newspaper.) Fifteen prominent black members of churches, universities, and charity organizations such as the King's Daughters, the Federation of Women's Clubs, and Ebenezer Third Baptist Church received invitations to the mayor's gathering at city hall to discuss creating a home where formerly enslaved people could live their senior years together. Mayor Wooldridge proposed hiring "an able-bodied housekeeper and cook" to assist in caring for those in the house, which he felt offered better living conditions than the elders had at the time.[31]

Three years later, A. C. Churchill of Nacogdoches tried to generate support for a home in Sherman, Texas, and published an article in the *Daily Sentinel*, "Promoting Ex-Slave Home." Using similar paternalistic notions, the article noted that "many of these old darkies are now unable to work and have no means of support, making them a charge upon the various communities of the satiate, and many of them suffer hardships." As during slavery, those who considered supporting such a home believed that it could be maintained with "strict accountability for all moneys contributed," and that as long as it is "rightly managed," this type of institution "would be a most worthy charity." One son of a former large Texas planter family sent a letter to the editor endorsing the plan because he believed that formerly enslaved people needed care "in their old age, and the last days on earth." He also stated that the formerly enslaved "were the backbone of our country."[32]

Efforts to care for elders paralleled the "colored convention movement" (a series of meetings that began in the 1830s and went well into the twentieth century where blacks met to address social justice issues), as well as the push for pensions for the formerly enslaved; both forms of activism gained momentum in Texas during Reconstruction but occurred in Northern communities as early as the 1830s.[33] From the 1870s to the mid-1880s, people of African descent in Texas and other parts of the United States addressed the needs of their communities seeking to recover from slavery, exercise their rights as citizens, and acquire medical care as they aged.

VALUATION OF ELDERLY ADULTS IN DEATH

Before efforts were made after slavery to care for superannuated people, enslaved elders were facing the realities of their inevitable death. When a Northern abolitionist had a conversation with a "chuckling old fellow," he asked the aged man if he wanted his freedom. To this, the old man replied, "I's would like to be free; but it's no use, massa—its [sic] no use, I's a slave, and I's been one sixty years, and I'speccs to die in bondage." Older enslaved people did not believe they would live to see the demise of the institution. Even the elderly wagoner who drove coffins to the burying ground knew his time was near. The same abolitionist encountered him sitting on top of a coffin "holding a broken piece of mirror" close to his wrinkled face as he shaved himself with a dull razor. When the abolitionist asked him about "driving the dead," the coachman acknowledged that everyone who had had this job before him had died shortly after due to "pestilence," but this did not stop him. Perhaps he liked the freedom of movement, the "benefits" of the job, or the closeness to death. He, too, was likely prepared to die.[34]

Life Insurance

Despite the fact that elderly enslaved people held low monetary values, given the natural aging process, some enslavers took out life insurance policies on them. The Southern Mutual Life Insurance Company offered policies for those between the ages of ten and sixty-five. Given that we know that some enslaved people lived much longer, like the centenarians buried at Laurel Grove, the age range suggests that those over sixty had little or no labor or income value for enslavers. The fact that some still carried value is a remarkable indicator of how the bodies of blacks were commodified at every age.

Looking specifically at those with the greatest appraisal values in this age range, there were forty-seven enslaved people between forty and sixty with values $1,000 or more. Enslavers took out short-term policies from six months, with premiums ranging from $10 to $95. Five of those valued over $1,000 were women: Priscilla, Emeline, Nancy, Harriet, and April. Priscilla had the highest price, $2,225. She was forty years old, and the policy on her life had a one-year term with a $95 premium at a rate of 4.5 percent. Although we do not know why these women had high values, they were likely skilled seamstresses, nurses, or cooks. No men in this age range had values as high as Priscilla's appraised value, suggesting that her enslaver greatly valued her labor. Forty-two-year-old Ellick was valued at $2,000 for a one-year premium at $80, with a 4 percent rate on the policy.

Other men, such as David (aka Davis), Peter, William, Isham, Prince Albert, and Dick, to name a few, had values greater than $1,000 and had policies until they reached age fifty-two. After this age, most insured enslaved people had market values between $250 and $800.[35]

These figures are telling. They suggest that the commodification of enslaved women extended well beyond their childbearing years, and for men, as long as they remained strong and able-bodied. To have a price of $800 in 1860, like fifty-one-year-old Charlotte, is equivalent to nearly $23,500 in 2014.[36] Given that appraisal value, we can understand why some enslavers chose to keep elderly enslaved people on their estate. They probably could not sell elderly women and men for that amount at the market, but they took out policies so that they could replace enslaved women like Charlotte if they died. Enslavers might also have recognized the soul values among the enslaved and understood that elders were revered within the plantation community. Finally, due to and perhaps in spite of years of hard labor, some enslaved people were in remarkably good shape, appearing physically younger than their age might suggest.

Isaac's Soul Value and Burial

When forty-plus-year-old Isaac took the stand, people marveled over his "muscular and active" physique. South Carolina residents saw him as "the very man a sculptor would select for a model" because of the curves of his muscles and the "great strength" he possessed. His intellect matched his physique, and he was respected as much as an enslaved person could be in an institution that sought to destroy the spirit of such an individual. But Isaac was different; he was "richly gifted" with "clear-headedness and nobleness of will"; his character garnered respect from the enslaved and the free. Isaac was a leader. Like Nat Turner, Dangerfield Newby, John Copeland, and John Brown, he, too, had tried to overturn the system of slavery decades earlier. When Isaac took the stand, he was not on an auction block; he was on the witness stand on trial for his life. Here, Isaac faced a jury not of his peers, but of an elite group of enslavers, men who questioned him about planning to lead a rebellion on July 4, 1816. Isaac had a soul value, and it was evident to all who interacted with him.[37] This internal, self-constructed value manifested itself as confidence, resolve, and belief in freedom. Those around him may not have recognized it, because they were distracted by the value of his brawn.

We learn of Isaac through the memory of a witness to his trial and execution, John C. Vaughan. A Kentucky newspaper editor, Vaughan grew up in South Carolina and remembered Isaac as a true hero. After being interrogated about the conspiracy he and his comrades had planned for six months, Isaac was found guilty, along with thirteen others, and scheduled to hang as punishment. Vaughan described Isaac as a "head man" who gained respect from his enslaver and the local minister before the discovery of his plan to rebel. He was so respected within his community that even "the severest patrol would take his word and let him go his way" if he was ever caught out without the written pass required of all enslaved people. Even though Isaac was in his forties when he planned the revolt, Vaughan marveled at his physical prowess, his religious fervor, and the moral and mental strength that gave him power over those around him.[38]

During the trial, Isaac tried to take the blame and spare the lives of his comrades: "I am the man," he told the court without any "hesitation in his manner." He spoke with confidence, courage, and resolve. When asked about the planned insurrection and pressured to testify against others, he refused and only repeated, "I am the man, and I am not afraid or ashamed to confess it." Again, Vaughan and others were shocked at his strength, "but no ingenuity, no promises, no threats, could induce or force him to reveal a single name." In response to repeated questioning, Isaac told the court, "You have me . . . no one other shall you get if I can prevent it. The only pain I feel is that my life alone is not to be taken." Then he apparently pointed to the other men on trial and stated, "If these . . . were safe, I should die triumphantly." When the court realized he would not implicate any others, they sent the minister whom Isaac knew intimately to meet with him in his cell in hopes of encouraging him to confess to additional details.[39]

The conversations between Isaac and his minister reveal Isaac's soul value on the eve of his death. The two talked for four hours that night. When asked to share the details of the revolt, Isaac spoke to his clergyman in a familiar language. "Master," he began, "will you, who first taught me religion, who made me know that my Jesus suffered and died in truth— will you tell me to betray confidence sacredly intrusted [sic] to me, and thus sacrifice other's lives because my life is to be forfeited?" Clearly, Isaac had a sense of his obligations to his fellow men. He was aware that his actions would lead to his death, but he valued the sacred confidence his comrades instilled in him. This intrinsic valuation of his soul was a model for his peers. He valued himself enough to sacrifice his life and protect his comrades. Isaac continued, "Can you persuade me, as a sufferer and a straggler for freedom, to turn traitor to the very men who were to help me?" According to the minister, he spoke in a calm voice with a nonthreatening demeanor and expressed "greatness of soul." The minister could not proceed with the questioning and acknowledged his own sin, stating that "for the first time in my ministerial life, I had done a mean . . . base act" and "felt myself to be *the* criminal."[40]

After a long silence, the minister tried once more to encourage Isaac to consider the ramifications, had he succeeded in leading a rebellion. He tried to get him to think about the bloodshed, the lives that would be lost, and whether he was capable of killing his enslaver and/or his minister. To this, Isaac responded, "I love old master and misses [and] I love you and yours, I would die to bless you any time . . . but you taught me that God was the God of black as well as white—that he was no respecter of persons." He reminded his minister of God's commandments in Matthew 22:36–40: "'Love the Lord your God with all your heart and with all your soul and with all your mind.' This is the first and greatest commandment. And the second is like it: 'Love your neighbor as yourself.' All the Law and the Prophets hang on these two commandments."[41] Then he educated his minister about the souls and lives of the enslaved, sharing what it was like to have a wife and children in bondage. Where was the equality in that arrangement, he inquired? He reminded his minister that he watched as others received an education and earned wages, while men of his race "could make nothing." After this statement, Isaac shared that he knew deep in his soul that there was no help for his wife, his children, his race, "except that we were free."[42]

The minister listened and faced the hypocrisy of his slaveholding brethren in their interpretations of God's commandments. Isaac continued, "God told me he could only help those who helped themselves," so Isaac preached "freedom" to his fellow enslaved people because they had been betrayed. Then he looked directly in his clergyman's face and said, "I tell you now, if we had succeeded, I should have slain old master and mistress and you first, to show my people that I could sacrifice my love, as I ordered them to sacrifice their hates, to have justice." After these chilling words, he pointed his shackled hand to his heart and said that God told him that he was right. For the second time during the conversation, the minister was overwhelmed, and he was ashamed of his conduct and humbled by Isaac's "transparent" and sincere words. Isaac's voice was "so commanding" that he saw Isaac as a hero, one whose "conscience was unstained by the crime." The minister ended the conversation with a prayer, holding Isaac's hands while tears streamed down his face. After they said "Amen" and squeezed one another's hands they stood, and Isaac, too, was moved to tears. "Master, I shall die in peace," he said through a strained voice, and then asked the minister to lead his wife and children "as you have led me—to heaven."[43]

When Isaac's "death-day" came, there was a large crowd to witness his hanging. Just as they had on the day Turner went to the gallows, the bystanders wanted to witness the execution of someone they considered a rebel. While Isaac and six others stood on the platform, he turned to them with the noose around his neck and said, "Be men . . . and die like men." Then he asked them to watch his example and follow his brother's lead after his death. His brother, too, stood on the platform that day. According to witnesses, "Isaac gazed intently upon the crowd." Some believed he was searching for his family. He said good-bye to his brother and the other men, but before the officer could pull the lever, Isaac faced his brother and said, "I'll die a freeman." He then "sprung up as high as he could, and fell heavily as the knotted rope checked his fall." His body convulsed and "his feet reached the plank on which he had stood." Isaac jumped to his death on his own terms, not because the floor fell from under him. His brother witnessed this brave act and shouted, "Let us die like him," and they all jumped to their death just as Isaac had. Their bodies hung in the air "the usual time," about thirty minutes, before being cut down. Isaac, his brother, and the five others were then "coffined and carted away to their burial place."[44]

We know that their bodies were laid to rest in an "out-of-the-way old field." But Isaac and his comrades did not die in vain. They had a resting

place, a spot to mark their presence in the world and a place to be remembered by those who loved them. After the bodies were placed in the
ground, Isaac's wife and children waited for the authorities to leave before approaching the grave of their beloved. No one but God knew "how
long the widowed one and the fatherless remained there, or what were
their emotions, but, next morning, a rough stake was found driven into
the earth where Isaac lay." A week later, on Sunday, his wife placed "a pile
of stones with an upright memorial . . . at the head of his grave." This site
was kept clean, weed free, and adorned with a wild rose until the day his
wife joined him.[45]

✦   ✦   ✦

Older enslaved people like Isaac still yearned for liberty and fought against
the idea of slavery, even though they spent nearly a half century in captivity.
Some, like Isaac, looked to the grave for spiritual release and found their
own way to freedom. Their soul values were so high at this age that they
balanced out the low market values and appraisals that planters assigned
to their bodies. When they died, some were buried, having no idea that
their bodies might once again be commodified. For many enslaved people,
another value came after death—ghost value—as their postmortem bodies went back into traffic. While their souls rested, their bodies were commodified and sold for more inspections and scrutiny; their postmortem
journeys are the subject of the final chapter in this narrative.

CHAPTER 6

Postmortem: Death and Ghost Values

AVERAGE VALUE OF CADAVERS: $0—$30 [$881 IN 2014.][1]

> *Do tell me, what is the cost of a fine, stiff [n_____r]?*
> —Fran Bowen to Dr. Wyman,
> Richmond Medical College, 1845[2]

> *It makes me feel very bad when I think of the way the graves of my race have been desecrated.*
> —Jim Burrell, janitor, Jefferson Medical College[3]

On a cold New York winter night, February 25, 1836, an audience of fifteen hundred people filled the City Saloon, anxiously anticipating the main attraction. Some had come from miles away and all had gladly paid the 50-cent admission fee for a show that promised to be like no other. Some arrived hoping to satisfy their long-held curiosity and wondered whether their theories would prove true. Others arrived not knowing what to expect. The saloon had been converted into a makeshift operating room for this special occasion, and the lights centered on a table in the middle of the stage.

The central figure in this drama, a deceased elderly enslaved woman named Joice Heth, lay atop the elevated table. She had died six days prior; her public autopsy was the main event that evening. The people surrounding her were Dr. David L. Rogers of Barclay Street Hospital, students, clergymen, *New York Sun* editor Richard Adams Locke, and lawyer Levi Lyman, who served as her "agent," along with the infamous showman P. T. Barnum. Nearly everyone present was male, and some reports suggest that the entire procedure was distasteful, described as a "bloodily invasive circus."[4]

While still alive, Heth had spent her last year on tour, advertised as a purportedly 161-year-old enslaved woman and the former nurse of George Washington. Barnum made $1,500 per week displaying her at halls and facilities throughout the mid-Atlantic and Northeast. She told stories and sang hymns as part of Barnum's "Freak Show." In seven months, he made roughly $42,000 from this orchestrated public spectacle. In contemporary times, that would be equivalent to $1,102,336.[5] As Barnum's property, Heth made nothing. Now, less than a week after her death, Barnum organized his last show, a public autopsy to determine her cause of death and true age. People who paid to see her while living marveled at the old soul. Barnum claimed she had lived a century and a half, and although she was blind, she remembered seeing the Red Coats during the American Revolution. She was also paralyzed and had use of only her right arm.

On stage, doctors and medical students felt the crevices of her wrinkles, gazed into her sunken eye sockets, and marveled at her internal organs. When Dr. Rogers cut her open, he and his team of medical professionals from the New York College of Physicians and Surgeons expected to see extreme ossification of the arteries near her heart if she was as old as Barnum claimed. Instead, however, she had the internal organs of a woman in her seventies and not older than eighty. Immediately, Barnum went on the defensive, blaming Heth for deceiving him. Local newspapers covered the autopsy; there was significant outrage that Barnum had deceived the public. Barnum had made a great deal of money off Heth when she was alive and even managed to collect fees for her very public display after she died.[6]

Organized autopsies differed from mob dissections, like those of Nat Turner and Shields Green. Although both autopsies and dissections educated medical students about pathologies in the human body, the former were typically state or locally sanctioned and often sought the cause of death in the case of alleged foul play. Determining the cause of death became a significant development that paralleled medical professionalization. In the nineteenth century, "The examination of the anatomy of very aged persons" was believed to be "one of the most curious and instructive studies in science."[7]

Physicians began publicly asserting their "expertise" in the field of medical jurisprudence in the opening decades of the nineteenth century at the New York College of Physicians and Surgeons (which eventually became a part of Columbia University), because physicians' findings were used in legal cases. Decades later, in 1853, medical practitioners in Gonzales, Texas, for example, performed a "post-mortem examination" of an enslaved boy named Jack to try to understand his cause of death. Approximately "13 hours after death," Drs. J. B. Logue, William Craig, F. M. Lyle, and W. T. Lockridge examined Jack's heart and found "a fibro adipose substance" or cyst in the "cavity of the right ventricle." They also found a second growth on "the left side of the heart extending 5 or 6 inches down the aorta." They noted that Jack had been "sick about 5 or 6 days" and complained about having "shortness of breath." In the end, the autopsy allowed them to determine that Jack had suffered from heart disease for "about 3 years standing."[8] In another case, from 1857, a Dr. Bennett of Bridgeport, Connecticut, conducted a postmortem on "a stout, healthy negro, eighteen years of age." We do not know if this man was ever enslaved, but we know that he suffered a traumatic injury after being stabbed with a "dirk-knife." Although it seemed as if he could recover from the injury, he died a few days later. During Dr. Bennett's postmortem exam, he discovered that the deceased man had a wound that was "sufficiently large to have produced instant death." Had the deceased rested as instructed and not climbed two flights of stairs, he would have had a chance of survival.[9]

These autopsies, which span from the 1830s to the eve of the Civil War, confirm the growing interest in cause of death, but they also illustrate the medical curiosity for understanding the human body (the heart, in particular). This curiosity was apparent in life and death. Measured examinations of the heart differed from the bodily dismemberment that occurred at the hands of mob violence. Mob dissections typically involved vigilante groups that took the law into their own hands, lynching, dissecting, and mauling the body of the deceased as a form of punishment.[10]

In the 1930s, when some of the last living formerly enslaved people were interviewed about their experiences under enslavement, they too recalled the medical curiosities of their bodies expressed in the form of "soundness." Once enslaved, Barney Stone of Kentucky noted that some doctors accompanied buyers on the eve of sales "to examine the slave's heart." If they were pronounced "sound," the "buyer would make an offer to the owner and if the amount was satisfactory, the slave was sold."[11]

Heth's public autopsy clearly gave new meaning to the monetary value of the dead. We know from the bellies of enslaved pregnant women that the financial value of their "future increase" was projected, but very little consideration has been given to the value of enslaved bodies after death, until now. Considering this topic brings us into a direct study of nineteenth-century medicine, medical education, the history of anatomy, and slavery.[12]

Dr. Rogers had students and colleagues standing by his side, watching his every move when he cut open Heth's body. Hands-on training was as important to medical education then as it is today, particularly at teaching hospitals. But historian of medicine Michael Sappol reminds us that "dissection for the purposes of medical instruction" had a completely different meaning than an autopsy. Typically, autopsies fell under the category of "medical jurisprudence," when questions surrounding the cause of death resulted in a hearing. Such procedures were "performed in a private room" with physicians who served as jurors; medical students could not weigh in on the case.[13] Perhaps people's curiosity about Heth's age justified their desire to pay for and watch the dissection. Some of the same individuals who paid to see her while she was living likely also paid to see her after death.

Dissections in public settings such as this, and in medical facilities for higher learning, occurred regularly in the nineteenth century, and the dissections of enslaved and formerly enslaved people represented a unique way to extend the profits of slavery beyond the grave. Heth arrives in the historical record as an aged woman loaned and purchased for display in popular cultural settings such as fairs, circuses, and live performances. Some argue that this was not only the result of her physical appearance but also her coerced complicity in her own exploitation. Clearly she participated in the public spectacle Barnum and Lyman created. She told stories and sang songs to entertain her audiences, and Barnum aided with publicity by sending anonymous letters to local newspapers before their shows. When Heth became ill, a Boston woman cared for her until she died on February 19, 1836. Her postmortem journey brought her corpse about 233 miles via carriage to the New York home of Barnum, where he allegedly "stored her" in a hallway for a few days and then hosted one final public performance in which Heth was the attraction. In addition to attending the autopsy, people paid for the newspapers that described the event, discussing Heth for months and years after she departed. Similar to the contemporary story of Henrietta Lacks, Heth's afterlife contributed to medical education.

This chapter examines the postmortem journeys of deceased enslaved people like Heth, as well as unknown cadavers, who were on display at medical schools for the benefit of higher learning. Because they were dead, the voices of the enslaved are barely represented here. Instead, I rely heavily on the perspective of physicians who handled their bodies. What follows is the story of the corpses of the enslaved bodies after death, bodies that became part of a clandestine cadaver trade that I believe paralleled other illegal forms of human trafficking. Formerly enslaved people and many others (black, white, and free) experienced a postmortem journey that few scholars consider. As one of the first to trace this history, with a particular focus on enslaved people and their cadaver journeys, I think that we have much more to learn about the life cycles of the enslaved. Their bodies experienced commodification after death. The fiscal values of their cadavers became tradable goods that were part of a clandestine traffic in bodies used for anatomical education.

During Heth's life and, arguably, in her death, audiences from all walks of life viewed her body for social purposes, as a form of entertainment, to satisfy their curiosities about the aged "African" body, and also to investigate Barnum's propaganda that asserted she was George Washington's elderly nursemaid. Other cadavers arrived at universities and medical colleges as part of an underground traffic in dead bodies—the domestic cadaver trade.

IDENTIFYING THE DOMESTIC CADAVER TRADE

Procuring bodies for medical instruction created an unusual problem for university faculty between the 1830s and 1880s. They needed bodies for dissection, but in most states, there were no legally sanctioned sources (aside from the gallows).

However, between 1760 and 1876, medical students likely participated in anywhere from an estimated 4,200 to 8,000 dissections. These statistics are more revealing when one considers that the only legal candidates for medical dissection were often unclaimed executed criminals and enslaved people with their enslaver's consent. This raises questions about where the bodies came from, and the role of enslavers in this process.

Some enslavers had the bodies of enslaved people dug up and sold, as Charlie Grant shared in his testimony (chapter 2). Other enslavers passively allowed the bodies of their deceased enslaved people to be harvested or exhumed. An unknown number of enslavers were also medical doctors who took the cadavers directly to the dissection table because they considered them their personal property. A number of corpses entered this market when stolen from burial grounds or the sites of enslavement on which they died. But not all enslavers supported this traffic, making this history difficult to trace. My focus here is on the cadavers in circulation, even when I cannot fully determine how they ended up on the dissection table. I know that a large number of medical specimens were obtained illegally, and that a significant proportion of them were of African descent; arguably many had once been enslaved.

Parts of the illegal activity involved purchasing cadavers through a clandestine market. In this setting, bodies sold for a range of prices, from $5 in most places to $30 in "Ohio and other states." Bodies were cheaper if it was easier "to procure the necessary supply of subjects," and they were more expensive when "it is difficult."[14] Just as in the domestic slave trade, in the cadaver trade, importing and exporting states depended on the enslaved population, the willingness of traders, and the ability to transport this unusual merchandise. Thus, before the passage of most statewide anatomy acts in the 1880s, "teachers of anatomy were driven to the undignified and illegal practice of encouraging and rewarding grave-robbing as the sole means of supplying the dissecting room." Some were directly involved in this practice, and others relied on professional resurrectionists, who stole fresh bodies from cemeteries at night and served as medical school janitors during the day. Dr. Daniel Drake, a physician from Kentucky, noted that "the 'resurrectionist' (grave robber) might be the college or hospital janitor, although often it was the student himself or even the professor of anatomy."[15] From this "material," taken by university janitors in the middle of the night, medical students learned "the structure of the [human] body."[16]

Tracing the origins, routes, and agents, I find that the traffic in enslaved bodies modeled itself after the transatlantic and domestic slave trade and is comparable to modern forms of human trafficking. In order to understand this network, however, we must consider the value of deceased people, outlined in previous chapters through ghost values, and the key people involved in facilitating "a traffic of dead bodies."[17] From private and public autopsies to an illegal cadaver trade, I will address the valuation and sale of formerly enslaved and some free black people after death.[18] Most of the cadavers were once enslaved, and neither death nor burial freed them from additional commodification and exploitation. Corpses of formerly enslaved people were technically the property of enslavers, institutions, or state agencies at the time of death, making it difficult or impossible for enslaved and free family members to claim the rights to their relative and ensure proper burial, or to prevent tampering after a body was laid to rest.

Cultivating a Corpse

The domestic cadaver trade was a highly organized transportation system. One way to understand it is to consider how it paralleled agricultural production. For this traffic to happen, a body had to be planted, harvested, and transported.

The cadaver trade functioned on a cyclical calendar, much as enslaved people's lives were governed by an agricultural calendar. As laborers, the life cycle of the enslaved followed the crop schedule. As cadavers, the lifespan of a body followed a decomposition schedule; proper preservation was important.

Like other forms of involuntary migration, the domestic cadaver trade was seasonal. The majority of body snatching occurred in the summer, fall, and early winter, just as coffles were transferred from the Upper South to markets in the Deep South, and as transatlantic ships made their voyages during specific months depending on the location, weather, and crop.[19] African merchants waited until harvest was done and crops were stored before they "sold enslaved farmers and provisions to coastal middlemen, who in turn, sold these captives to ship captains" headed to New World plantation communities in North and South America as well as the Caribbean.[20] Fall weather proved ideal for domestic travel and for grave digging, before frozen ground revealed snow-tracked footsteps and such work became nearly impossible. Brisk fall nights offered suitable temperatures for preserving corpses; the summer months were challenging because hot weather sped up decomposition. Thus, most bodies were stolen, sold, and prepared for dissection during cooler months. Anatomy demonstrations that involved dissections often occurred during the winter and concluded at the onset of spring.

These rather unusual trading systems make sense when understood through the metaphor of cultivating crops and corpses. In January, agricultural laborers working with cotton prepared the fields for planting. Cadavers were also prepared before being placed in the ground, but this work, often done by family members or close associates, occurred throughout the year, as people died daily.[21] In March, enslaved laborers put cotton seeds in the ground; after planting came the "lay by" stage, in which the crop was given time to incubate and grow. Burial represented the planting phase of a cadaver, but in order to cultivate a corpse, it had to be exhumed. In other words, the "lay by" season for a cadaver was less than seventy-two hours after burial because it took seven to ten days to completely "anatomize" a corpse before "the body became too decomposed to be useful for study."[22] Harvesting marked the next important stage for cotton crops and cadavers. The cotton harvest lasted from the summer to the early fall. Cadavers were often harvested or exhumed in late summer, fall, and the early winter months. Following the harvest, the crop or, in this case, cadaver had to be packaged and prepared for the market. The process of producing a good crop or cadaver involved highly specialized packaging. These "products" had to make it to their destinations intact, well preserved, and ready for the process that turned a corpse into a specimen. Cotton bales and bags protected fibers by keeping them clean. Cadaver bags, also made of cotton, functioned the same way for short transports, but for further distances that involved shipping, bodies were placed in large casks filled with preservation liquids such as whiskey or brine. At the market, planters and brokers sold the raw crops and the smuggled cadavers. When the "fresh" body arrived at a medical college, it was removed from its packaging, set on a table-like assembly line, "manufactured" as a specimen, and used for

Bodies were put in cadaver bags for transfer.

dissection until complete decomposition ended the cycle.

The causes of death of an enslaved person varied, and so did the way their bodies entered the market. Some were executed, sold, or stolen, others buried and exhumed, and some were unclaimed and legal candidates for dissection. The once-enslaved body now had a different purpose; it was manufactured into a valuable commodity that would be used to train medical professionals in the halls of some of America's leading institutions, including Dartmouth College, Harvard University, Northwestern University, the University of Chicago, the University of Virginia, the University of Maryland, and Virginia Commonwealth University.[23] At these colleges, the harvest process was completed and the corpse was fully manufactured for anatomical education. Just as the raw cotton produced by enslaved people was manufactured into cloth, and then transformed into aprons covered with rubber and worn by physicians and their students in the dissecting rooms, the once-enslaved body underwent a similar process as a way for medical profesionals to better understand the human body.

Schools were dependent on cadavers, whether formerly enslaved or not. However, given the illegal nature of the trade in the early to mid-nineteenth century, members of the medical community proceeded with caution and participated in an underground market to obtain these unusual goods. In their opinion, they had no alternative, because "the number of legally available corpses was woefully inadequate."[24] It was, however, legal to dissect executed criminals and unclaimed persons, so almshouses, hospitals, and prisons worked closely with physicians.[25] Although denied humanity while enslaved, after cultivation and manufacturing the corpse-turned-specimen was now more human than before as it was used to understand the intricacies of the human body. This ghost value enabled the bodies of the enslaved to generate money for enslavers after death. Determining the racial identity and social status of the cultivated corpses is difficult; however, it is clear through the historical record that the majority were African Americans.[26]

Major medical men in the United States played key roles in the domestic cadaver trade. They were the orchestrators of this grand symphony, while enslaved and free janitors served as the conductors. These men were of great medical stature and were well known in their communities as local physicians and leaders. They were also men who encouraged and participated in an illegal trade in deceased people. Their training overlapped and so did their methods. Rather than operating in a triangular trade, the doctors involved in the domestic cadaver trade created an intricate web that had recognizable patterns. First, many of them were trained at the same institutions; second, they relied on European methods of dissection; and finally, they recognized that an ample supply of cadavers was crucial to anatomical training. Some early American physicians did part of their training in Europe, where members of the upper-class elite killed and dissected poor citizens who had few legal avenues of protection. This web of doctors appears in the historical literature.[27]

By tracing physicians and their protégés' academic genealogies, the trade in dead bodies becomes clear. The point here is not to demonize these medical practitioners, but to paint a historical picture based on the records.[28] Thus, when placed in the context of the global history of anatomical education, the cadaver trade functioned along familiar routes, and the advancement of higher learning served as the primary object. The value of cadavers to nineteenth-century medical education clearly supports the idea that ghost values were a necessary part of the trade. Physicians were not always trying to obstruct justice; many were doing as their mentors had trained them. Yet the disrespect of African American life, as well as the lives of the poor and disadvantaged, also comes to the fore.

Looking specifically at anatomical education in the United States, I uncovered an intellectual genealogy with Philadelphia roots and a reach that went as far west as Texas, as far north as Massachusetts, and as far south as Louisiana, Mississippi, and Alabama. Tracing the physicians and their protégés illustrates the importance of a normalized traffic in dead bodies. To begin, all roads lead to and from Philadelphia.

PHYSICIANS AT NORTHERN MEDICAL SCHOOLS

Northern medical schools had a slight advantage over their Southern counterparts because anatomical education in America began in the North. Dr. William Shippen Jr. gave the first anatomy lecture in the colonies at the University of Pennsylvania in 1762. In an advertisement to announce the lectures, he explained that he would address all parts of the human body. However, because the public was opposed to dissection at this time, he had to reassure them, three years later in another newspaper advertisement, that the bodies he dissected were from people who committed suicide or were publicly executed.[29] In actuality, Shippen "instructed his students in the ways and means of body-snatching," and his rooms at the university "were filled with cadavers . . . no grave was safe against his predatory plans."[30]

One year later, a man in New York City became one of the earliest identifiable cases of an African American dissection in the colonies.[31] This marked the beginning of medical education, particularly the dissection of the dead. It also spurred the clandestine business of sending bodies and body parts to physicians and colleges, creating a traffic in human remains that still exists today in the form of underground organ trade on the "black market."

In 1770, Shippen was accused of body snatching and publicly defended himself in the *Pennsylvania Chronicle*. "To the Public," he began, "I hear," that residents were "terrified by sundry wicked and malicious reports of my taking up bodies from the several burying grounds in this place." These reports were false, he explained, and "propagated by weak prejudiced persons, or intended to injure my character." Further, he wanted the public to know that by "declaring in the most solemn manner," he "never" did nor would he ever "directly or indirectly" take a "subject from the burying ground belonging to any denomination of Christians whatever." How he determined faith after death he did not clearly articulate, but those buried in church-sponsored grounds likely confirmed their faith before death. The Christianity argument—that stated one could enslave Africans regardless of their faith—was also used to justify slavery in the sixteenth century and later.

Shippen closed his statement with a defense of his practice, stating that he taught anatomy for the "public good" and that he "always will preserve the utmost decency with regard to the dead." He promised readers that "none of your house or kindred shall ever be disturbed in their silent graves, by me or any under my care." Finally, he invited readers to review an included affidavit by one of his students, Joseph Harrison, as further evidence of his legitimate practices.[32]

The fact that Dr. Shippen paid to place an advertisement in a local paper suggests that these allegations were indeed serious. The studies of anatomy and dissection were not highly favored at this time, and physicians like Shippen had to be careful about their activities. Members of the medical profession generally agreed that dissection was necessary, but it took some time to convince the larger public.

Some doctors learned how to identify and acquire bodies for dissection from their classmates. In 1796, Dr. John Collins Warren of Harvard University shared that he started the business of "getting subjects" for dissection while in college. Describing the practice, he explained that he and his co-conspirators "found the grave" and commenced "uncovering the coffin by breaking it open." Next, they "took out the body of a stout young man, put it in a bag and carried it" away. Despite nearly getting caught, the corpse was "taken up" and "drove off to Cambridge." Two people stayed at the gravesite to complete the important task of filling the grave in order to avoid detection in the morning. The next day, Warren showed his father (John Warren), the founder of Harvard Medical School, the cadaver he had stolen and the elder "saw what a fine healthy subject it was" and was pleased at the quality but even more so that this particular body "lasted the course through."[33] The elder Warren had "dissected and demonstrated the structure of lower animals and studied the bones of the human skeleton" in his day.

When the younger Warren (John Collins) joined the faculty (1815–1847), he faced the challenge of finding cadavers for dissection. Rumors of body snatching were common, and he said that he was personally attacked for his activities. However, in 1831, Warren led the charge to pass the first anatomical law in the United States, which established parameters for the "proper acquisition of cadavers."[34] As noted, with the seasonality of the cadaver trade, bodies procured in the late fall were ideal for use during the winter lecture courses. Warren's stolen cadaver discussed earlier was exactly what the school needed that year. Ironically, when he died, he made special instructions for his postmortem body, requesting to have his bones "carefully preserved, whitened, articulated and placed in the Medical College near my bust," because he wanted physicians to advance their craft by studying his body.[35] Fifty years later, physicians at Harvard were still involved in trafficking cadavers, black bodies in particular.[36]

Just before Thanksgiving in 1845, Francis Bowen, a Harvard-trained philosopher and editor of the *North American Review*, sent a letter to Dr. Jeffries Wyman at Hampden-Sydney Medical College (Richmond, Virginia) inquiring about cadavers. The two old friends had been writing to one another for some time. "You speak of taboo crops and the price of [n_____r]s," Bowen remarked, but because he wanted to be certain, he added, "Of course, you meant the price of *dead* [n_____r]s, they being the only commodity that you trade in." Dr. Wyman was not a slave trader, nor was he a plantation owner. He was a physician who used cadavers in the classroom and was in the business of sending cadavers north to colleagues at medical schools, such as Harvard where he received his degree. "Do tell me, what is the cost of a fine, stiff [n——r]?" Bowen continued, "one that will *cut up fat* and that doesn't smell strong enough to be *nosed* a mile off?" Clearly, he wanted to avoid detection, given the illegal nature of the trade and hoped that the decaying body would not emanate strong odors. In closing, he asked his friend, "Do you have a *price* current for such merchandise?"[37]

Nearly all of the nineteenth-century medical schools and colleges in Georgia, Ohio, Massachusetts, New York, and Virginia participated in this clandestine trade because doctors wanted subjects for dissection. According to the history of Harvard Medical School, "Body-snatching and the rise of modern anatomy went together."[38] The field of medicine depended on cadavers for instruction, forcing doctors and their protégés to rely on this illegal trade.[39] It relied on a wide network of agents, brokers, and buyers, as well as material to transport the "goods," chemicals to mask the odor, and individuals to facilitate the traffic.

Bowen made a specific inquiry about African American cadavers, ones that "cut up fat," meaning that they were fresh, with thick skin. This characteristic was important for instruction purposes because overused cadavers had thin, leathery skin and did not make good teaching tools. Physicians at the University of Virginia had complained about "inferior subjects" and even returned ones that were not packaged properly.[40]

As the web of influence grew and the hunger for medical education continued, faculty trained their students to continue instructing others. Moving to the Midwest, one of Dr. Shippen's students, Dr. Daniel Drake, became a leading physician in Kentucky and Ohio. Drake first trained under Dr. Goforth in Ohio and learned to practice medicine by age twenty. He arrived in Cincinnati or Losantiville in 1800, as "its first student of medicine" and started his medical training in December.[41] Other doctors in Cincinnati included Robert McClure, John Sellman, and John Cranmer (also spelled Dranmore), all of whom may have been involved in the cadaver trade before the legalization of dissection.

After completing his formal training in 1816, Drake received his MD from the University of Pennsylvania and practiced in Cincinnati. Drake is known as being "the first active medical faculty [member] west of the Allegheny Mountains." Two years later, he founded and incorporated the Medical College of Ohio.[42] After creating a medical department at Cincinnati College (1819), he worked at Transylvania University (Lexington, Kentucky) and then Jefferson Medical College in Philadelphia from 1830 to 1831. Sometime in 1831, he returned to Ohio to develop the medical department at Cincinnati College. One of his former students noted that Drake was so competent that he could be compared to the famous Philadelphia doctor, Benjamin Rush, also a politician and a signer of the Declaration of Independence. However, reflecting on Drake, former apprentice William Barbee noted that Drake always asked his students about "some anatomical fact."[43] Given the scarcity of medical men in Ohio at the time, one wonders if Drake could have viewed and/or taught with parts of Nat Turner's dismembered body.

Drake had strong opinions about slavery. In his travels, he witnessed everyday life in slave and free states. In 1839, he accepted a chair at Louisville Medical Institute and continued training students. A little more than ten years later, he discussed slavery in a series of letters to Dr. John Collins Warren of Harvard. Rather than dissection, he seemed distracted with emancipation and colonization. This distraction makes sense because he wrote around the time of the Compromise of 1850, which in part included a "fugitive slave clause" that made Northerners culpable for not returning runaways. Warren and Drake supported the Union, but were not considered abolitionists. From his travels throughout the North and South, for example, Drake firmly believed that slave states should remain pro-slavery and that free states should remain free. "In the State Governments," he wrote, "and in them only, resides the power which can annihilate the causes of agitation, and quiet the tempest they have raised." He felt that Northern states "should shut out all emancipated and fugitive slaves; and the States of the South, with equal uniformity, should forbid all emancipation."[44] Given these reflections, he was clearly neither friend nor foe to the enslaved. If anything, he seemed concerned about the presence of free blacks. These attitudes become important when we study the domestic cadaver trade as they provide insight into the minds of the medical men who were involved and suggest that their practices were for the benefit of instruction as opposed to recreational or experimental demonstations.

The US medical profession lagged behind its European counterparts, particularly in terms of material and human items for medical museums and anatomy instruction. However, several physicians received training in Europe in the eighteenth and nineteenth centuries because of a growing enthusiasm for medical knowledge.[45] By the third decade of the nineteenth century, "no school in our country has as yet collected such a Museum as to be sufficient for the instruction of the lectures of the professors."[46] The faculty at Jefferson Medical College in Philadelphia, especially Dr. Granville Sharp Pattison, demonstrator of anatomy, wanted to remedy this shortcoming. Having studied in London and worked at the University of Maryland, Pattison came to Jefferson Medical College with the hopes of capitalizing on the number of "liberally supplied" corpses one could find in and around an urban center such as Philadelphia.[47] The

City of Brotherly Love was "celebrated for the facilities it affords to the medical students," who went there in droves seeking an education. The same facilities that attracted students drew the attention of physicians such as Pattison.

Founded in 1824 by the Pennsylvania legislature, by 1836 the school had admitted its largest class, 354 students, since its opening. About 32 percent of the student body came from Southern states, and a handful came from Ireland, Barbados, and Canada. However, the majority were from the North. The college boasted: "The number of students in attendance during the last session was not exceeded by that of any other Medical School in the United States." Their students spent time "in the offices of intelligent Practitioners," as the faculty recruited Dr. Robley Dunglison from the University of Virginia and Dr. Granville Sharp Pattison from the University of Maryland. They believed that no good medical school could function without strong faculty and a state-of-the-art museum.[48]

John Barclay curated the museum at Jefferson Medical College, which contained "healthy and morbid anatomical specimens" or body parts of considerable value. The school janitor, William Watson, had been hired in the fall of 1828 for $18 per month. In his application letter, he added that his payment should occur monthly from November through April. His duty was to "prepare the use of two rooms in the basement [for dissection and] two little cellar apartments," where he could live rent free. He was also responsible for taking "charge of the Building and Air the Rooms and Brush them off occasionally . . . [and all the] necessary . . . scrubbing and washing of the basement story."[49] It was his responsibility to keep the area clean and well ventilated.

The college acquired some cadavers, both intact and dismembered, after soliciting material from "friends" who might have come across unusual specimens of morbid anatomy in their practice. To transport these items, "all that is necessary is merely to have them removed from the body and placed in a vessel of whiskey." Drawing the "old whiskey" off and adding fresh amounts to the cask could salvage large specimens kept in "spirits for a fortnight." These rather straightforward instructions, published openly in the college announcement of lectures, suggest that transporting bodies and body parts for anatomical display was quite common before the mid-nineteenth century. Although extralegal, physicians needed material to teach their students, and the school's reputations and recruitment often rested in these vivid solicitations.[50]

In an 1833 lecture, Pattison cautioned students to "guard against over-estimating the talents and the reputation of those Members of your profession" who lived at a distance. Having trained in Europe, he felt justified in his remarks, so he reminded students not to view European physicians as "idols," because Jefferson Medical College also had a wonderful faculty including Dr. Phillip Syng Physick and Dr. George M'Clellan who "are not inferior to any of their most gifted brethren in Europe." He wanted them to look for "eminence in your own profession or in other walks of life," because it was not necessary "to go from home" or "to leave your own Country."[51] Students, as a result, were fortunate to have a "distinguished" group of physicians and surgeons to teach them. A hospital and almshouse nearby added great diversity to the cases that the physicians at Jefferson Medical College examined. "The supply of subjects for dissection" was "abundant even to profusion," making Philadelphia the center of medical training.[52]

Although urban doctors believed that large cities meant an ample supply of subjects for dissection, population demographics did not necessarily correlate to an excess of "dead bodies." State and local legislation restricted the means of acquiring corpses. For example, historian Michael Sappol states that "the first law to sanction dissection in the United States" was enacted in New York in 1789. Referred to as an "Act to Prevent the Odious Practice of Digging up and Removing for the Purpose of Dissection, Dead Bodies Interred in Cemeteries or Burial Places," this legislation required a surgeon to be present to claim the body if the judge declared that dissection was part of the sentencing. It also outlawed body snatching. In Massachusetts, "only those killed in a burl or those executed for such a homicide could be dissected." It was also customary for "judges in some of the other states . . . to decree dissection as part of the death sentence."[53]

Just a few years before the Heth autopsy, faculty members at Jefferson Medical College published their "Annual Announcement of Lectures." In this circular, they made it clear that "dissection, and dissection alone, can make a *man* an Anatomist." Advertising their facilities, faculty, and lectures was an important recruitment tool for medical schools hoping to attract a good class of students. Jefferson Medical boasted about its facilities, claiming to have admirable theaters "for the purposes of effective teaching" that are "large, well-ventilated, and so constructed, that the most minute demonstrations can be distinctly seen from the most distant benches."[54] It did not have to convert a saloon, as was done in Heth's case, to study the human body. JMC was proud to have state-of-the-art facilities.

The faculty at Jefferson Medical College operated under the medical harvesting schedule previously described to optimize bodily preservation and university instruction. As noted, bodies ideally needed to be exhumed within twenty-four hours of burial, no more than seventy-two hours postmortem and ten days before complete decomposition. The bodies had to be transferred to medical schools quickly and/or placed in preservation liquids. Schools stocked their shelves with these specimens, as is evident in JMC's supplies.[55] Once the bodies reached their destination, via shipment, rail, or carriage, those on the receiving end had to prep them for dissection.

From Pennsylvania and Ohio to Massachusetts, physicians and their protégés were in conversation about medicine and slavery. Sons of the South went north to matriculate through medical degree programs and stayed in communication with their (often) planter-class families. Sometimes Northerners went south to work at universities. During his short time at Hampden-Sydney in Richmond, Dr. Wyman made occasional references to slavery. "I feel more & more convinced," he wrote a Boston colleague, "that in the system of Slavery where everything connected with it is accursed, the slave & master are both sufferers." He was not impressed with the South and felt that slavery was a "vile system [that] must be done away with."[56] Others took pride in working at Southern institutions.

PHYSICIANS AT SOUTHERN MEDICAL SCHOOLS

Southern medical schools and colleges competed with Northern institutions. For too long, their sons had been traveling above the Mason-Dixon Line to pursue their academic dreams at elite Northern universities such as the University of Pennsylvania, Harvard, Dartmouth, and others. In order for Southern institutions to excel, they needed to demand that their physicians maintain a high level of respectability.

According to the sentiment in the late 1820s, the medical student was a "student all his life," and schools should enforce reasonable fees. In an address to the Medical Society of Georgia, Dr. Alexander Jones added that physicians should be *"polite, virtuous, charitable, hospitable, kind, benevolent* and well educated gentlemen." Placing physicians just one mark below clergymen, he suggested that doctors needed official training and that it did not have to occur in Philadelphia, an indictment against the University of Pennsylvania and Jefferson Medical College. In some cases, Southern students who went north were not encouraged to maintain their virtuous upbringings, Jones suggested, because Northern institutions were more concerned with increasing their numbers as opposed to "giv[ing] the school respectability and standing." Diplomas were distributed liberally "without regard to merit." Thus, on the eve of a watershed in anatomical education, Jones encouraged potential students to obtain a medical education in the South, in order to "free up the profession from such lumber, by setting up a purer standard of medical character."[57] Too many leading anatomists received their education in Philadelphia, and even though their influence reached international fame, regionalism remained important in the South.

Physicians in South Carolina harbored strong opinions about regionalism. The Palmetto State established a medical board in 1817 and a medical college in Charleston in 1823. At the opening lecture for the fourth class of students at the Charleston Medical College, Dr. Samuel Dickson reminded them of their high calling and encouraged them to apply the "pious language" of Milton by participating in "devout prayer to the eternal spirit . . . industrious and select reading, steady observation and insight into . . . all affairs." He took pride in measuring students by these standards. He closed by reminding them that "in selecting the Medical Profession . . . [they] have not chosen a life of ease and indolence," because the path in front of them included "roughness and difficulty."[58] Thus, by the first three decades of the nineteenth century, students of medicine had opportunities to learn in Northern and Southern institutions. If they chose to go north, they paid lecture fees, which included twenty dollars at the University of Pennsylvania, ten dollars at Jefferson Medical College, and a "moderate" fee at facilities in New York. Remaining close to home saved money and supported their local and state governments, and for some, gave them more access to formerly enslaved bodies.

Certain laws gave enslavers the right to donate or sell enslaved people "dying from natural causes" for the use of anatomical studies.[59] Enslavers were even known to advertise them, as can be seen in the notices from Dr. T. Stillman of South Carolina, who sought sick, disabled, diseased, and nearly dead enslaved people. In an ad placed on October 12, 1838, in the *Charleston Mercury*, Stillman requested the following:

> To PLANTERS AND OTHERS.—Wanted *fifty negroes.* Any person having sick negroes, considered incurable by their respective physicians, and wishing to dispose of them, Dr. S. will pay cash for negroes affected with scrofula or king's evil, confirmed hypocondriasm [sic], apoplexy, diseases of the liver, kidneys, spleen, stomach and intestines, bladder and its appendages, diarrhea, dysentery, &c. The highest cash price will be paid on application as above.[60]

That he was willing to pay the "highest cash price" confirms the need for medical subjects. It also suggests that the value of enslaved bodies for medical research was established according to a different price scale than enslaved bodies valued for physical labor in plantation fields, factories, and homes. The diseased body in a medical setting had value for research and education and was often displayed in museums, but a diseased or unsound body in a market setting for labor carried little monetary value.

Advertisements placed in newspapers by Southern physicians searching for diseased enslaved bodies confirm that these practices were not unusual. On May 29, 1839, Dr. King of New Orleans posted a detailed ad in the *Picayune* similar to his colleague's in South Carolina.[61] In the ad, King listed the diseases that he was interested in, and the curiosity in women, perhaps in their childbearing years, ones with "female diseases," confirms the interest in women's bodies previously discussed (in chapter 3). King also posted this ad in Arkansas, South Carolina, Kentucky, and Mississippi newspapers.

Regional pride drove some physicians to specific recruiting methods. Dr. Paul Eve of the Medical Institute of Georgia encouraged Southern students to attend schools close to home rather than in New York, Philadelphia, Baltimore, Lexington and Charleston. To accommodate higher learning, the college extended its instruction period from the customary four months to six months (October–April). It nurtured the development of the medical profession for the first thirty years of the nineteenth century and acknowledged the charge of the noble physician to always be "ready, to act without being officious, to be attentive without being too familiar, to be kind without being too yielding, to proportion the pleasures of society without neglecting study, to treat all claiming the professional fraternity with due regard and circumspection without exhibiting partialities or inattentions." Like Dr. Jones, Eve also believed Southern practitioners had a higher calling.[62]

Twenty years later, Southern physicians used nationalism as well as religious sentiment to encourage Southerners to seek medical degrees close to home. It is no surprise that the North/South divide increased on the eve of the Civil War. For example, the Savannah Medical College had an all-Southern medical class for the 1857–1858 session. Of the twenty-five students, all but two were from Georgia, with the exceptions of one student from South Carolina and another from Florida. The college boasted of its "large, well lighted and ventilated" dissecting rooms, which contained "every desirable convenience." Students could "rest assured" that there was an "abundance of material furnished for dissection." Tickets to lectures cost $5, while the demonstrator of anatomy received $10 lecture fees. In the opening remarks of his commencement address, attorney George A. Gordon emphasized "*the necessity of encouraging and promoting the success of this and kindred Institution[s]*" [emphasis in original] to maintain its patriotic support of medical education in "slaveholding States." He also conferred on the graduating class power and influence "almost to that of Divinity" and reminded them that their medical training was the root of their influence. He chastised Southerners who went to Northern colleges for not "fostering and developing our schools at home." He also likely intended to discredit the University of Pennsylvania and Jefferson Medical College when he noted, "The antiquity of a college is not an index of its excellence" and that "the nearer home you bring the great laboratories of truth, the wider must be their dissemination among our own people." The entire address was a call to stay in the South and share their gifts with their communities because they were a "peculiar people in every respect." The South was "peculiar in soil, peculiar in her climate, peculiar in her diseases," but most importantly, "the South needs the energy of her own sons—and no others—to shape the course of her destiny." By 1859, there was a mass exodus of Southern students from Northern medical schools, particularly the University of Pennsylvania and Jefferson Medical College.[63]

The growing tension between the North and South had clearly reached the halls of medicine. However, physicians in both regions worked together to develop a domestic cadaver trade. Perhaps the quest for medical knowledge trumped regionalism. Cooperation between Northern and Southern physicians increased as US physicians competed with their European counterparts, ultimately fueling the traffic in bodies used for dissection. The actions of the Medical College of Georgia provide a great deal of insight into this cadaver trade.

Body Snatching

In 1839, the Medical College of Georgia in Augusta purchased $100 worth of cadavers from a New York source. Anatomical "subjects" at that time cost approximately 75 cents each; therefore, it is likely that the school received 130 cadavers through this transaction. The subjects were "shipped in casks of brine or whiskey" and placed on a "coastal steamer" to Charleston, along the same routes as shipments of living enslaved people. Three years later in 1842, Dr. Newton, the demonstrator of anatomy, took a trip to Baltimore "to secure subjects for the coming year." He probably traveled the Atlantic seaboard along the same shipping lanes as domestic and transatlantic slave ships. These ships would have been outfitted with a small crew and raw goods being sent north for manufacturing. To take such a voyage, Newton had to make arrangements in advance, and the items he purchased had to be prepared for transportation. He would need casks to transport the bodies and whiskey or lime for preservation. He also knew that popular sentiment did not support dissection, so he used discretion in conversations with enslavers and "next of kin."[64] Some enslavers in Norfolk, nearly two hundred miles from the University of Virginia, did not want their enslaved people's graves tampered with; others simply did not care. The same patterns existed in Georgia.[65]

From 1848 to 1852, the Medical College of Georgia used "resurrection slaves named Joe, King, Peter, Jackson, John and Edmund" to rob graves from local cemeteries. It brought in sixty-four subjects for dissection, equivalent to "16 subjects per term."[66] These enslaved men were given wages or modest fees for their services, which included grave robbing and then reinterment after the medical students and faculty were finished with the dissection. They acquired bodies in South Carolina and Georgia.

Eventually, by the 1850s, the Medical College of Georgia (MCG) faculty relied on one enslaved man to conduct this business. On January 6, 1852, seven members of the medical faculty purchased Grandison Harris from a Charleston, South Carolina, auction block. Known as a member of the Gullah community, the thirty-six-year-old Harris was bought for $700, and valued at $753, equivalent to $22,125 in 2014. Faculty members each owned one-seventh of his person and could sell their share if they left the school.[67] His official title was "porter," but the faculty purchased him for one purpose: to supply the school with subjects for dissection. Those who knew him said he "was good." We do not know the race and status of all those he procured; some were free blacks. Members of the African American community had mixed feelings about him.[68] We do know that he stole bodies from Cedar Grove Cemetery, which was reserved for poor and black residents; the cemetery was not fenced. Harris learned to read and write, searched obituaries for potential subjects, and sat in on anatomy lectures. Some referred to him as a "teaching assistant," and "students respected his expertise." He became knowledgeable about dissections and, over time, perfected his craft. One scholar described him as being responsible for all the preparations necessary for acquiring, preparing, displaying, and disposing of human specimens.[69]

Once he identified a potential corpse, he went to Cedar Grove Cemetery at night and dug "down to the upper end of the box"; then he smashed it "with an axe" and drew the subject out, placed it in a sack, and carted it to the college. By employing Harris, the Medical College of Georgia saved money, because it no longer had to hire enslaved people to do this work, nor did it have to purchase cadavers from sources in South Carolina, Maryland, New York, and Massachusetts, as they had done before Harris's arrival.[70]

Harris was fully integrated into MCG, and he appears frequently in school records. Faculty made note of his activities, including his wages, room and board, supplies, and payments for acquiring dissection subjects from 1853 through 1857. At a glance, he appears in about 25 percent of the faculty account records. Harris received $6.75–$10.00 in monthly wages from the college.[71] Over this four-year period, he was paid a total of $412 for forty-one subjects collected. He likely needed supplies for his clandestine activities, so in December 1854, the faculty paid $4 for "containing subjects and cover" and, on another occasion, purchased a wheelbarrow. Likewise, on January 17, 1856, the school paid $66.67 for whiskey, which was probably used to preserve cadavers.[72]

After years of collecting subjects for dissection, Harris had also been traveling back and forth to South Carolina to see his family. In 1858, the dean of the college returned to the Charleston auction block and purchased Harris's wife, Rachel, and son, George, for a total cost of $1,250, equivalent to $37,083 in 2014.[73] Again, this represented another financial decision, because owning the entire family "kept Grandison Harris off the railroad between Augusta and Charleston," a journey that cost the school twelve dollars each time. Rachel worked as a cook and laundress, while George learned about his father's business. Although we do not know much about Rachel and George, we can speculate that she washed the sheets, blankets, aprons, and rags used in the dissecting rooms. Postslavery photographs of black laundresses at medical colleges show unnamed women with brooms behind medical students performing dissections. We know, from the testimonies of medical students themselves, that the smells and substances involved were not pleasant. We can only imagine that George aided his parents in their work, which was customary at the time. In a photo of the MCG anatomy class taken in the early twentieth century, an unidentified African American adolescent is present. Could this be Grandison and Rachel's son George? The family spent their lives at the college where they lived and worked.[74]

Harris was so well known and respected that he appeared in many graduating class photos alongside newly minted doctors. The Harris family remained connected to the medical college even after slavery. Like many of his peers, Harris was caught and jailed in the 1880s and later released. Newspaper reports of the incident noted that he had been "exhuming bodies from the city cemeteries . . . for some time" and that Harris had been sending bodies "in trunks to Atlanta for medical colleges."[75] In 1904, the school minutes made the following remarks about their "faithful old servant, and friend, Grandison Harris," who was described as "too decrepit for the [janitorial] work." The minutes comment that his son George is "too trifling to be kept in the position" of janitor. In 1905, the faculty voted to pay Harris a monthly ten-dollar pension for the rest of his life. In June 1911, a few months before his death, the faculty arranged for his care at a home near the Freedmen's Hospital. The "Registrar report" indicated that "Harris was in a most deplorable condition . . . and in great need of medical attention." The same physicians and students he served for much of his adult life agreed to have a nurse administer his care as he aged. A Professor Wilcox moved to have Harris "placed in a house adjoin the Lamar Hospital" with a "nurse . . . to give him all the necessary attention." This motion was seconded and carried.[76] Harris died in 1911, at age ninety-five. Ironically, he was laid to rest in the same cemetery, Cedar Grove, in which he had conducted his business of cadaver stealing.

Harris's actions were revisited seventy-eight years postmortem, when construction workers found the cadavers of close to four hundred people in the basement of the Old Medical College on Telfair Street. Some of the bones "had specimen numbers written on them," and workers found vats full of whiskey that held the remains of "body parts." It is believed that Harris played a central role in procuring these corpses. He had served as the college cultivator and the university manufacturer of cadavers in a clandestine trade. The 1989 discoveries of Harris's actions resulted in conversations among anthropologists, activists, physicians, historians, and community members.[77] For nearly a decade, anthropologists and bioarchaeologists studied the remains. Then, in 1998, the bones were returned to Augusta in a sealed 2,500-pound vault, "so that their slumber won't get disturbed again."[78]

By the 1830s, the domestic cadaver trade was highly organized in Georgia and other Southern states, such as Maryland and Virginia. The trade, however, crossed the entire United States, and bodies were sent from the South to the North. In September 1830, for example, Dr. Nathan Ryano Smith of the University of Maryland wrote to Dr. Parker Cleveland of Brunswick, Maine, about the traffic in cadavers. "It will give me pleasure," he wrote, "to render you any assistance in regard to subjects." Smith believed his colleague would "rely upon having them," so he "immediately invoke[d] Frank," his highly skilled "body snatcher." Smith was so confident in Frank's skills that he boasted about their large source base: "We get them here without any difficulty at present." Such language suggests that there may have been an earlier time when it was challenging to acquire a corpse. Despite their current success, he remained guarded about the fact that cadavers were being shipped out of Baltimore. For the time being, he would package and ship three bodies "in barrels with whisk[e]y."[79]

Frank and Smith worked well together. Frank helped "stock" the anatomy lab's inventory, and he received "$5 for a large body; $2.50 for a small [one]." He "would steal into the graveyards at night, carrying with him a shovel, sack, and meat hook," the customary tools of the trade. "When he came upon a freshly covered grave, he would carefully remove stones and pebbles placed on top" and then he "dug down only to the head of the coffin." At this point, he "broke open the flimsy pine box and grabbed the body under the eye socket or the chin with a meat hook." This "process took less than 30 minutes," and like other grave robbers, Frank harvested the cadaver by removing it from the ground and placing it in a bag, so he could transport it to the processing facility, in this case, the University of Maryland. "Frank's work was completely sanctioned by the medical school," and evidence shows that Smith and Frank worked with other institutions in the Northeast.[80] Such practices were important to those interested in the body trade, as we saw earlier in the letters between Drs. Wyman and Bowen and in the tactics used by Harris at the Medical College of Georgia. Recall that Bowen requested bodies that couldn't "be nosed a mile off."

Smith had difficulty transporting corpses through the larger Northern cities. Complaining about the high risks in Baltimore and New York City, he claimed, "The stories in New York in regard to the moving of persons in the street have been repeated here." As a result, some people believed they were put to death "for dissection," in other words, killed so they could be used as spcimens. These fears reached those working in shipyards, and Smith concluded, "If the business was not conducted in the most prudent manner, our College would be destroyed per our heads and our lives placed in imminent danger." To be clear, he said, "If I were to be detected in conniving the transportation of dead bodies from this city, it would ruin me at once and drive me from B[altimore] in less than a week." Given the climate in Baltimore at the time, Dr. Smith apologetically said, "I have done everything that I could," however he did not have any "subjects for dissection" to share.[81] Just like other trading systems, the domestic cadaver trade yielded seasons of growth and seasons of low activity. Despite natural ebbs and flows, this traffic clearly involved transportation routes in both the North and the South.

On April 9, 1836, Dr. Granville Sharpe Pattison of Jefferson Medical College in Pennsylvania spent $78.25 on "subjects for dissection," which he purchased from an agent in Baltimore.[82] It is possible that his colleague was Dr. Smith, but the surviving letters are not always forthcoming with regard to such controversial activities. Given the fee, we can safely assume that he purchased more than one cadaver and that there were already established trade routes. We don't know whether the bodies of those purchased were black or white, or at one time enslaved or free.

Similar transactions between physicians and body snatchers occurred in Virginia, and just as at the Medical College of Georgia, an African American janitor secured the cadavers. The activities at the University of Virginia in the 1840s and 1850s provide extensive details about the cadaver trade. Dr. John Staige Davis became a demonstrator of anatomy in 1845 and was later appointed professor in 1855–1856. Like many nineteenth-century physicians, he received some of his training in Philadelphia, "the medical capital of the nation." He remained on the faculty at the University of Virginia for thirty years, until his death in 1885. In correspondence with medical professionals in Richmond, we learn that the cadaver trade was in full swing by the mid-1840s, with Davis's assistance. He worked with a covert team of people who harvested cadavers for medical research, transporting bodies from Richmond to Charlottesville, where the they were sold to university faculty.

Davis's letters reveal that this trade was highly organized and structured as a fully functioning business. His transactions included price negotiation, product specialty, compensation for missed shipments and delays, as well as a set of agreed-upon fees for shipments. He traded cadavers via steamboat, carriage, and ships to people in and around Virginia, such as Dr. Lewis Minor of Portsmouth Naval Yard Hospital, James L. CaBell of Carter Islands, and H. L. Thomas of Richmond. In a letter from Thomas in the summer and early fall of 1849, there is a discussion of "criminal cadavers" and the desire to pay $20 per subject, and references to "resurrectonists." On November 27, for example, Thomas wrote about "booty men" and asked for the "first material that dies . . . no matter who else wants it."[83] The men worked with Thomas White, the white body snatcher responsible for collecting and transporting subjects.

Davis had an excellent reputation for teaching, and the University of Virginia anatomy students were known to be well trained in this field. The strength of the program relied on allowing students to perform "individual dissections." As a result, Davis needed to acquire approximately twenty-five cadavers per year. Given that it was illegal to dissect the dead in Virginia and in most other states, depending on how cadavers were received, Davis relied on an underground market. Because of the proximity to slavery and the knowledge of domestic slave trade routes, the domestic cadaver trade flourished in this region. According to one scholar, it was easier to secure bodies in the South because of the large enslaved population and because enslavers had legal authority over black bodies. This important point explains why enslaved people became postmortem commodities and why Charlottesville and Richmond were key trade cities.[84] The region is also not far from the Southampton and Harpers Ferry rebellions, confirming the possibility of increased traffic in cadavers in the aftermath of those two events.

In transactions with Minor, Davis worked with Thomas White, who received a hundred dollars for putting bodies in well-secured liquor or oil barrels. The men had a "memorandum of the agreements" with specifications for the "subjects." The barrels were large enough to contain his "favorite article of the trade," so long as they were "good subjects, properly shipped." In one shipment, Minor agreed to pay "$32 for two adults and two children." However, the most interesting involved a "prime subject," a "coloured woman," who was scheduled to be buried, and a "newborn child." In December 1850, Minor wrote to Davis that he had seen White and that White had sent the "case mentioned in his last letter," namely, the colored woman.[85]

Davis probably competed for cadavers with Dr. Jeffries Wyman at Hampden-Sydney College. Wyman mentioned these illicit activities in a letter to his colleague Dr. David Humphreys Storer at Tremont Medical School in Boston. Apparently, two Boston students "got into some hot water for stealing a body." In a letter to Storer, Wyman acknowledged that case and he shared a similar incident that had taken place in Virginia. "*Our* students do the thing in a manner somewhat different," he explained. After the police had received and buried a body, fifteen to twenty students "turned out the next night with dirks pistols bowie knives [etc.] and went to work very coolly to dig up the body." They told the police "that it would be done peaceably if no resistance was offered." The bold nature of their threat to the police suggests that these medical students were willing to "fight it out" if necessary.[86] The fact that they came prepared with digging instruments as well as weapons confirms that they were ready to kill for this body. In the end, they worked through the night, and there was "no opposition" from the police. Such incidents place the fight for bodies in context and suggest that these exchanges were common in the 1830s and 1840s. Thus, when medical students dug up John Copeland and Shields Green in the late 1850s in the aftermath of the John Brown raid, their entitlement and quick possession of the bodies were not unexpected. The students were simply acting in accordance with common extralegal practices.

Looking specifically at the trade routes between Richmond and Charlottesville, it is clear that this traffic was highly organized. Although the two cities were only seventy-one miles apart, in the nineteenth century, the trip took two days by carriage.[87] Even though physicians traded cadavers of the enslaved, "there were never nearly enough legal slave bodies to go around, creating a demand for other sources," such as free blacks.[88] Dr. Lewis Minor of the Navy Yard Hospital worked with Davis to remedy this: "They closely monitored black funerals because they had to act

Richard H. Whitehead's University of North Carolina School of Medicine anatomy students during a dissection staged outdoors, Raleigh, circa 1890. Notice the African American janitor sits on a bucket in front of an African American man who is being dissected.

within four days," because of decomposition and travel. "Three experienced persons could move in at night," according to one description, "remove the body, and rearrange the soil and flowers within an hour." As the cultivation process continued, the harvested corpse was then placed in a barrel "tightly packed in bran and shipped by boat to Richmond," and then transferred by rail for the journey to Charlottesville. The following shipping rates applied:

Adults	$12
14 years being considered adult age	
Subjects from 4–10	$8
Mother and infant	$15
Infants from birth to 8 years	$4[89]

This highly organized system transported formerly enslaved and free black corpses throughout Virginia. The pricing system reveals some interesting patterns. Deceased mothers with their infants carried the highest price, in contrast to the values given to living mothers and their offspring. As noted earlier, some enslavers did not want "breeding wenches" in their homes, but deceased mothers and infants offered medical students the ability to study the reproduction process and women who were lactating. These price patterns also confirm that by age fourteen, after reaching their first menarche, most girls were considered adults. Just like any market activity, these rates were negotiated, as some physicians tried to avoid extra charges such as "freight rates" and premiums for quality cadavers.[90]

As Grandison Harris served at the Medical College of Georgia, Chris Baker served at Virginia Medical College (which began in 1838 as the medical department of Hampden-Sydney College in Richmond; in 1854, it became the Medical College of Virginia and severed its ties to Hampden-Sydney; in 1860, it became a state institution and later Virginia Commonwealth University) in Richmond, and he likely was involved with the corpse cultivation utilized by Drs. Davis, Wyman, and Minor. Baker was born in the 1840s to parents owned by the university, just as George Harris was. Some accounts suggest that he was born in the basement of Egyptian Hall, the place where he would later prepare exhumed bodies. His father worked for the university and probably taught Baker his craft. Over the years, he became knowledgeable about human anatomy, and medical students and faculty respected him. Dr. Charles Robbins, emeritus professor of the medical college, shared that he knew Baker and "held him in high esteem." Robbins remembered his father, Billie, who had taught Chris his "trade." Chris lived with his wife, Martha, and son, John, "in the basement of the Egyptian Building."[91] Like Grandison and, perhaps, George Harris, Baker also appeared in class pictures, and we have direct evidence about him from local newspapers. Baker's description contains racial undertones, common in the 1880s. He is described as a "little well-made darky, with gingerbread skin and slightly rheumatic legs."

Baker "and a party of students" robbed graves at night. Despite the nature of his work, many found him happy and even "more cheerful in the presence of six or eight corpses than any man in Richmond." After collecting the corpses, he brought them to the dissecting room to prepare them for the processing stage of cultivation. When a reporter visited Baker in the 1880s, he noted, "The odor from the cadavers is simply frightful," adding, "New students tumble over by the dozens when they hear their first lecture." Baker lived in "the little ante-chamber," which was connected to the dissecting room. "To a casual observer," his room might have been un-settling, given the shelves of pickled body parts in jars throughout. "When I read the labels on those jars," the reporter recalled, "my hair stood on end." Baker had one for "HEARTS," another for a "SPINAL CORD," and "a third LIGAMENTS VERTABRAE." During the reporter's visit, a student came to the dissecting room to complain about one of the ca-davers. "The skin had worn off the body in several places, and the young man" and Baker agreed that it was a "poor subject."[92] After this casual con-versation, Baker apparently went back to showing the reporter around the facilities, where he learned more about the corpse preparation and manufacturing processes.

When Baker arrived on campus with a "fresh subject," he took the body to the basement "pickling vat." Here he used lime as a chemical preservative before moving the cadaver to the dissecting table. "After the bodies have been dissected," he then prepared the remains for skeletal articulation. As described earlier (chapter 4), this process involved boiling the bones in a "caldron . . . not the least bit suggestive of a witch's kettle." Baker was "a first-class skeleton manufacturer" because he could clean "the bones" of a dead man and fix "them up for mounting." This was not an easy or "pleas-ant task," and after he was done with the remains, he buried them and students were prohibited from "exhibit[ing] or expos[ing] them." Given that dissection was not legal during Baker's time at the Medical College of Virginia, "the material used had to be stolen." The college purchased a "few corpses . . . from northern hospitals, but they were hard to obtain." Likewise, the "premium on dead men" was "so high that the institution re-ally could not afford to buy them."[93] Baker's story about body snatching in Richmond confirms the presence of the trade in cadavers.

Similar to Grandison Harris at the Medical College of Georgia, Baker remained on campus even after slavery ended. In December 1882, he and two others were caught at a cemetery and indicted by a grand jury for grave robbery. He was jailed for a short period before the governor pardoned him. Even after this incident, Baker aided in collecting the body of Solo-mon Marable, an African American Virginian hanged for the alleged mur-der of Lucy Pollard in the summer of 1896. After the jail-room hanging,

Chris Baker is one of the known black resurrectionists employed by the Medical College of Virginia in the late nineteenth and early twentieth centuries.

Marable's cadaver was sent to the medical school for dissection. Local black ministers fought unsuccessfully for the return of Marable to his wife for proper burial. Baker assisted with the embalming and storage of the body. Given his role in this high-profile murder case, it's not surprising that Baker still appeared at the college in the 1890 census, listed as the "Anatomical man." He lived at the university until his death in 1919.[94]

Baker's legacy differed from those of blacks and whites because he was not a part of either community. People, regardless of race, had mixed feelings about Baker. Among the white medical community, he was celebrated and honored in life and in death. Former students reflected

Chris Baker posing with the students of the Medical College of Virginia, 1899–1900.

on his influence on their careers. One professor from the MCV, John Brodnax, wrote the following poem in his honor:

TO OLD CHRIS
To thee, who mindless of the helpless dead,
These crude, unpolished lines are for you penned;
Who'll daily sit in age, with hoary head,
And scrape their bones, unthinking of your end.

While you pursue your ghastly, ghoulish trade,
Does no compunction ever come to you?
That as these cadavers, you were made,
And may have to receive this treatment, too.

Yet, let us in good feeling, you protect,
And all have one kind word to say to you;
That the ghouls are the students, who dissect,
And will give you this after task to do.

For science 'tis aimed, yet you get no part
In what is gained, and they the honors bear;
In co-partnership, you share not their art,
But in day by day must sit and cut and pare.[95]

Brodnax tried to separate Baker from medical students and wanted him to understand that he would not receive much credit for the work he completed.

Free blacks also had mixed thoughts about Baker. Legend has it that when the African American community saw him in town, they feared that he had come to collect their bodies. Black parents told their children to run and hide when they saw him. Imagine the level of isolation he experienced. Yet when he died, he was given a decent burial, and members of the medical community eulogized him.[96]

Baker is buried in Evergreen Cemetery in Richmond. But his life, like many others in this book, does not end at death. His history has been resurrected along with the bones of some of the very people he brought to the dissection room more than 130 years ago. But I digress; we will return to Baker soon. For now, it is important to remain in the nineteenth century and to examine the religious thoughts of other leading citizens.

Despite the actions of medical students and faculty in the North and the South, some abolitionists, including Lucretia Mott, believed physicians, students, and their staff needed to respond to a higher calling. Mott addressed the oppression of the enslaved and the free in an 1849 lecture at the Cherry Street Meeting House in Philadelphia. A religious antislavery activist, Mott started her remarks with an invocation: "My prayer is that this occasion may be blessed," she began, "both to the hearers and to the speakers." After acknowledging the grace of God and identifying the temptations of vice present in any city, she appealed to students regarding the abolition of slavery. She shared her interpretation of equality and mankind and urged the students to consider their faith and examine their hearts during moments of solicitude and prayer. Mott wanted the physicians to humbly submit themselves to a divine father and asked that they remain "obedient to the heavenly vision." Continuing, she urged them to "be obedient to the truth" so they could "become wiser than" their teachers. One of her objectives that evening was "to speak plainly" to "the prevailing errors and sins of the times." As she addressed the topic of slavery, she asked the audience to become "advocates for the oppressed." [97]

Many in the audience were doctors who at some point had been caught or arrested for grave robbing, despite having had a legitimate rationale—to advance medical education. Were Mott's words prophetic? Did she appeal to the students because she knew there was something "evil" about slavery and, possibly even worse, a cadaver trade? Did her presence instill in anatomy professors a fear of getting caught? History tells us that slavery ended in 1865, but the trade in deceased African Americans, many formerly enslaved, continued until the 1880s.

ANATOMY LEGISLATION IN THE 1880s

Over the years, in communities throughout the United States, residents became weary of physicians' activities and rioted or had doctors arrested. For example, when Dr. Shippen's activities were discovered, his accusers "suspected that he kept vats in which he disposed of the bones and fragments of the bodies" in order to cover up his activities.[98] Slanderous newspaper campaigns ensued and, according to historian Michael Sappol, a "Sailor's Mob" disrupted Shippen's anatomy class in 1765.[99] New Yorkers started a doctor's riot in 1788, when a group of young children saw a medical student wave a dismembered arm outside the New York Hospital. Another riot occurred when relatives visited their loved ones' graves and found the deceased bodies missing. A visit to the teaching facility of Dr. Richard Bayley and his protégé Wright Post in New York City revealed "corpses [of] both black and white in various stages of dissection and dismemberment." After being dragged into the street, the physicians and their students were placed in "protective custody."[100] After these events, doctors began fleeing to find safety elsewhere, and the city of New York passed an act (1798) that made grave digging for the purpose of dissection illegal. Yet the demand for cadavers continued to outweigh the supply. With this in mind, the body trade continued before, during, and after emancipation.

The police arrested Jefferson Medical College faculty in the early 1880s, indicating that grave robbing for medical purposes remained steady for much of the nineteenth century. Under the tutelage of Dr. Samuel, medical students robbed Lebanon Cemetery, a black-owned burial ground in Philadelphia. Three men were arrested, and Dr. William Smith Forbes was charged with conspiracy; later he was freed on $5,000 bail. One body snatcher who worked for Forbes said that he received $2.50 per body. This is the same amount that Charlie Grant, who was formerly enslaved, received for exhuming the cadaver of an enslaved infant and delivering it to Dr. Johnson in Virginia, and similar to the rates paid to Frank in Maryland.

By the 1880s, as the cadaver trade had stretched across the United States, several cases of public exposure led to anatomy legislation in nearly every state. "Grave Plunderers in Richmond, VA and Philadelphia PA" was the opening line of "Medical Items and News" in the December 1882 edition of the *Medical Record*, a trade journal for doctors. Bodies that had been laid to rest in Oakwood Cemetery had, according to the article, been "systematically robbed for a long time" and were used as subjects for dissection by the Virginia Medical College. This underground practice had finally been exposed when "two medical students and two colored persons were arrested at the cemetery."[101] One of the "colored" persons was Chris Baker; the other, a man named Caesar Roane.

Nearly 250 miles away, Jim Burrell, the "colored" janitor from Jefferson Medical College, feared for his life after he talked with a local reporter about the domestic cadaver trade. His employer, Dr. Daniel E. Hughes, was on the faculty at Jefferson Medical and sanctioned the body snatching from Lebanon Cemetery. After the story was published in the *Philadelphia Press*, the same month as the *Medical Record* story, medical students began to jeer at Burrell in the street and threatened him on campus. One remarked, "Jim you are a d—fool . . . you got yourself in a bad scrape with that tongue of yours." After a day of chastisement, Burrell concluded that his "life was in danger." He claimed he was not "frightened at their threats," but did worry that the students "might hurt me in some way." As a result, he decided to "resign my place at once for it [cannot be] safe for me to continue to perform duties under these circumstances."[102]

News items like these were increasingly common in the 1880s and 1890s. These years marked a time when grave robbers were caught, exposed, and indicted. In some cases, they were indicted and sentenced. Both Baker in Virginia and Burrell in Pennsylvania were convicted, but then pardoned by their respective governors. These African American men did not act alone. They worked for institutions of higher learning and under the tutelage of major medical faculty such as Dr. Forbes, in Pennsylvania, and Dr. Hughes, in Virginia. Not only was the practice of a clandestine cultivation of corpses widespread, it was orchestrated through an intricate network of physicians tracing, as we have seen, to the 1820s and 1830s. This blemish on medical history evolved with the development of the medical profession.

Although Massachusetts was the first state to establish an anatomy act (1831), which forbade the illegal collection of cadavers, followed by New York (1854), it was another thirty years until the rest of the country developed such legislation. Before Pennsylvania's ban in 1867, three medical schools in the state had developed a system to distribute evenly among them the unclaimed bodies of prisoners and almshouse residents.[103] The Pennsylvania law left the distribution process in the hands of the coroner, but some felt that he "persistently disregards and disobeys the law"; thus,

Solomon Marable was transported in a whiskey barrel and sent to Chris Baker, who embalmed and stored Marable's body until further arrangements were made regarding who owned his body and how to dispose of or bury it.

some physicians felt justified in their illegal activity. The 1867 legislation, for example, "directs that unclaimed bodies shall be given to the medical colleges in proportion to the number of students," but the almshouse did not have enough cadavers, and medical schools continued to find other means of acquiring bodies—namely, through grave robbing. The quality of the cadavers was another common problem, as everyone sought fresh "subjects" for dissection. "Nearly all the cases of unknown persons that" the coroner possessed had to undergo a "postmortem" examination or autopsy. Medical students and faculty disliked this practice because an autopsy "mutilates a body, and the colleges refuse to take them unless they are perfect and uncut."[104]

Local newspapers, as we have seen, reported cases of grave robbery; some ministers even preached about the problem during Sunday sermons. The Reverend T. Doughty Miller told his black congregants that the public exposure of body snatching contained an ironic twist. "Many scientists and philosophers have written long and learned arguments," he began, "to demonstrate the fact that, as a race, we were not really human beings." The American public saw African Americans as "slaves—merchandise." But the discovery of grave robbing for dissection in university settings, particularly the cadaver trade, has now "spoken for" African American "manhood" by "selecting the bodies of those declared by so many to be mere animals, as models upon which to base the study of human anatomy." Continuing, he reminded his congregation that they were not inferior "because of color." In fact, "the sam[e] bones, ligaments and sinews run alike through the human frame, despite the outside hue."[105]

When body-snatching cases were discovered, both local and national newspapers took notice. Shocked, one reporter wrote, "I scarcely know what to say concerning the horrible disclosures" made public by the arrests of faculty, staff, and students of Jefferson Medical College. The reporter was disgusted with the practice that he called "the terrible . . . trafficking with the dead." Sympathizing with African American outrage, he wrote that he could not "blame them" for being agitated by "the desecration [that] has been going on for years."[106]

This decade marked a watershed of arrests, including that of Grandison Harris at the Medical College of Georgia. Like Baker, he was caught grave robbing and was apprehended on December 13, 1881. News of his arrest appeared in a New Haven, Connecticut, newspaper: "Grandison Harris (colored) was arrested at Augusta, GA yesterday for exhuming bodies from the city cemeteries, which for some time has had been sending in trunks to Atlanta for medical colleges."[107] In response to this case and the riots that occurred in Philadelphia in 1883, state legislatures began passing anatomy acts to regulate the acquisition and distribution of cadavers.

In 1884, the Virginia legislature established an anatomical review board to regulate the cadaver trade and to equalize the distribution process of bodies for medical education. Just as in Pennsylvania, the goal was to evenly distribute them "among the state's three medical schools for dissection."[108] The impetus for this new legislation was the discovery of Baker, his assistant, and two medical doctors with a "fresh subject."

Georgia legislators passed the Anatomical Act a few years later in 1887. It included statutes that defined more clearly the 1867 law that sought to protect "cemeteries and burying places in this state, and to prevent and punish the unauthorized use and traffic in dead human bodies." Twenty years later, this new legislation established a "Board for Distribution of Bodies" as well as for the "Delivery of Certain Bodies," with a host of other regulations outlining the terms for disposing of a body.[109] As the industry became institutionalized, university and school officials were forced to keep better track of their cadaver acquisitions. They did so in registers that eerily mirrored plantation ledgers. These documents contained information on the cadavers such as the name, sex, race, place of birth, occupation, and cause of death. They also noted where the bodies came from and which school they were delivered to, as well as the associated costs. The regulation of this once clandestine traffic is now a more visible part of our historical record.

Clandestine cadaver cultivation practices were so common in 1880 that no region of the country was untouched by this trade. In 1883, when Johns Hopkins Medical School opened, "the 1,200 medical students in Baltimore's medical schools had to rely on this informal source of supply." In Boston, scandals regarding the trade occurred when "resurrection men" supposedly tanned human hides "for gloves and slippers," reminiscent of techniques used on Nat Turner's corpse. New York reports, also from the 1880s, note that "medical schools have for the instruction of their 495 freshmen, the pick of the 30,000 unknowns who die annually." The corpses are "placed in plain coffins and hauled by barge to one of the East River islands for burial." On the opposite coast, in San Francisco, "an anonymous doctor makes the rounds of poorhouses, jails, reformatories, public hospitals and asylums," searching for unclaimed cadavers. In the end, he "selects 30 to 40 specimens for the 472 medical students of Stanford and the University of California." As in the 1840s, "the transportation, preservation and storage" included specific fees, in this case, "$10 per cadaver."[110]

Clearly, the body trade reached medical schools throughout the United States in the postslavery era and expanded the pool of potential specimens to members of the lower socioeconomic classes. Some schools competed for cadavers, just as medical students had in the aftermath of the John Brown raid. However, it is no surprise that the most well-known scandal occurred in Philadelphia, involving Dr. William Smith Forbes of Jefferson Medical College.

In 1882, Dr. Forbes and four others were caught grave robbing as part of a ring that involved collaboration between the university and cemetery officials at Lebanon Cemetery. The reporter, Louis N. Megargee, found Frank McNamee and three accomplices "hauling a wagon-load of six bodies to the Hospital." When Megargee stopped and questioned the men, he saw that the six bodies, "all, as it happened, Negroes," were uncovered. When the story appeared in local papers the next day, racial tensions arose, and "the Negro population roused to a blood-thirsty pitch." As the story unfolded, the public learned that Dr. Forbes had paid McNamee "to rob the graves." Anatomists throughout the city faced intense scrutiny, as many explained that they "labored under a constant need of more bodies." Some defended Forbes's actions, claiming that the cadaver supplies from hospitals, alms- houses, prisons, and morgues were inadequate to serve the needs of medical education. A trial ensued and all four men confessed that Forbes orches- trated the corpse harvesting at Lebanon Cemetery. They were convicted and sentenced to ten years, while Forbes was held for trial on $5,000 bail.[111]

During the hearing, countless witnesses came forward in Dr. Forbes's defense, asserting his prominence as one of the leading anatomists. He de- nied the charges and claimed that he had assumed the cadavers had come from the "House of Correction." The case revealed that Forbes paid Mc- Namee between $5 and $8 per body, with an average of 150 bodies per year. In the end, Forbes was acquitted of the charges and released from jail. This case led to the official legalization of dissection in Pennsylvania through the Anatomy Act of 1883.[112]

Despite the assertion that "few medical colleges directly engaged in the practice of grave robbing," the findings presented here suggest the con- trary.[113] Medical school account books, anatomy professors' personal letters, newspaper accounts, and miscellaneous receipts prove that the traffic in dead bodies stretched as far north as New Hampshire and as far south- west as Texas. The domestic cadaver trade was so active in the nineteenth century that physicians feared their own bodies would be exhumed after they died.[114]

BURIAL RIGHTS

Dr. Samuel D. Gross, who was trained by Dr. John Eberle at Jefferson Medical College and spent some time at the Medical College of Ohio, addressed this fear in his autobiography. Early in his career, he suffered poor health and had difficulty sleeping because he was "harassed by horrid dreams." To calm himself, he "kept a light burning all night" in his room for fear of dying "in the dark." One night, he dreamed that his "grave was being dug" and that he "saw people at work throwing up the earth and getting ready to deposit all that was mortal" of him. He "awoke suddenly, jumped up hastily," and adjusted his lamp. He eventually gained "self-possession," despite waking up in a deep sweat."[115] Dr. Gross's fear was validated by the activities of physicians and their students. He quite likely knew about the grave robbing and possibly witnessed and/or participated in it. Therefore, he left specific instructions regarding his body upon death.

Gross was not the only doctor or family member of a physician who had specific thoughts about the afterlife of their bodies. For example, on the death of his colleague Dr. Breckenridge of Kentucky, Dr. Gross requested a "postmortem examination," but the late doctor's wife had an "unconquerable objection" to any such procedure. [116] Her objection is quite understandable, given the history of grave robbing and illegal dissections that occurred in the 1830s through the 1850s. The cultivation of corpses benefited the medical profession, and Gross made his desires clear to a number of people. His wishes are reflected in newspaper accounts of his death.

On May 8, 1884, the *New York Times* announced Dr. Gross's death and his desire to be cremated. "Another Body to be Cremated: The Remains of Dr. Samuel D. Gross to be Reduced to Ashes" was the headline. At this time, in the early 1880s, cremation represented a new way to dispose of bodies. This method only became a real possibility in the United States in 1876. Even though there were "two recorded instances of cremation before 1800, the real start began in 1876 when Dr. Julius LeMoyne built the first crematory in Washington, Pennsylvania." This is the same facility where Gross's remains were sent "to be reduced to ashes." In 1884, "the second crematory opened in Lancaster, Pennsylvania, and, as was true of many of the early crematories, it was owned and operated by a cremation society. Other forces behind early crematory openings were Protestant clergy who desired to reform burial practices and the medical profession, which was concerned with health conditions around early cemeteries."[117] By the turn of the twentieth century, two dozen such institutions were fully operational.

Gross's body arrived at the crematory accompanied by his son, A. Haller Gross, and a Dr. Horowitz, who were present to ensure the late physician's last wishes were properly executed. Dr. Gross favored incineration and had even published pamphlets on the topic. Apparently, while living, he frequently "said he did not desire his body to be buried in the grounds and to have his bones tossed about after years." His will contained specific instructions on the disposal of his remains, which included an autopsy and a modest funeral, followed by cremation. His death caused unrest in the medical community because his colleagues did not feel comfortable with Gross's decision to be cremated, and for some reason, the family delayed public announcements of his death, adding to the frustration of his colleagues. Dr. Ewing Mears and Professor J. M. Dacosta performed an autopsy that Gross had agreed to before his death, while Dr. Hewson, also present, produced the report stating that Gross had "a very large brain" and his primary organs were in "healthy" condition for a man of his age. Like Turner, Gross's brain was examined to determine a connection between cranial size and personal characteristics of the deceased person. However, because of his insight and knowledge of the cadaver trade, Gross's remains "were sealed up and sent to Washington" to prepare for the cremation. During his modest funeral, the Reverend George Currie, rector of St. Luke's Protestant Episcopal Church, gave the last rites. After incineration, his ashes would be kept in the family vault at Woodland Cemetery. Finally, Dr. Gross's wife, who preceded the late doctor in death, was "cremated in the same furnace."[118]

It is important that we consider Gross's burial rites because he practiced medicine at a time when medical discovery was at its peak and the cadaver trade was in full operation. That he could have his body disposed of as he wished, have a postmortem autopsy, have his remains sealed during transport, request cremation in the same furnace as his wife, and have his ashes placed in a family vault at a designated cemetery, all represent the privileges a man of his class and stature had at his disposal. For many enslaved and free blacks, and poor whites who died in the nineteenth century, this was not the case. As chattel property, enslaved people had no "rights" to their burial customs, let alone their bodies.

Albert Wilson Monroe, an African American porter at the University of Pennsylvania, is an exception. He worked at the university for most of his adult life and was given an honorable funeral that was well attended by hundreds of people. He had come to work at the university around age thirteen in 1854 and was known as the "errand boy under the charge of the College 'janitor.'" Monroe worked with two different janitors, including Francis Dick, later Frederick Dick. In this capacity, he "did the menial work of keeping College Hall [dissecting rooms] clean and orderly." He became the university janitor who locked and unlocked the doors to College Hall, rang the college bell, lit fires, delivered mail, and collected lab fees from medical students. Nicknamed "Pomp" (short for Pompey) by medical students, he was close to generations of physicians and even appeared in class photos, just as Harris had at the Medical College of Georgia and Baker at the Medical College of Virginia. Like his counterparts, Monroe took care of the buildings that housed the medical department and "often slept in a bunk in the basement." During the day, he attended lectures and served as an assistant during procedures and experiments. He never married, and when he died in 1904, university officials held a special funeral in his honor.

The service included an elaborate program with "honorary pallbearers, drawn from the junior and senior classes," a hearse, and a public viewing attended by "hundreds of alumni." The funeral took place in the College Hall chapel, the same building in which he labored during his fifty years of service at the university. The chapel, "filled with flowers," had a "standing-room only crowd of faculty, alumni, students and others." The Reverend Dr. Jesse Y. Burk conducted the service, and a professor of music played the organ "to accompany the University's best singers." Following the program, the "body was then carried from the Chapel as the college bell tolled fifty times," and Monroe was finally laid to rest in Merion Cemetery in Cynwyd, Pennsylvania. Much of the pomp (no pun intended) and circumstance resembled the services held for Dangerfield Newby and the other followers of John Brown reinterred in North Elba, New York, in July 1899. To commemorate Monroe's life, the University of Pennsylvania created the "Albert Wilson Monroe Scholarship" in honor of "a faithful servant and loyal friend."[119]

Regardless of Monroe's involvement in the cadaver trade, we know that he maintained the facilities at the first medical institution in the United States. He may or may not have assisted in grave robbing, but he certainly helped provide support and services for fifty years of medical education that was dependent on cadavers for hands-on training. He differed from other janitors and resurrectionists, such as Harris and Baker, in that his death involved an elaborate service and is commemorated in university records.

•   •   •

Recognizing the domestic cadaver trade allows us to connect the overt and covert medical education in nineteenth-century United States to contemporary forms of organ and human trafficking. Through the cultivation and processing of bodies 150 to 200 years ago, we learn that the orchestrators of this web were men of distinction. Well-trained physicians, many who knew one another, corresponded through letters and publications in college circulars and medical journals. They discussed the illegal acquisition of bodies, many formerly enslaved people and free blacks. However, they could not do their work without help from janitors, students, or professional grave robbers. These individuals, like Grandison Harris, Chris Baker, and Albert Wilson Monroe, aided in acquiring "subjects for dissection," and completed a host of janitorial tasks at their respective institutions. Also known as "night prowlers," these men were highly skilled and respected by medical practitioners. They mastered the craft of grave robbing and were publicly acknowledged in life and in death.

Harris, Baker, and Monroe, along with an Irishman named Frank in Baltimore and William Watson in Philadelphia, cultivated corpses and facilitated traffic in dead bodies. This cadaver trade continues today in the form of underground organ markets.[120]

The public outcry over dissection in England in the 1830s resulted in the British 1832 Anatomy Act. US physicians outside Massachusetts continued the practices for fifty more years until US legislation restricted anatomical dissection. After a series of arrests of doctors and body snatchers in the 1880s, other states passed legislation and joined Massachusetts (1831) in passing anatomy acts, clarifying the avenues for procuring legal subjects for dissection under specific circumstances. Such legislation occurred in states including Pennsylvania (1883), Virginia (1884), and Georgia (1887).

Today, people can choose to donate their organs, but fees are involved. For example, Mercer University in Macon, Georgia, covers "the costs for transportation, embalming and cremation" if the donor lives within a fifty-mile radius. Those who live outside this perimeter are "responsible for costs of transport[ing]" cadavers "to the Mercer University School of Medicine." Just as Dr. Davis of the University of Virginia negotiated freight charges in Virginia with Drs. Minor and Wyman, Mercer University provides a formula to estimate transportation costs. On its website, the university suggests that the family of the deceased "multiply the distance from the lo-cation to Macon in miles by $2.25/mile."[121] At least the fees are now clearly publicized, and family and friends can rest assured that their loved ones' wishes have been granted. This was not true for the enslaved, free blacks, and poor whites.

Even in graves, the souls and spirits of the enslaved rested lightly. Would they be exhumed, reburied, and/or removed? Enslaved and free blacks worried about their corpses being disturbed after death. Returning to the story of Joice Heth in her final hours, we learn that she was buried in a mahogany casket, one that Barnum felt was honorable. This was cer-tainly a more respectable, better-quality type of wood for a casket than a pine box. We know nothing of her funeral, except that Barnum stated in his autobiography that her remains were removed to Bethel, Connecticut, and buried "respectably."[122] What did he mean by "respectably," given her exploitation in life and death? She had already been dissected. Was she truly at rest?

The contemporary case of Henrietta Lacks, whose cancerous cells were taken without her consent, confirms that even after death, bodies and body parts are still sometimes in circulation. Lacks's HeLa cells continue to ad-vance medical research in human and animal bodies. Today, we can try to determine whether our bodies or body parts will continue to serve medical research or the life of another human being by checking "donor" on our driver's license. However, the Lacks case confirms that we are still not in complete control of our bodily materials, particularly blood after it is drawn or "waste" after surgery. We simply do not know how it's used, recycled, or disposed. We can thank medical research for showing us possibilities, and we can acknowledge the unknown, unnamed, enslaved, and free blacks, and poor whites who aided in this process. Despite the fact that enslavers made a spectacle of the deaths of the enslaved, we can still lay them to rest. We do so by honoring their memories and tracing their postmortem journeys. The stories in this book remind us that the circle of life exceeds time and space, and that the life cycle of the enslaved is much longer than we realized. May the bodies and souls uncovered here rest in peace.

The Afterlives of Slavery

The valuation and division of slaves among contending heirs was a most important incident in slave life.

—Frederick Douglass[1]

Black lives are still imperiled and devalued by a racial calculus and a political arithmetic that were entrenched centuries ago. This is the afterlife of slavery.

—Saidiya Hartman[2]

What do we make of this legacy of souls and ghosts in circulation? How do we understand the ways enslaved people responded to this history of bodies and souls in circulation? As always, I turn to them for the final word, first to Elizabeth Keckley and then to a descendant of Nat Turner. Keckley shares, "At the grave, at least, we should be permitted to lay our burdens down, that a new world, a world of brightness, may open to us. The light that is denied us here should grow into a flood of effulgence beyond the dark, mysterious shadows of death."[3] For her, death would be a resting place, one free of the burdens of the here and now, a place to let in God's spiritual light. The descendants of Nat Turner shared this belief, as Lucy Turner noted, "sometimes, there is a Victory in the Grave, which leads to a bright, eternal Heaven, where Faith, Hope, Charity, Love, and Justice, shall last forever and forever, without ceasing."[4] Understanding the soul values of the enslaved and their descendants provides a window into their concepts of life and death. For some, their bodies would remain in circulation years after their last breath.

.   .   .

The internal and external values of human chattel examined in this book resonate today in recent discoveries of bones dating back to slavery. A construction project at Virginia Commonwealth University (VCU) in 1994 led to the discovery of several unidentified remains of African American cadavers. Like the remains found at the Medical College of Georgia, the VCU remains were sent for study to the Smithsonian Institution in Washington, DC. Forensic anthropologists have been examining the remains of about twenty-six unnamed African Americans that Baker likely collected. Now, with the help of Professor Shawn Utsey, there is a movement to return the remains to Virginia and lay them to rest. On January 10, 2014, the Virginia General Assembly issued Senate Joint Resolution 84, "Recognizing the training of nineteenth-century physicians in Richmond," and acknowledging the work of Chris Baker. The university is currently preparing for a "fitting memorial to commemorate the contributions of Richmond's African Americans whose bodies were stolen for anatomical dissection and the furtherance of science and medical research."[5]

The VCU case speaks volumes about ghost values and documents some of the history offered in this book. We now know more than ever that a trade in cadavers occurred and that historians like Ruth Richardson were correct in describing the process. She found human beings "compressed into boxes, packed in sawdust, packed in hay, trussed up in sacks, roped up like hams, sewn in canvas, packed in cases, casks, barrels, crates, and hampers; salted, pickled or injected with preservative." This was the work of folks like Grandison Harris, Chris Baker, and many other resurrectionists who came before them or followed after. People put price tags on corpses and "carried them in carts and wagons, in barrows and in steam-boats." They were "dismembered and sold" sometimes into pieces and placed in an underground "red market" that exists today.[6]

Ghost values of the formerly enslaved cultivated to populate this market remind us that death did not end their commodification. Their bodies were sold and remained in circulation decades and, in some cases, centuries after their deaths. For some, like Shields Green, Joice Heth, and Nat Turner, their remains (or parts of them) ended up being crucial to medical instruction, suggesting that postmortem histories tell us different stories about their lives than when they were living.

·   ·   ·

This book ends where it began, with an enslaved man in prison. And yet not quite. As you will see in the story of Mingo, it ends with the recognition of soul values that led to freedom. Mingo was a poet and possibly was influenced by Shakespeare. While in prison for liberating himself, he inscribed the following poem on one of the beams in his cell:

Good God! and must I leave them now—
My wife, my children, in their woe?
'Tis mockery to say I'm sold—
But I forget these chains so cold,
[...]
Dear wife, they cannot sell the rose
Of love, that in my bosom glows.
Remember, as your tears may start,
They cannot sell th' immortal part!
[...]
Thou sun, which lightest bond and free,
Tell me, I pray, is liberty
The lot of those who noblest feel,
And oftest to Jehovah kneel?
[...]
I feel high manhood on me now,
A spirit-glory on my brow;
I feel a thrill of music roll,
Like angel harpings, through my soul [...]

In the opening lines, Mingo expressed grief about being separated from his family. He challenged the institution of slavery as a mockery to him and many other enslaved people, because their souls were invaluable. While he acknowledged the realities of his enslavement, Mingo offered a sensory description of his cold shackles. But he also did what most enslaved people did: he drew strength from his inner spirit, focused on God, and viewed his condition "above the sky." He kept his spirit intact, preserving his love for his family and his God. Turning to his wife, he instructed her to find peace in the fact that neither their love nor their souls could be sold. He reminded her that even in the face of anguish, their union eclipsed captivity. More important, for him, there was an inner spirit that could not be commodified, a place deep in his heart that enslavers could not control. This "immortal part" was sacred and owned by self and spirit. Mingo shifted to comparisons between the enslaved and free, emphasizing the spirit expressed through feeling and kneeling. He used the metaphor of kneeling, which signals supplication, a position of humility and deference to a higher power.

From his perspective, humankind operated under the same sun and all were equal in the sight of Jehovah, Allah, or the name one called their maker. Mingo rose above to assert his humanity and his value as an incandescent spirit. He mentioned "touching Isaiah's lips with fire," drawing on prophetic imagery from biblical scripture. He likened himself to the anointing granted in Isaiah's commission.[7] Although favored by God, Mingo struggled with the notion of justice, given his enslaved status. Thus he prayed and fled that night and was killed by bloodhounds. He left us with words to describe how he felt on the eve of his death. Mingo valued his life, his wife, and his children. And he went to glory assuring them that enslavers could never sell their "immortal part."[8]

Despite being traded as commodities from the womb to the grave, enslaved people's understanding of their soul values transcended the external values placed upon their bodies. And with this realization, their souls were at peace.

POSTSCRIPT

On October 6, 2016, while this book was in production, Richard Hatcher, former mayor of Gary, Indiana, confirmed what I suspected, that he was in possession of the alleged skull of Nat Turner. DNA testing ensued and the descendants await confirmation. If the outcome is affirmative, then the family will have some closure, and Nat Turner's body and soul will be reunited with his people just as he said it would, "Somehow, Somewhere, Someday!"

Acknowledgments

With a grateful and humble heart, I have many people and institutions to thank for helping this book come to fruition. I received fellowships from the Ford Foundation, the American Council of Learned Societies, and the National Endowment for the Humanities, as well as internal funding from Michigan State University and the University of Texas at Austin as an Institute for Historical Studies fellow.

The libraries and staff members at more than twenty archives are the heart of this project. I owe special thanks to Michael Sappol of the National Library of Medicine and F. Michael Angelo at the Scott Memorial Library at Thomas Jefferson University. The former read two chapters, and the latter was my research angel. Library fellowships from the College Physicians of Philadelphia, the Massachusetts Historical Society, and the Library Company of Philadelphia (Program in African American History) shaped this book in many ways.

While on fellowship at the National Humanities Center, I received tremendous support from Eliza Robertson, Jean Houston, Josiah Drewry, and Marian Wason. I benefited from two classes of fellows (2007–2009) and an exceptional staff who made sure my research needs were met. I am thankful for meeting new colleagues and friends, including Paula Michaels and Heather Williams, who read most if not all of this manuscript in draft form.

At the University of Pennsylvania, the College of Physicians of Philadelphia Medical Library, the Library Company of Philadelphia, and the Pennsylvania Hospital, I received research assistance from Stacey Peeples, Erica Armstrong Dunbar, Krystal Appiah, and Nicole Jonic. In Boston, I conducted research at the Harvard University archives, the Countway Medical Library (with help from Jack Eckert), and the Massachusetts Historical Society (with the assistance of Dan Hinchens, Conrad Wright, and Kate Veins). I also met with Robert Margo of the National Bureau of Economic Research to clarify the direction of some of my economic analysis.

I wish to thank Richard Behles of the University of Maryland Medical Library; Laura Clark Brown and John White of the Southern Historical Collection at the University of North Carolina; Linda McCurdy, Elizabeth Dunn, Janie Morris, and Karen Jean Hunt at the Duke University archives; Lynette Stoudt of the Georgia Historical Society; Lee Shepard and Angie Boyer of the Virginia Historical Society; and Jane Aldrich, Mary Jo Fairchild, and Karen Stokes of the South Carolina Historical Society, as well as staff archivists at the North Carolina State Archives and the South Caroliniana Library.

This book came to life because of my agent, Cecelia Cancellaro, and my editor at Beacon Press, Gayatri Patnaik. Their wisdom, expertise, and editorial prowess and flare were the perfect combination. Through them, I found a home at Beacon Press with a phenomenal staff, including Helene Atwan, Rachael Marks, Tom Hallock, Alyssa Hassan, Bob Kosturko, Louis Roe, Pamela MacColl, Caitlin Meyer, Beth Collins, Susan Lumenello, Marcy Barnes, and Alyson Chu.

Stanley Engerman and the late Robert Fogel were extremely generous to donate years of original research material. They deserve a level of gratitude that I cannot fully express in words. John McCusker helped with the currency conversions, while Randy Fotiu, Jewel Ward, and Nate Marti spent countless hours organizing the data set for this book. Alan Olmstead and Peter Lindert provided research advice at different stages. I also appreciate Joyce Chaplin, Joshua Rosenblum, and Jonathan Pritchett for their scholarship and for entertaining questions about price data. Rick Steckel helped me think about age and health categories early in the research process.

Talitha LeFlouria, Sowandé Mustakeem, and Ava Purkiss deserve extra special thanks for their research support at the Greenblatt Medical Library at Augusta University and the Tompkins-McCaw Medical Library at Virginia Commonwealth University, Harvard University, and the

University of Virginia, respectively. I am also grateful to Isabel Wilkerson, who read drafts of this manuscript and provided excellent advice on the writing process.

Research for chapter 6 was funded in part by a travel grant from the F. C. Wood Institute for the History of Medicine at the College of Physicians of Philadelphia.

I am fortunate to work at a university that has rich archives, such as the Dolph Briscoe Center for American History. Thank you, Margaret Schlanky, Brenda Gunn, and Aryn Glazier for pulling, copying, and digitizing sources as I needed them. Colleagues in History, African and African Diaspora Studies, and other units on campus have been invaluable. Madeline Hsu, Denise Spellberg, Martin Kervorkian, and Jacqueline Jones read the proposal and drafts of chapters. Cherise Smith, Dawna Ballard, and Meta DeEwa Jones served as virtual writing and accountability partners, and I could not have completed this book without their support and friendship. Kali Gross, Tiffany Gill, Randy Diehl, Alan Tully, Edmund T. Gordon, Lisa Thompson, Jennifer Wilks, Jennifer Keys Adair, Keisha Bentley-Edwards, Tshepo Masango Chery, Frank Guridy, Keffrelyn Brown, and Anthony Brown talked though ideas and provided feedback as this project took shape. I also appreciate support from Terrence Moline, Michael Stevenson, David Lobenstein, Deborah Douglass, Teresa Puente, Angela Rich, Chere Atkins, Melba Vasquez, Taniel McKelvey, Hilary Bergman, Sheila Marie Hunter, Robyn McCarty, Samantha Bee, and the Adair, Bell, Bermiss, and Henry families.

Pero G. Dagbovie, Jennifer L. Morgan, Leslie Harris, Barbara Krauthamer, Wilma King, Brenda Stevenson, Calvin Schermerhorn, Heather Williams, and Cynthia Yaudes read parts if not all of this work. I thank them for countless hours helping me work through ideas at different stages. I also appreciate conversations with Erica Armstrong Dunbar, Jessica Millward, Kennetta Hammond Perry, LaShawn Harris, Amrita Myers, Jim Downs, Catherine Clinton, and P. Gabrielle Forman. I am equally grateful to those who served on conference panels or were in the audience when I presented portions of this work: Walter Johnson, Ed Baptist, Sharla Fett, Sasha Turner Bryson, Jessica Marie Johnson, Vanessa Holden,

Stephanie Jones-Rogers, Peter Wood, David Barry Gaspar, Adrienne D. Davis, Harry Watson, Seth Rockman, and Sven Beckert.

Student research assistants shaped, read, and assisted with this book. Thank you, Lauren Williams, Simonne Lawrence, Brittny O'Neal, Nik Ribianszky, Jenifer L. Barclay, Terry Brock, Andrew Dietzel, Nedra Lee, Jermaine Thibodeaux, Kate Shelton, Chyna Bowen, Nakia Parker, Signe Fourmy, Rachel Winston, Ron Davis, Lauren Henley, Maria Hammack, Mikayla Harden, and Elizabeth Eubanks.

My family and friends kept me sane, and I appreciate their patience with this project. Thank you, Dona C. Edwards, Jana Perry-Henry, Adriane Hopper Williams, Andrea Lewis, Tina Rogers-Brown, Tisa McGhee, Iva Mills, T'Leatha Suitt-Johnson, Monica Bailey, and Reina Davis. I appreciate the Houstons, Bullards, DeWits, Peelers, Rameys, and Berrys. My brother Dave and his family allowed me to stay at "Ramey-East" on my many trips to Philadelphia. My husband, Lisbon, lived with this book as long as our son, Ben, has been in this world. I thank the two of them for supporting, uplifting, and believing in me. More important, they allowed me to talk about the enslaved people who brought life into our home. I dedicate this book to my parents and cousin who have been by my side in spirit and in truth—to God be the glory.

Eighteenth Century

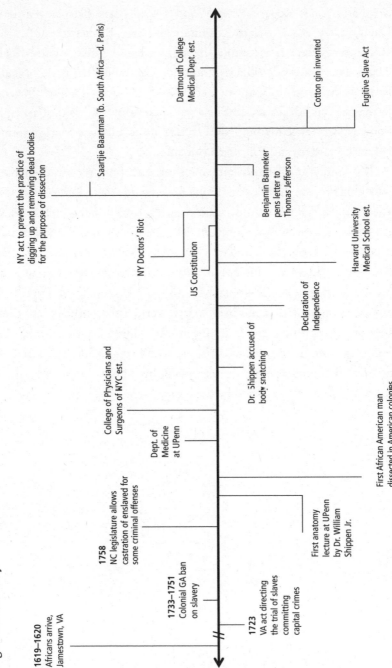

1619–1620
Africans arrive,
Jamestown, VA

1733–1751
Colonial GA ban
on slavery

1758
NC legislature allows
castration of enslaved for
some criminal offenses

1723
VA act directing
the trial of slaves
committing
capital crimes

First anatomy
lecture at UPenn
by Dr. William
Shippen Jr.

NY act to prevent the practice of
digging up and removing dead bodies
for the purpose of dissection

Saartjie Baartman (b. South Africa—d. Paris)

Dartmouth College
Medical Dept. est.

Cotton gin invented

Fugitive Slave Act

NY Doctors' Riot

US Constitution

Benjamin Banneker
pens letter to
Thomas Jefferson

Harvard University
Medical School est.

College of Physicians and
Surgeons of NYC est.

Dept. of
Medicine
at UPenn

Dr. Shippen accused of
body snatching

Declaration of
Independence

First African American man
dissected in American colonies

Nineteenth Century

Medical Dept., Cincinnati College, est.

Medical College of OH est.

American Medical Association est.

Southern Mutual Insurance Co. est., Athens, GA (later SMLIC)

Plessy v. Ferguson

Chris Baker born

Turner skull allegedly displayed, College of Wooster (OH)

Medical Dept., Transylvania University, est.

Hampden-Sydney College Medical Dept. (VCU Medical Center) est.

SC Medical Board est.

Grandison Harris's wife and son purchased by MCG

First US crematory built by Dr. Julius LeMoyne

University of MD School of Medicine est.

Medical College of GA est.

US Civil War

GA Anatomical Act

MA Anatomy Act

Grandison Harris purchased by MCG

Charleston Medical College est.

Dangerfield Newby killed, Harpers Ferry

Chris Baker and others indicted for grave robbery

Southampton Rebellion

TX Medical Association est.

Thomas Jefferson Medical College est.

John Brown executed, Charles Town, VA

VA Anatomy Law

Nat Turner hanged

Jane Elkins executed, TX

John A. Copeland and Shields Green executed, Charles Town, VA

UVA Medical Dept. est.

Joice Heth died, days later dissected, NYC

NY "Bone Bill"

Memorial service for Copeland and Green, Oberlin, OH

Dangerfield Newby and six others reinterred

Medical School Valley of VA (Winchester) est.

Twentieth and Twenty-First Centuries

- Tuskegee syphilis study
- Henrietta Lacks's mortal life
- Chris Baker laid to rest, Richmond, VA
- World Health Organization est.
- Grandison Harris died
- HeLa cells, obtained w/o consent and used
- Albert Monroe Wilson, UPenn janitor, laid to rest

- VCU discovery of human remains in abandoned well
- MCG discovery of human remains
- First revision, UAGA
- Uniform Anatomical Gift Act (UAGA)
- MCG human remains reinterred
- Harvard University discovery of remains near Holden Chapel
- Yale, Slavery & Abolition report

- Health Insurance Portability and Accountability Act (HIPAA)
- Second revision, UAGA
- Brown University president Ruth Simmons est. Steering Committee on Slavery and Justice
- UVA est. President's Commission on Slavery and the University
- Saartjie Baartman's remains repatriated, South Africa

- William & Mary est. Lemon Project
- Harvard and Slavery: Seeking a Forgotten History pamphlet
- Nat Turner's Bible displayed, National African American Museum, Washington, DC

Additional materials are available at http://www.drdainarameyberry.com.

Note on Sources: A History of People and Corpses

My journey to this history has been long, eye-opening, and difficult. Trained as a social historian, I am naturally drawn to the experiences of people. Yet enslaved people were also property, and scholars have been grappling with this reality for decades. I first started examining what I called "slave prices" in my first book, *Swing the Sickle for the Harvest Is Ripe: Gender and Slavery in Antebellum Georgia*. However, the material differed so much from the rest of the work that the editors suggested I use it for another project. *The Price for Their Pound of Flesh* is the result.

My conception of prices changed while on fellowship at the National Humanities Center in North Carolina. While there, I participated in a Duke University symposium, where I met economics scholar Stanley Engerman (University of Rochester). I had just delivered a paper about the dual valuation of the enslaved as commodities and people when he approached me and said that he had been waiting for thirty years for someone to write this book. In 1974, Engerman and the late Robert Fogel (then at the University of Chicago) published one of the most controversial and path-breaking studies of the economics of slavery, *Time on the Cross: The Economics of American Negro Slavery*. Fogel and Engerman were among a small group of scholars using cliometrics to interpret American slavery. Cliometrics involves the use of large statistical databases drawn from population censuses, parish records, probate material, and so on. *Time on the Cross* was controversial in many ways, in particular because the authors did not consider the experiences of the enslaved within that system. Even so, it remains one of the foundational studies of the economics of slavery.

My work merges the economic patterns of enslaved appraisals and sales with the testimonies of the enslaved. It illustrates the ways in which black people were commodified from birth through death—and beyond (some enslaved bodies were harvested as cadavers for nineteenth-century medical education). I also argue that enslaved people held internal values, soul values that often escaped commodification. Such a multidimensional discussion of external values is long overdue. I hope that readers will interpret this material as context for twentieth-century controversies, such as the Tuskegee syphilis experiment (1932–1972) and the 1950s case of Henrietta Lacks, the unwitting source of an immortal cell line for medical research.

Some will be uncomfortable with my discussion of enslaved people in connection with livestock, rape, and forced breeding. However, enslaved people spoke about these difficult connections as realities. My job is to present the history as it is written and spoken. Historians Karl Jacoby and Mia Bay provide a space for me to grapple with these ideas. Jacoby eloquently argues that even when enslaved people made analogies between themselves, cattle, and other animals, they did so to "underscore the dehumanizing features of slavery."[1] I wholeheartedly agree, and my book offers evidence of enslaved people strongly responding to their dehumanizing commodification. They valued themselves so much that they risked their lives to claim their personhood. Expressing themselves through "soul values," enslaved people clung to humanity, dignity, decency, and freedom. At the same time, when they died, some of them were placed in circulation as part of a cadaver trade. Their bodies held worth beyond death; I call these "ghost values."

A rather unusual aspect of capitalism and slavery, deceased human chattel has hardly appeared in the historiography of slavery. Yet several scholars address suicide, murder, compensation for executed enslaved people, and burial practices in their work.[2] My contribution to death culture is deliberately transnational as I address Saartjie Baartman, the South African woman used for medical research in the early nineteenth century, to link her experiences to women like Joice Heth, an enslaved woman who was studied in the 1830s.

ECONOMISTS AND HISTORIANS

Economists and historians have discussed slave prices since the early twentieth century, but it was not until 1999 that historian Walter Johnson encouraged thinking about what it meant to be a person with a price.[3] Social historians and economists have done great work on slave prices dating back to 1918. Today, more than a dozen scholars continue to analyze and interpret market values and appraisals of enslaved people. But the two fields have not always been in agreement. The 2014 publication of Edward Baptist's *The Half Has Never Been Told* unleashed a firestorm of debate about the relationship between capitalism, slavery, and violence.[4] I enter this conversation with a modest background in economics. My focus is simple and relies on both quantitative and qualitative data, but my primary objective is to insert the voices of the enslaved into the ongoing conversation about their value. Searching for their voices has been the primary thrust of this work that compares enslaved people's soul value with sale and appraisal information for a large data set of monetary values (N = 64,193).

Even though history books are peppered with commentary from the enslaved, few scholars allow them to enter conversations about their commodification. Social historians Walter Johnson, Edward Baptist, and Calvin Schermerhorn use enslaved narratives in their work, as do many others. But published narratives are usually privileged over those collected orally in the 1930s. Others are distracted by the debate about the validity of narratives as a reliable source. Many economists (and many historians) do not employ narratives, claiming that the narratives contain bias and that they are interested in the quantitative rather than qualitative. I believe bias is evident in every source, from plantation letters to enslaved testimonies as well as medical reports and physicians' lectures. Therefore, I look for the voice of the enslaved in a host of records, including published narratives from *Documenting the American South*; edited collections such as John Blassingame's *Slave Testimony*, James Redpath's *The Roving Editor*, William Still's *The Underground Railroad*; and the Works Progress Administration collection of more than 2,500 narratives housed at the Library of Congress and available online. During my ten years of research, I read most of the published narratives that appeared in the nineteenth and early twentieth centuries, beginning with the work of Solomon Bayley and William Grimes, published in 1825, up to the narrative of Thomas L. Johnson, published in 1909. Putting debates aside, my objective was to let the enslaved lead my journey into their thoughts, comments, and feelings about commodification.

DATA

The data in this book are from a large sample that I use to analyze the economic value of the enslaved. The Berry Slave Value Database, as I call it, derives from more than thirty years of research donated by Robert Fogel and Stanley Engerman (N =55,756), as well as Civil War data from Robert Margo (N=1,213). Fogel and Engerman's research comes from probate records housed in the Family History Library in Salt Lake City, Utah, that include mainly appraisals (roughly 90 percent). I add figures to their work culled from a decade in the archives researching enslaved people's values. The Berry segment of the data is the most diverse, in that I searched multiple sources, including plantation records, diaries, trading company records, bills of sale, receipts, auction reports, insurance companies, titles, deeds, gifts, court records, medical records, and virtually any written document I could find that included name, age, sex, monetary value, and year data (N = 8,437). Readers can view the list of the more than twenty archives I accessed across the United States in the notes section. I also consulted with John McCusker, an expert on the history of currency, and received guidance on how to convert all the data to 1860 dollars using the David-Solar estimates found in the *Historical Statistics of the United States*.[5] At one point, the composite Berry Slave Value Database contained information on nearly ninety thousand enslaved people from the Upper and Lower South, from birth to death.[6] However, just before publication, I omitted the Margo data because I was not able to determine whether the figures were in Confederate greenbacks or US dollars. This is unfortunate because I spent nearly three years working on trading patterns and pricing during the Civil War and consulted several Civil War historians, but because the data were so scattered and conversion tables needed to be done monthly based on occupation patterns, I simply did not have all the necessary information. The best evidence of how enslaved prices changed during the war comes from the work of Jonathan Pritchett and Charles W. Calomiris.

Readers will not find ghost values and soul values included in my data set, even though they appear throughout the text. I deliberately decided not to add such values to the larger database because ghost values represent an act of commodification with which I was not comfortable, given the years of exploitation that enslaved people experienced. As for soul values, from what I was able to discern, they were sometimes infinite and incalculable.

PLANTATION RECORDS

I rely on the records of several large plantations to capture enslaved appraisals and sales. Cane Brake (Adams County, Mississippi) and Airlie (East Carroll Parish, Louisiana) plantations, owned and operated by the Carson family, provide vivid valuation patterns, as Dr. James Green Carson kept meticulous records of enslaved appraisal values at the beginning and end of the year for more than a hundred enslaved people. Extant lists from Cane Brake include the years 1856 to 1858. In 1861, Carson moved the family to Airlie Plantation in Louisiana and appraised all 180 enslaved people. In addition to the data for the Carson properties, I use an 1850 appraisal of the 150 enslaved people at Bayou Boeuf Plantation (Rapides Parish, Louisiana), as well as newspaper advertisements of large sales, to capture the differences between market values (sales) and projected values (appraisals). I also consulted records of the following traders of enslaved people: Tyre Glynn, Isaac Franklin, John Armfield, and A. and J. McElveen, among many others, to analyze sale patterns of the domestic slave trade.

Although the experiences of those on small- to medium-sized farms and in industrial spaces represent circumstances equally important to our understanding of commodification during slavery, I mainly cite large plantations, even though the values of those on small farms are incorporated in the Berry Slave Value Database. Both Stephanie McCurry and Wilma Dunaway remind us that the experiences of those on small farms contain additional data about enslavement and sales. Dunaway's online archive, for example, offers quantitative material about enslaved children's prices on a companion website, http://scholar.lib.vt.edu/faculty_archives/mountain_slavery/tables.htm, in Table 8.5, "Profitability of Mules and Slave Children," showing that the value of children age five and under increased from $100 to $150 for males and from $90 to $130 for females.[7] Considering diverse locations, whether plantations or small farms, is important for our understanding of the institution and the monetization of enslaved people. Some might wonder about the enslaved people who never experienced sale. Their experiences also appear in this book because most enslaved people received appraisal values whether or not they were sold.

INSURANCE RECORDS

Slave life insurance represented one way to secure enslavers' investment in enslaved people, and many chose this option to protect themselves from potential loss. This practice was not new nor was it unique to one state. Investing in insurance was a global phenomenon, with a scale ranging from individual to statewide or national policies. Some of the earliest evidence on insuring enslaved people appears in literature on the transatlantic slave trade, describing buyers who insured their cargo prior to transport to New World communities. Given the risky nature of travel by boat and the high mortality rates during the Middle Passage, insurance offered financial protection for any loss "at sea." Rather than wait until an enslaved person died to seek legal routes to recover the value, enslavers and traders purchased life insurance policies on enslaved people in case they died. They used firms and hired agents to help them identify the best policy with an appropriate premium. Through these transactions, we have another rich indicator of enslaved people's economic values. These policies included the monetary value of the enslaved, the age, the term limit, the percentage, and the premium for each individual policyholder. Some enslavers chose short terms consisting of six months, while others extended policy terms from one to five years and beyond. Such policies guaranteed reimbursement for the value of the enslaved regardless of the mode of death, with the exception of suicide.[8] Readers will notice that the appraised values for enslaved people in these records are much higher than those found in probate records and estate inventories.

In the year 2000, the California state legislature passed SB 2199 to identify and "make available to the public" all the policies that had related to slavery for existing insurance companies. This paved the way for other states, such as Illinois (in 2002), Iowa (in 2004), and Maryland (in 2012), to follow suit with similar bills. These public reports shed light on the monetary value of the enslaved in life and at their projected deaths.[9] Around the same time as the enactment of the California legislation, Walmart made national news when employees learned that the company took out life insurance policies without their consent in an effort to protect itself and profit from their deaths.[10] The Walmart example is not dissimilar to enslavers' practice of purchasing insurance to protect themselves from potential or pending financial loss, particularly for enslaved people who worked in industrial settings such as coal mines, factories, and mills.[11]

As valuable as these data are, what we know about slave insurance comes mainly from the California registry or the records of the Baltimore Life Insurance Company, which insured enslaved people from the 1830s through the Civil War. The work of Sharon Murphy, Karen Ryder, and Michael Ralph relies on these records. Each of these scholars, along with Josiah Nott, Eugene Genovese, and Todd Savitt, shapes the conclusions about slave life insurance, arguing that we have little evidence south of the Potomac River.[12] In 2004, however, I discovered an archival goldmine and found over four thousand policies from throughout the South written by Southern Mutual Insurance, which later merged with the Southern Mutual Life Insurance Company (SMLIC) and is still in business today. Although some historians referenced SMLIC based on scattered newspaper advertisements and brief correspondence from agents, to date no scholar has analyzed the SMLIC records offered in this manuscript. I spent months placing this material in a readable format so that I could analyze the patterns of insurance on various enslaved people. As with all the data used in this book, I have made access to these records available on my personal website, http://www.drdainarameyberry.com.

MEDICAL RECORDS

While not a new source, medical records reveal much about the institution of slavery. I am certainly not the first historian to review this work, given the scholarship of William Dostie Postell, Todd Savitt, Stephen Stowe, Sharla Fett, and Peter McCandless, to name a few. Much of this book has been influenced by conversations with, and the scholarship of, historian Michael Sappol, who encouraged me to search for the history of bodies traded. I recall him telling me that it would be like finding a needle in a haystack to search the records of anatomy professors. He was right. I spent six years in the medical archives researching anatomy professors, their lecture notes, account books, and official publications, such as university catalogues, announcements of lectures and fees, and alumni magazine publications from medical schools in the North and the South. From here, I went into specific records such as autopsies, coroner's reports, receipts, supplies, anatomical preparations, and dissection room notes. I uncovered documents that had not been viewed since the 1870s and read the notes of professors seeking to understand the human body. Enslaved and free blacks are prevalent in these records, including clinical reports and testimonies. I studied the artists who attended public dissections, reviewed their drawings, and found evidence of black bodies everywhere. As a result, I created a "family tree" of physicians and their students to trace these men's trajectories of influence on the medical profession. This material is also available on my website, http://www.drdainarameyberry.com, for those interested in studying nineteenth-century physicians. Just as this book was in production, a number of studies on slavery reached the shelves, which I anticipate *The Price for Their Pound of Flesh* will be in conversation with, including Christina Sharpe, *In the Wake: On Blackness and Being* (Durham, NC: Duke University Press, 2016), and Marisa Fuentes, *Dispossessed Lives: Enslaved Women, Violence, and the Archive* (Philadelphia: University of Pennsylvania Press, 2016).

◆   ◆   ◆

I hope my work is the first of many in which the enslaved voice is central to conversations about what happened to enslaved bodies. This intervention is tremendously important, because some of those bodies that circulated two hundred years ago are only now being prepared for burial in Virginia. I believe we will find more bodies in the ground as well as evidence in the archives, and it is our responsibility to lay them to rest so their souls will have everlasting peace.

Notes

ARCHIVES CONSULTED [WITH ABBREVIATIONS]

Albert and Shirley Small Special Collections Library, University of Virginia (Charlottesville)—UVA

Calvin M. McClung Historical Collection, Knox County Public Library (Knoxville, TN)

Charles Patterson Van Pelt Library, University of Pennsylvania (Philadelphia)

College of Physicians of Philadelphia—CPP

David M. Rubenstein Rare Book and Manuscript Library, Duke University (Durham, NC)

Dolph Briscoe Center for American History, University of Texas at Austin—DBCAH

Filson Historical Society (Louisville, KY)

Francis A. Countway Library of Medicine, Harvard University (Cambridge, MA)

Georgia Archives, University System of Georgia (Morrow)

Georgia Historical Society (Savannah)

Harvard University Archives (Cambridge, MA)

Harvard University Special Collections (Cambridge, MA)

Health Sciences and Human Services Library, University of Maryland (Baltimore)—HS-HSL

Huntington Library (San Marino, CA)

Inter-University Consortium for Political and Social Research (Ann Arbor, MI)—ICPSR

Jefferson Medical College (Philadelphia)—JMC

Library Company of Philadelphia

Library of Congress (Washington, DC)—LOC

Library of Virginia (Richmond)—LVA

Massachusetts Historical Society (Boston)—MHS

National Archives and Records Administration (Washington, DC)

National Library of Medicine, National Institutes of Health (Bethesda, MD)—NLM

New York Public Library (New York, NY)

Oberlin College Special Collections (Oberlin, OH)

Research Library & Municipal Archives, City of Savannah (Savannah, GA)

Robert B. Greenblatt, MD, Library (Augusta, GA)—GML

Schomburg Center for Research in Black Culture (New York, NY)

Scott Memorial Library, Thomas Jefferson University (Philadelphia)

South Carolina Historical Society (Charleston)—SCHS

South Caroliniana Library, University of South Carolina (Columbia)

Southern Historical Collection, University of North Carolina (Chapel Hill)—SHC

Southern Mutual Life Insurance Company Archives—SMLIC

State Archives of North Carolina (Raleigh)

Tompkins-McCaw Library for the Health Sciences, Virginia Commonwealth University (Richmond)—TMCC

University Archives, Louisiana State University (New Orleans)

University Archives and Records Center, University of Pennsylvania (Philadelphia)—UPENN

Virginia Historical Society (Richmond)

AUTHOR'S NOTE

1. Dave Harper, *Slave Narratives: A Folk History of Slavery in the United States from Interviews with Former Slaves* (hereafter referred to as *Slave Narratives*), *Missouri Narratives*, vol. 10 (Washington, DC: Library of Congress [LOC]/WPA [Works Progress Administration], 1941), 165.

PREFACE

1. James Baldwin, "Amen," c. 1983, 1985, in *Jimmy's Blues and Other Poems* (Boston: Beacon Press, 2014).

INTRODUCTION

1. Figures given here and to start chapters 2 through 5 are from the Berry Slave Value Database, available at the author's website, http://www.drdainarameyberry.com; raw data stored at the ICPSR, https://www.icpsr.umich.edu/icpsrweb/landing.jsp.

2. "To Thomas Jefferson from Benjamin Banneker, 19 August 1791," Founders Online, National Archives, http://founders.archives.gov/documents/Jefferson/01–22–02–0049 [last update: December 30, 2015]. Source: *The Papers of Thomas Jefferson*, vol. 22, *6 August 1791–31 December 1791*, ed. Charles T. Cullen (Princeton, NJ: Princeton University Press, 1986), 49–54.

3. "The Position of England. British and American Views," *Christian Recorder*, April 19, 1862.

4. J. W. C. Pennington, *A Narrative of the Events of the Life of J. H. Banks, an Escaped Slave, from the Cotton State, Alabama* (Liverpool: M. Rourke, 1861), 33. Hereafter, *Narrative of J. H. Banks*.

5. Ibid., 11.

6. Wilma King, *Stolen Childhood: Slave Youth in Nineteenth-Century America* (1995; repr., Bloomington: Indiana University Press, 2011), 71.

7. Pennington, *Narrative of J. H. Banks*, 33.

8. Ibid., 41.

9. All quoted material in this paragraph comes from Pennington, *Narrative of J. H. Banks*, 81.

10. Ibid.

11. Ibid., 82.

12. Alain Locke, "Values and Imperatives," in *The Philosophy of Alain Locke: Harlem Renaissance and Beyond*, ed. Leonard Harris (Philadelphia: Temple University Press, 1991), 31–50.

13. George P. Rawick, ed., *God Struck Me Dead: Religious Conversion Experiences and Autobiographies of Negro Ex-Slaves* (Fisk University, 1941; repr., Westport, CT: Greenwood Publishing Company, 1972), 34.

14. First quotation comes from Locke, "Values and Imperatives," 38, emphasis in the original. The second quote is taken from Vincent Brown, "Social Death and Political Life in the Study of Slavery," *American Historical Review* 114, no. 5 (December 2009): 1231–49, quoted material on 1236. My definition of soul values builds on the work of Locke and Brown, as well as on that of Nell Painter, Orlando Patterson, and, most recently, Ramesh Mallipeddi. See Painter, "Soul Murder and Slavery: Toward A Fully Loaded Cost Accounting" in *Southern History Across the Color Line*, Painter, ed. (Chapel Hill: University of North Carolina Press, 2002), 15–39; Patterson, *Slavery and Social Death: A Comparative Study* (Cambridge, MA: Harvard University Press, 1982); and Mallipeddi, *Spectacular Suffering: Witnessing Slavery in the Eighteenth-Century British Atlantic* (Charlottesville: University Press of Virginia, 2016).

15. Daina Ramey Berry, "'Broad Is da Road Dat Leads to Death': Human Capital and Enslaved Mortality," in *Slavery's Capitalism: A New History of American Economic Development*, ed. Sven Beckert and Seth Rothman (Philadelphia: University of Pennsylvania Press, 2016).

16. Rawick, *God Struck Me Dead*, 78.

17. Ruth Richardson, *Death, Dissection and the Destitute* (1987; repr. Chicago: University of Chicago Press, 2002), 72.

18. Robert Blakely and Judith Harrington, eds., *Bones in the Basement: Postmortem Racism in Nineteenth-Century Medical Training* (Washington, DC: Smithsonian Institution Press, 1997); Michael Sappol, *A Traffic of Dead Bodies: Anatomy and Embodied Social Identity in Nineteenth-Century America* (Princeton, NJ: Princeton University Press, 2002); and Harriet A. Washington, *Medical Apartheid: The Dark History of Medical Experimentation on Black Americans from Colonial Times to the Present* (New York: Doubleday, 2007). A group of bioarchaeologists is also doing novel work in this area. See Kenneth C. Nystrom, ed., *The Bioarchaeology of Dissection and Autopsy in the United States* (New York: Springer International Publishing, 2016).

19. Richard C. Wade, *Slavery in the Cities: The South, 1820–1860* (New York: Oxford University Press, 1964), 171.

CHAPTER 1

1. Thomas R. Gray, ed., *The Confessions of Nat Turner, the Leader of the Late Insurrection in Southampton, Virginia* (Baltimore: Lucas & Deaver, 1831), 7, available online at *Documenting the American South*, docsouth.unc.edu/neh/turner/turner.html.

2. James Redpath, *The Roving Editor: Or, Talks with Slaves in the Southern States* (New York: A. B. Burdick Publisher, 1859), 39.

3. "Slave Auction in South Carolina," *Frederick Douglass' Paper*, February 16, 1855.

4. Robert Falls, *Slave Narratives, Tennessee Narratives*, vol. 15 (Washington, DC: LOC/WPA, 1941), 13.

5. Tempe Herndon, *Slave Narratives, North Carolina Narratives* 14, no. 1 (Washington, DC: LOC/WPA, 1941), 284–90, quote on 288.

6. "Mr. Clay on Slave Breeding," *National Era*, August 22, 1859.

7. Josephine Howell, *Slave Narratives, Arkansas Narratives*, vol. 2, pt. 3 (Washington, DC: LOC/WPA, 1941), 339.

8. Mollie Williams, *Slave Narratives, Mississippi Narratives*, vol. 9 (Washington, DC: LOC/ WPA, 1941), 158.

9. Theodore Dwight Weld and the American Anti-Slavery Society, *American Slavery as It Is: A Testimony of a Thousand Witnesses* (New York: American Anti-Slavery Society, 1839), 110–11.

10. *City Gazette* (Charleston, SC), April 30, 1798.

11. Darold Wax, "New Negroes Are Always in Demand: The Slave Trade in Eighteenth-Century Georgia," *Georgia Historical Quarterly* 68, no. 2 (Summer 1984): 193–220.

12. Jed Handelsman Shugerman, "The Louisiana Purchase and South Carolina's Reopening of the Slave Trade in 1803," *Journal of the Early Republic* 22, no. 2 (Summer 2002): 263–90.

13. Gwendolyn Midlo Hall is the exception. She has a searchable online database of enslaved values based on ethnicity, gender, and decade. See *Ibiblio*, http://www.ibiblio.org/laslave /calcs/prices.html, accessed January 15, 2011; and Gwendolyn Midlo Hall, *The Louisiana Slave Database, 1719–1820* (Baton Rouge: Louisiana State University Press, 2000). Hall's database contains detailed information for approximately one hundred thousand individuals and price data for about twenty thousand.

14. U. B. Phillips, "Slavery—United States," in *Encyclopedia of Social Studies*, vols. XIII–XIV, ed. Edwin R. A. Seligman and Alvin Johnson (New York: MacMillan Company, 1934), 84–90.

15. Daina Ramey Berry, "'We'm Fus' Rate Bargain': Value, Labor, and Price in a Georgia Slave Community," in *The Chattel Principle: Internal Slave Trades in the Americas, 1808–1888*, ed. Walter Johnson (New Haven, CT: Yale University Press, 2004), 55–71; and Daina Ramey Berry, "'In Pressing Need of Cash': Gender, Skill and Family Persistence in the Domestic Slave Trade," *Journal of African American History* 92, no. 1 (Winter 2007): 22–36.

16. Manuel Fraginals, Herbert Klein, and Stanley Engerman call attention to the skill premium, the ambiguity of enslaved people's ages, and the female childbearing premium; see Fraginals, Klein, and Engerman, "The Level and Structure of Slave Prices on Cuban Plantations in the Mid-Nineteenth Century: Some Comparative Perspectives," *American Historical Review* 88, no. 5 (December 1983): 1201–18, esp. 17n and 49n. Enslaved women's financial value increased during childbearing years; see Berry, "'We'm Fus' Rate Bargain,'" and Ashley N. Coleman and William K. Hutchinson, "Trade Restriction and Factor Prices: Slave Prices in Early Nineteenth Century U.S.," Working Paper No. 05-W21, Vanderbilt University Department of Economics (August 2005): 1–35.

17. Jacqueline Jones, "Race, Sex, and Self-Evident Truths: The Status of Slave Women During the Era of the American Revolution," in *Women in the Age of the American Revolution*, ed. Ronald Hoffman and Peter J. Albert (Charlottesville: University Press of Virginia, 1989), 293–337, especially 296–97.

18. Richard Sutch, "Slave Population Table Bb214," in *Historical Statistics of the United States, Millennial Edition Online*, ed. Susan B. Carter et al. (Cambridge, UK: Cambridge University Press, 2006), 2–381.

19. For discussions of colonial and Revolutionary ages of first birth, see Cheryll A. Cody, "A Note on Changing Patterns of Slave Fertility in the South Carolina Rice District, 1735–1865," *Southern Studies* 16 (1977): 457–63; Allan Kulikoff, "A 'Prolifick' People: Black

Population Growth in the Chesapeake Colonies, 1700–1790," *Southern Studies* 16, no. 4 (1977): 391–428; Allan Kulikoff, *Tobacco and Slaves: The Development of Southern Cultures in the Chesapeake, 1680–1800* (Chapel Hill: University of North Carolina Press, 1986); Russell R. Menard, "The Maryland Slave Population, 1658–1730: A Demographic Profile of Blacks in Four Counties," *William & Mary Quarterly* 3rd. series, vol. 32 (1975): 29–54; Jennifer L. Morgan, *Laboring Women: Reproduction and Gender in New World Slavery* (Philadelphia: University of Pennsylvania Press, 2004); Philip D. Morgan, "Black Society in the Lowcountry, 1760–1810," in *Slavery and Freedom in the Age of the American Revolution*, ed. Ronald Hoffman and Ira Berlin (Charlottesville: University Press of Virginia, 1983), 83–141; and James Trussell and Richard Steckel, "The Age of Slaves at Menarche and Their First Birth," *Journal of Interdisciplinary History* 8 (Winter 1978): 477–505.

20. Kenneth Morgan, "Slave Sales in Colonial Charleston," *English Historical Review* 113, no. 453 (September 1998): 905–27, quoted material on 919. See also Menard, "The Maryland Slave Population, 1658 to 1730."

21. William Andrews, ed., "Narrative of the Life of Moses Grandy," in *North Carolina Slave Narratives: The Lives of Moses Roper, Lunsford Lane, Moses Grandy, & Thomas H. Jones* (Chapel Hill: University of North Carolina Press, 2003), 156–86.

22. Ibid., 176.

23. Ibid.

24. Ibid. This method of concealment might remind readers of another North Carolina enslaved woman, Harriet Jacobs, who hid in her grandmother's attic crawl space for seven years. See Jacobs, *Incidents in the Life of a Slave Girl: Written by Herself*, ed. Lydia Maria Child (Boston: Privately published, 1861), 149, available online at *Documenting the American South*, http://docsouth.unc.edu/fpn/jacobs/jacobs.html.

25. Richard Sutch, "The Breeding of Slaves for Sale and Westward Expansion of Slavery, 1850–1860," Institute of Business and Economic Research, Berkeley, CA, 1972; and Michael Tadman, *Speculators and Slaves: Masters, Traders, and Slaves in the Old South* (Madison: University of Wisconsin Press, 1989).

26. Hall's database is extremely useful here because she also examines female price patterns. In particular, she divides "slave value" by decade, gender, and origin. In her sample of male and female values (including African, American, Caribbean, and Anglo origins), Hall offers prices from 1770 to 1810 with a data set of 19,455, of which 8,379 were women. Hall found that women's economic values increased in the 1770s and 1780s, slightly decreased in the 1790s, and surpassed the 1780s figures in 1800 and 1810.

27. Stephanie M. H. Camp, *Closer to Freedom: Enslaved Women and Everyday Resistance in the Plantation South* (Chapel Hill: University of North Carolina Press, 2004).

28. Although I am not totally comfortable with these terms, I am using them in this chapter as they are reflected in the literature. My definition of skilled women includes agricultural and nonagricultural laborers who "had the ability to do any form of work well." See Daina Ramey Berry, *Swing the Sickle for the Harvest Is Ripe: Gender and Slavery in Antebellum Georgia* (Urbana: University of Illinois Press, 2007), 9 and passim. "Fancies" are most recently defined as "neither precisely black nor white, and neither field labor nor cooking and cleaning, but rather the 'fancy' of the market for selling the right to rape a special category of women marked out as unusually desirable." See Edward Baptist, "'Cuffy,' 'Fancy

Maids,' and 'One-Eyed Men': Rape, Commodification, and the Domestic Slave Trade in the United States," *American Historical Review* 106, no. 5 (December 2001): 1642–43. Breeders were enslaved women (and men) used to reproduce and provide additional enslaved laborers for the plantation workforce. For recent literature on fancies, see Richard Follett, *The Sugar Masters: Planters and Slaves in Louisiana's Cane World, 1820–1860* (Baton Rouge: Louisiana State University Press, 2005), 55–75; Sharony Green, *Remember Me to Miss Louisa: Hidden Black-White Intimacies in Antebellum America* (DeKalb: Northern Illinois University Press, 2015); and Diane Miller-Sommerville, "Moonlight, Magnolias, and Brigadoon; or 'Almost Like Being in Love': Mastery and Sexual Exploitation in Eugene D. Genovese's Plantation South," *Radical History Review* 88 (Winter 2004): 68–82.

29. Frederic Bancroft, *Slave Trading in the Old South* (1931; repr., Columbia: University of South Carolina Press, 1996), 328–30.

30. Berry Slave Value Database.

31. For a detailed discussion of derogatory naming patterns, see Daina Ramey Berry, "'Buck,' 'Pussy,' 'Angus,' and 'Wench': Naming, Sexuality, and Personality in the Slave South," paper presented at the Organization of American Historians annual meeting, March 19, 2011.

32. *City Gazette and Daily Advertiser* (Charleston, SC), May 2, 1798.

33. Fannie Moore, *Slave Narratives, North Carolina Narratives*, vol. 11, pt. 2 (Washington, DC: LOC/WPA, 1941), 127–37, quote on 131.

34. Ashley N. Coleman and William K. Hutchinson, "Determinants of Slave Prices: Louisiana, 1725 to 1820," Working Paper No. 06-W24, Vanderbilt University, Department of Economics (December 2006), http://www.vanderbilt.edu/econ/wparchive/working06.html.

35. Berry, *Swing the Sickle*, 77–84; Sutch, "The Breeding of Slaves for Sale and the Westward Expansion of Slavery"; and Richard Sutch, "Slave Breeding," Social Science Working Paper No. 593, California Institute of Technology, Pasadena, 1986.

36. E-mail conversation between author and Jennifer L. Morgan, April 23, 2011.

37. "Auction block" is used here as a metaphor for sale, as some women experience sale through other methods such as private transactions, legal deeds, mortgages, and transfers.

38. *Virginia Chronicle and Norfolk and Portsmouth General Advertiser*, March 9, 1793.

39. Berry, *Swing the Sickle*, 104–28.

40. See *Pennsylvania Packet and General Advertiser*, February 5, 1784. Likewise, James Glentworth advertised "A Negro Wench, American Born," *Pennsylvania Packet and Daily Advertiser*, November 23, 1786.

41. *New-York Gazette*, April 27, 1761.

42. *New-York Gazette*, April 3, 1758.

43. *New-York Gazette*, January 23, 1775.

44. *Pennsylvania Packet and General Advertiser*, February 5, 1784, and August 15, 1786. A "health strong" New Jersey woman experienced sale, along with her five- and six-year-old sons and four-year-old daughter, "on account of breeding too fast." See *New Jersey Journal*, April 27, 1791.

45. "A Slave Auction in Richmond, VA," *National Era*, March 24, 1853. Emphasis in the original.

46. Hannah Jones, *Slave Narratives, Missouri Narratives*, vol. 10 (Washington, DC: LOC/WPA, 1941), 216.

47. Frances Ellen Watkins Harper, "The Slave Mother," in *Poems on Miscellaneous Subjects* (Boston: J. B. Yerrinton & Son, 1854).

48. John Collins, "The Slave-Mother" (Philadelphia: Pennsylvania Anti-Slavery Fair, 1855).

49. Berry Slave Value Database.

50. *Virginia, Maryland, Pennsylvania, & New-Jersey Weekly*, February 25, 1775.

51. *Charleston Morning Post and Daily Advertiser*, November 4, 1786.

52. Benjamin Drew, *A North-Side View of Slavery: The Refugee* (1856; repr., Reading, MA: Addison-Wesley, 1969), 199.

53. *City Gazette and Daily Advertiser* (Charleston, SC), October 28, 1793.

54. Drew, *A North-Side View of Slavery*, 177.

55. Betty Cofer, *Slave Narratives, North Carolina Narratives*, vol. 11, pt. 1, "Negro Folklore of the Piedmont" (Washington, DC: LOC/WPA, 1941), 165–75, quote on 171.

56. Bill Simms, *Slave Narratives, Kansas Narratives*, vol. 6 (Washington, DC: LOC/WPA, 1941), 8.

57. Adams escaped to Canada and provided her testimony upon arrival. It appears that she was interviewed in or around 1855 and believed that, at that time, she was seventy or eighty years old. Drew, *A North-Side View of Slavery*, 237.

58. Ibid., 237.

59. Ibid., 237.

60. Ibid., 237.

61. Ibid., 237.

62. Fishwick's Adm'r. v. Sewell, Maryland Court of Appeals 4 H. & J. 393; 1818. The others listed with Dinah included Fanny, Phyllis, John, Paul, Moses, Susannah, Pat, Isaac, Charles, Nelly, Sally, John, Sampson Tom, Nancy, Kit, Anna, and Harriott.

63. Ibid.

64. Ibid.

65. According to the data set, the highest value at this time was $225, and Dinah's value far exceeds this figure. I suspect that she was a valuable servant and that her ability to give birth or that she had healthy children justified her high value.

66. Moses Grandy never mentioned his mother's name in the narrative, and for the purpose of this discussion, I will occasionally refer to her as "Mother." The act of temporarily naming her is not meant to disrespect her memory in any patronizing way. Instead, it is used as both a respectful gesture and literary convenience. The latter and former work in conjunction as a way to provide a voice to one of many unnamed black women in the historical record. I am not suggesting that historians rename nameless historical figures; however, I am supporting the notion that these once invisible women become visible when we tell their stories and acknowledge their presence.

67. Andrews, "Moses Grandy," 159.

68. Ibid.

69. Ibid.

70. James Redpath, "The Slave-Mother's Reply," in Redpath, *The Roving Editor*, 44–45.

71. John Theophilus Kramer, *The Slave-Auction* (Boston: Robert F. Wallcut, 1859), 8–9.

72. Redpath, *The Roving Editor*, 251.

73. "Abolitionist Song," from *A Collection of Miscellaneous Songs, from the Liberty's Minstrel, and Masons's Juvenile Harp* (Cincinnati: Cincinnati High School, 1854), Oberlin College Special Collections.

74. Lina Hunter, *Slave Narratives, Georgia Narratives*, vol. 4, pt. 2 (Washington, DC: LOC/WPA), 262.

75. Grandy's reference to death is most likely an inference to the high infant mortality rates at this time. Andrews, "Moses Grandy," 159.

76. Bancroft, *Slave Trading in the Old South*, 19. In the footnote on p. 19, Bancroft explains that, of at least 288 advertised individuals, none were born in Africa.

77. Morgan, *Laboring Women*, 83.

CHAPTER 2

1. Pennington, *Narrative of J. H. Banks*, 29.

2. Ethan Allen Andrews, *Slavery and the Domestic Slave-Trade in the United States* (Boston: Light & Stearns, 1836), 147.

3. Nehemiah Adams, *South-Side View of Slavery: Three-Months at the South in 1854* (Boston: T. R. Marvin and B. B. Mussey & Company, 1854), 64–70.

4. Ibid., 69.

5. Sigmund Freud, *Beyond the Pleasure Principle* (1920; repr., Whitefish, MT: Kessinger Publishing, 2010); D. W. Winnicott et al., *Babies and Their Mothers* (Reading, MA: Addison-Wesley, 1987); and Travis Wright, "Learning to Laugh: A Portrait of Risk and Resilience in Early Childhood," *Harvard Educational Review* 80, no. 4 (Winter 2010): 444–63.

6. Several slave narratives used the term "cried off" in place of "being sold." See, for example, the narratives of W. L. Bost, Adaline Johnson, Charlotte Willis, and Emma Barr. Historian Calvin Schermerhorn also recognized this descriptive word choice. Schermerhorn, *The Business of Slavery and the Rise of American Capitalism, 1815–1860* (New Haven, CT: Yale University Press, 2015).

7. Chaney Spell, *Slave Narratives, North Carolina*, vol. 11, pt. 2 (Washington, DC: LOC/WPA, 1941), 306–8; and Harriett Hill, *Slave Narratives, Arkansas Narratives*, vol. 2, pt. 3 (Washington, DC: LOC/WPA, 1941), 258.

8. Frederick Douglass, *My Bondage and My Freedom, Documenting the American South*, http://docsouth.unc.edu/neh/douglass55/douglass55.html, 207; Annie L. Burton, *Memories of Childhood's Slavery Days* (Boston: Rose Publishing Company, 1909), 3; Elizabeth Keckley, *Behind the Scenes: Or, Thirty Years a Slave and Four Years in the White House* (New York: G. W. Carleton & Co., Publishers, 1868), 18–19; and King, *Stolen Childhood*.

9. James Mellon, ed., *Bullwhip Days: The Slaves Remember; An Oral History* (New York: Avon Books, 1988), (first quotation) 149, (second quotation) 41.

10. Douglass, *My Bondage and My Freedom*, 38–39.

11. Mingo White, *Slave Narratives, Alabama Narratives*, vol. 1 (Washington, DC: LOC/WPA, 1941), 413–14.

12. Thomas A. Foster, "The Sexual Abuse of Black Men Under Slavery," *Journal of the History of Sexuality* 20 (September 2011): 445–64.

13. Douglass, *My Bondage and My Freedom*, 39.

14. Horace C. Grosvenor and American Reform Tract and Book Society, *The Child's Book on Slavery; or, Slavery Made Plain* (Cincinnati: American Reform Tract and Book Society, 1857), 6–7, 9, 20, 22, and 24.

15. Keckley, *Behind the Scenes*, 28–29.

16. Ibid., 23–24.

17. Eugene D. Genovese, *Roll, Jordan, Roll: The World the Slaves Made* (New York: Vintage, 1976), 503.

18. King, *Stolen Childhood*, introduction and xx.

19. Redpath, *The Roving Editor*, 245–50.

20. Marlida Pethy, *Slave Narratives, Missouri Narratives*, vol. 10 (Washington, DC: LOC/WPA, 1941), 279.

21. See forthcoming work of Stephanie Jones-Rogers, *Lady Flesh-Stealers, Female Soul Drivers, and She-Merchants: White Women and the Economy of American Slavery* (New Haven, CT: Yale University Press, forthcoming); Thavolia Glymph, *Out of the House of Bondage: The Transformation of the Plantation Household* (New York: Cambridge University Press, 2008).

22. Kramer, *The Slave-Auction*, 8.

23. Charles Ball, *Fifty Years in Chains; Or the Life of an American Slave* (New York: H. Dayton, Publisher, 1859), 10–11. See also Edward Baptist, *The Half Has Never Been Told: Slavery and the Making of American Capitalism* (New York: Basic Books, 2014).

24. W. L. Bost, *Slave Narratives, North Carolina Narratives*, vol. 9, pt. 1 (Washington, DC: LOC/WPA, 1941), 140–41.

25. Ibid., 139–40.

26. Kramer, *The Slave-Auction*, 36–37.

27. Martha King, *Slave Narratives, Oklahoma Narratives*, vol. 13 (Washington, DC: LOC/WPA, 1941), 170.

28. Berry, "'We'm Fus' Rate Bargain'"; Berry, "'In Pressing Need of Cash'"; and Thomas D. Russell, "Articles Sell Best Singly: The Disruption of Slave Families at Court Sales," *Utah Law Review* (1996): 1161–1209.

29. *Savannah Republican, February 8, 1859.*

30. Berry, "'In Pressing Need of Cash' and '"We'm Fus' Rate Bargain.'" See also Q. K. Philander Doesticks, "Great Auction Sale of Slaves at Savannah, Georgia, March 2d and 3d, 1859," *New York Tribune*, March 9, 1859; Kwesi DeGraft, "Unearthing the Weeping Time: Savannah's Ten Broeck Race Course and 1859 Slave Sale," *Southern Spaces*, February 18, 2010, http://www.southernspaces.org/2010/unearthing-weeping-time-savannahs-ten-broeck-race-course-and-1859-slave-sale (accessed June 12, 2015).

31. Bost, *Slave Narratives*, 140.

32. Hardy Miller, *Slave Narratives, Arkansas Narratives*, vol. 2, pt. 5 (Washington, DC: LOC/WPA, 1941), 74.

33. King, *Stolen Childhood*; and Tiffany M. Gill, "Hair and Headdresses," in *Enslaved Women in America: An Encyclopedia*, ed. Daina Ramey Berry (Santa Barbara, CA: Greenwood, 2012).

34. John J. Ormond, Arthur P. Bagby, and George Goldthwaite, *The Code of Alabama* (Montgomery: Brittan and De Wolf, 1852), 390–93, quote on 392.

35. B. F. French, *Historical Collections of Louisiana, Embracing Many Rare and Valuable Documents Relating to the Natural, Civil and Political History of That State* (New York: Wiley and Putnam, 1846), xliii, 94.

36. Brett Josef Derbes, "'Secret Horrors': Enslaved Women and Children in the Louisiana State Penitentiary, 1833–1862," *Journal of African American History* 98 (Spring 2013): 277–90, quote on 277. See also Michele Lise Tarter and Richard Bell, eds., *Buried Lives: Incarcerated in Early America* (Athens: University of Georgia Press, 2012).

37. Derbes, "'Secret Horrors,'" 280.

38. Glenn McNair, "Slave Women, Capital Crime, and Criminal Justice in Georgia," *Georgia Historical Quarterly* 93 (Summer 2009): 135–58; Susan E. O'Donovan, "Universities of Social and Political Change: Slaves in Jail in Antebellum America" in Tarter and Bell, *Buried Lives,* 124–48; and Betty Wood, "Some Aspects of Female Resistance to Chattel Slavery in Low Country Georgia, 1763–1815," *Historical Journal* 30 (September 1987): 603–22. For post-emancipation patterns of incarcerated women, see Talitha LeFlouria, *Chained in Silence: Black Women and Convict Labor in the New South* (Chapel Hill: University of North Carolina Press, 2015).

39. All quoted material in this paragraph comes from Andrews, *Slavery and the Domestic Slave-Trade in the United States,* 146–47.

40. "Visit to a Slave Auction," *New York Tribune,* January 30, 1855, emphasis in original.

41. Cane Brake Plantation Records, 1856–1858, DBCAH.

42. In 1856, the total population was 154, but in 1858, Carson owned 162. Given the birth information, it appears that only two enslaved people were purchased.

43. Sharla Fett, *Working Cures: Healing, Health, and Power on Southern Slave Plantations* (Chapel Hill: University of North Carolina Press, 2002).

44. See Kenneth F. Kiple and Virginia H. Kiple, "Slave Child Mortality: Some Nutritional Answers to a Perennial Puzzle," *Journal of Social History* 10 (Spring 1977): 284–309; Richard Steckel, "A Dreadful Childhood: The Excess of Mortality of American Slaves," *Social Science History* 10 (Winter 1986): 427–65; Michael P. Johnson, "Smothered Slave Infants: Were Slave Mothers at Fault?," *Journal of Southern History* 47 (November 1981): 493–520; William Dosite Postell, *The Health of Slaves on Southern Plantations* (Baton Rouge: Louisiana State University Press, 1951), esp. 111–28; and Steven Stowe, *Doctoring the South: Southern Physicians and Everyday Medicine in the Mid-Nineteenth Century* (Chapel Hill: University of North Carolina Press, 2004), 211.

45. James G. Anderson, "Dr. James Green Carson, Ante-Bellum Planter of Mississippi and Louisiana," *Journal of Mississippi History* 18 (October 1956): 243–67, quote on 247.

46. Ibid., 249.

47. Ibid., 254, 256, and 258.

48. Andrews, "Moses Grandy," 8–9.

49. Elizabeth Poole, "The Slave Boy's Death," in *The Liberty Bell* (Boston: American Anti-Slavery Society, 1844), 132–34.

50. See Genealogical Committee of the Georgia Historical Society, *Laurel Grove South Cemetery,* vol. 1, October 12, 1853, to November 30, 1861 (Savannah: R. J. Taylor Jr. Foundation, 1993); and Leslie Harris and Daina Ramey Berry, *Slavery and Freedom in Savannah* (Athens: University of Georgia Press, 2014), 116–18.

51. Alice Duggan Gracy and Emma Gene Seale Gentry, comp., *Travis County, Texas: The Five Schedules of the 1860 Federal Census* (Austin: Gracy and Gentry, 1967), 70–72.

52. See Caitlin C. Rosenthal, *From Slavery to Scientific Management* (Cambridge, MA: Harvard University Press, forthcoming); and Caitlin C. Rosenthal, "Slavery's Scientific Management: Masters and Managers," in Beckert and Rothman, *Slavery's Capitalism*.

53. "Advertisements," in Thomas Affleck, *The Sugar Plantation Record and Account Book No. 2*, 3rd ed. (New Orleans: Weld & Company, 1851); Cane Brake Plantation Records, 1856–1858, DBCAH.

54. *Second Annual Report of the Southern Mutual Life Insurance Company for the Year 1856* (Columbia, SC: Edward R. Burton, 1857), 22.

55. Bethany Veney, *The Narrative of Bethany Veney: A Slave Woman* (Worcester, MA: n.p., 1889), 10.

56. Stephen Duane Davis II and Alfred L. Brophy, "'The Most Solemn Act of My Life': Family, Property, Will, and Trust in the Antebellum South," *Alabama Law Review* (2011): 757–810, quote on 799.

CHAPTER 3

1. Thomas Smallwood, *A Narrative of Thomas Smallwood: Giving an Account of His Birth— The Period He Was Held in Slavery—His Release—and Removal to Canada, etc. Together with an Account of the Underground Railroad* (Toronto: James Stephens, 1851), 52, available online at *Documenting the American South*, http://docsouth.unc.edu/neh/smallwood /smallwood.html.

2. Lucy A. Delaney, *From the Darkness Cometh the Light or Struggles for Freedom* (St. Louis: J. T. Smith Publishing, 1891), 10.

3. Kramer, *The Slave-Auction*, 13–15.

4. In all likelihood, Joseph and his counterparts lived on Waterloo, Southdown, and Hollywood plantations, operated by the Minor family, or on the two sugar plantations on Bayou Boeuf owned by the Lewis Thompson family. See Minor Family Papers, 1763–1900, SHC; William J. Minor Collection, LSU; J. Carlyle Sitterson, "The William J. Minor Plantations: A Study in Ante-Bellum Absentee Ownership," *Journal of Southern History* 9 (February 1943): 59–74; "The Transition from Slave to Free Economy on the William J. Minor Plantations," *Agricultural History Society* 17 (October 1943): 216–24; and Lewis Thompson Papers, 1723–1895, SHC.

5. Kramer, *The Slave-Auction*, 31.

6. Rawick, *God Struck Me Dead*, 23.

7. Maya Angelou, "I Know Why the Caged Bird Sings," in *The Complete Collected Poems of Maya Angelou* (New York: Random House, 1994), http://www.poetryfoundation.org /poem/178948.

8. John W. Blassingame, *Slave Testimony: Two Centuries of Letters, Speeches, Interviews, and Autobiographies* (Baton Rouge: Louisiana State University Press, 1977), 516–17.

9. See Allan D. Austin, *African Muslims in Antebellum America: Transatlantic Stories and Spiritual Struggles* (New York: Routledge, 1997); Sylviane A. Diouf, *Servants of Allah: African Muslims Enslaved in the Americas* (New York: New York University Press, 1998); Michael Gomez, *Exchanging Our Country Marks: The Transformation of African Identities*

in the Colonial and Antebellum South (Chapel Hill: University of North Carolina Press, 1998); Walter Rucker, *The River Flows On: Black Resistance, Culture, and Identity in Early America* (Baton Rouge: Louisiana State University Press, 2008); and Jason R. Young, *Rituals of Resistance: African Atlantic Religion in Kongo and the Lowcountry South in the Era of Slavery* (Baton Rouge: Louisiana State University Press, 2011).

10. Georgia Writer's Project, *Drums and Shadows: Survival Studies Among the Coastal Georgia Negroes* (1940; repr., Athens: University of Georgia Press, 1986).

11. Merriam-Webster Dictionary online, http://www.merriam-webster.com/dictionary/puberty.

12. "American Vanity," *Christian Recorder*, April 19, 1862.

13. Solomon Bayley, *A Narrative of Some Remarkable Incidents in the Life of Solomon Bayley, Formerly a Slave in the State of Delaware, North America* (London: Harvey and Darton, 1825), 31–32, SHC (hereafter referred to as "Narrative of Solomon Bayley," SHC).

14. Loren Schweninger, "Solomon Bayley," in *African American Lives*, ed. Henry Louis Gates Jr. and Evelyn Brooks Higginbotham (New York: Oxford University Press, 2004), 59–60.

15. Friends of Freedom, *The Liberty Bell*, 34–35.

16. Walter Johnson, *Soul by Soul: Life Inside the Antebellum Slave Market* (Cambridge, MA: Harvard University Press, 1999), 20.

17. King, *Stolen Childhood*, 233.

18. See "Note on Sources." See also Stephanie Smallwood, *Saltwater Slavery: A Middle Passage from Africa to American Diaspora* (Cambridge, MA: Harvard University Press, 2007), chap. 2, quote on 36.

19. Blassingame, *Slave Testimony*, 395.

20. Still's *The Underground Railroad* was first published in 1872 (repr. New York: Arno Press, 1968). Drew's work, *A North-Side View of Slavery*, appeared in 1856.

21. Blassingame, *Slave Testimony*, 426.

22. Ibid., 427–29. See also editorial comments and lengthy letters in Still, *The Underground Railroad*, 188–202.

23. Still, *The Underground Railroad*, 188–202.

24. Berry, *Swing the Sickle for the Harvest Is Ripe*, and Baptist, *The Half Has Never Been Told*.

25. See Dan S. Hale, Kayla Goodson, and Jeff W. Savell, "USDA Beef Quality and Yield Grades," *Meat Science*, Texas A&M, http://meat.tamu.edu/beefgrading/, accessed October 31, 2015; and "How the USDA Grades Beef," Prime Time Top Ten USDA Prime Steakhouses, http://www.primesteakhouses.com/how-usda-grades-beef.html, accessed October 31, 2015.

26. Broadsides are replete with this language. See "Auction Notice, Credit Sale of a Choice Gang of 41 SLAVES!," Schomburg Center for Research in Black Culture, New York, NY, http://digitalcollections.nypl.org/items/510d47df-a264-a3d9-e040-e00a18064a99, accessed February 1, 2016; "An Unusually Prime and Orderly Gang of TWENTY-ONE NEGROES . . . ," Hutson Lee Papers, MSS 11–260–02–03, SCHS; "At Private Sale . . . Prime Wench," *Southern Patriot*, November 27, 1839.

27. Blassingame, *Slave Testimony*, 431.

28. Ibid., 438–39; and Drew, *A North-Side View of Slavery*, 131–32, emphasis added.

29. Blassingame, *Slave Testimony*, 406.

30. Ariela J. Gross, *Double Character: Slavery and Mastery in the Antebellum Southern Courtroom* (Princeton, NJ: Princeton University Press, 2000), 125.

31. Redpath, *The Roving Editor*, 247.

32. Ibid., 10 11.

33. Ibid., 252. Another woman chopped off her hand at the site of sale. See Jesse Torrey, *American Slave Trade; Or, An Account of the Manner in Which the Slave Dealers Take Free People from Some of the United States of America* (London: J. M. Cobbett, 1822), 72.

34. Juriah Harriss, "What Constitutes Unsoundness in the Negro?," *Savannah Journal of Medicine* 1 (September 1858): 145–52; and S. L. Grier, "The Negro and His Diseases," *New-Orleans Medical and Surgical Journal* 9 (1853): 752–63.

35. Brenda Stevenson, "Gender Convention, Ideals, and Identity Among Virginia Slave Women," in *More Than Chattel: Black Women and Slavery in the Americas*, ed. David Barry Gaspar and Darlene Clark Hine (Bloomington: Indiana University Press, 1996); and Adrienne D. Davis, "Don't Let Nobody Bother Yo' Principle: The Sexual Economy of American Slavery," in *Sister Circle: Black Women and Work*, ed. Sharon Harley (New Brunswick, NJ: Rutgers University Press, 2002).

36. Jenifer L. Barclay, "Mothering the 'Useless': Black Motherhood, Disability, and Slavery," *Women, Gender, and Families of Color* 2, no. 2 (Fall 2014): 115–40; "Reproduction and Motherhood" in Berry, *Enslaved Women in America*; Morgan, *Laboring Women*; Deirdre Cooper Owens, *Medical Superbodies: Slavery, Race, and the Birth of American Gynecology* (Athens: University of Georgia Press, forthcoming); and Sasha L. Turner, "Home-Grown Slaves: Women, Reproduction, and the Abolition of the Slave Trade, Jamaica 1788–1807," *Journal of Women's History* 23 (Fall 2011): 39–62.

37. Several scholars write about Saartjie Baartman, too many to name here. Some of the more recent publications include Clifton Crais and Pamela Scully, *Sara Baartman and the Hottentot Venus: A Ghost Story and a Biography* (Princeton, NJ: Princeton University Press, 2009); Sadiah Qureshi, "Displaying Sara Baartman, The 'Hottentot Venus,'" *History of Science* 43 (2004): 234–57; and Anne Fausto-Sterling, "Gender, Race, and Nation: The Comparative Anatomy of Hottentot Women in Europe, 1815–1817," in *Deviant Bodies: Critical Perspectives on Difference in Science and Popular Culture*, ed. Jennifer Terry and Jacqueline Urla (Bloomington: Indiana University Press, 1995).

38. John Roberton, "On the Period of Puberty in Negro Women," *Edinburgh Medical and Surgical Journal* 58 (1842): 112–20, quoted material on 112, 113, 115, 117, and 119; courtesy of NLM.

39. Berry, *Swing the Sickle*; and Berry, *Enslaved Women in America*.

40. HS-HSL; Trussell and Steckel, "The Age of Slaves at Menarche and Their First Birth"; Stephen C. Kinney, "'A Dictate of Both Interest and Mercy'? Slave Hospitals in the Antebellum South," *Journal of the History of Medicine and Allied Sciences* 65 (2010): 1–47.

41. Louise Oliphant, "Folk Remedies and Superstition," in *Slave Narratives, Georgia Narratives*, vol. 5, pt. 2 (Washington, DC: LOC/WPA, 1941), 285. I wish to thank Talitha LeFlouria for calling my attention to this source.

42. Fett, *Working Cures*; Dorothy Roberts, *Killing the Black Body: Race, Reproduction and the Meaning of Liberty* (New York: Vintage, 1997); and Marli F. Weiner with Mazie

Hough, *Sex, Sickness, and Slavery: Illness in the Antebellum South* (Urbana: University of Illinois Press, 2012).

43. Oliphant, "Folk Remedies and Superstition," 285.

44. J. R. C. Carroll, "Cases of Menstrual Derangement in Negro Women," *Southern Medical and Surgical Journal* 6 (April 17, 1860): 332–37; courtesy of NLM.

45. "Extensive Sale of Choice Slaves," Broadside Collection, DBCAH.

46. Letter from Thomas Henderson, May 18, 1841, Natchez Trace Collection, box-4Jc114c, DBCAH.

47. Garner's story is the basis for Toni Morrison's novel *Beloved*. See also Mark Reinhardt, *Who Speaks for Margaret Garner? The True Story That Inspired Toni Morrison's* Beloved (Minneapolis: University of Minnesota Press, 2010); and John H. Morgan, "An Essay on the Causes of the Production of Abortion Among Our Negro Population," *Nashville Journal of Medicine and Surgery* 19 (August 1860): 1.

48. Morgan, "An Essay on the Causes of the Production of Abortion Among Our Negro Population," 117–23.

49. "The Case of a Negro Woman Who Performed the Caesarean Operation on Herself," *London Medical Journal* 6 (1785): 372–73.

50. Jacobs, *Incidents in the Life of a Slave Girl: Written by Herself*, 44.

51. Veney, *The Narrative of Bethany Veney*, 8.

52. Foster, "The Sexual Abuse of Black Men Under Slavery," 445.

53. John Cole, *Slave Narratives, Georgia Narratives*, vol. 4 pt. 1 (Washington, DC: LOC/WPA, 1941), 228.

54. Laura Thornton, *Slave Narratives, Arkansas Narratives*, vol. 11, pt. 6 (Washington, DC: LOC/WPA, 1941), 326.

55. Jones-Rogers, *Lady Flesh-Stealers, Female Soul Drivers, and She-Merchants*.

56. Oscar Felix Junell, *Slave Narratives, Arkansas Narratives*, vol. 11, pt. 4 (Washington, DC: LOC/WPA, 1941).

57. Davis, "Don't Let Nobody Bother Yo' Principle."

58. Coleman and Hutchinson, "Determinants of Slave Prices in Louisiana, 1720 to 1820"; David Eltis and Stanley Engerman, "Was the Slave Trade Dominated by Men?," *Journal of Interdisciplinary History* 23 (Autumn 1992): 237–57; and Sutch, "The Breeding of Slaves for Sale and the Westward Expansion of Slavery." For the historiography of breeding and practices in the Caribbean, see Gregory Smithers, *Slave Breeding: Sex, Violence, and Memory in African American History* (Gainesville: University Press of Florida, 2012), and Eddie Donoghue, *Black Breeding Machines: The Breeding of Negro Slaves in the Diaspora* (Bloomington, IN: AuthorHouse, 2008).

59. Douglass made this remark in a speech that was later published in the *Sheffield Mercury*, September 12, 1846. See *Documenting the American South*, http://docsouth .unc.edu/neh/douglass/support5.html, accessed February 15, 2016.

60. A.S.D., "On Raising Negroes," *Southern Agriculturist* (February 1838): 77–80; and "Rules for Breeding," *Southern Cultivator* 2 (August 1844): 126. See also Amy Dru Stanley, "Slave Breeding and Free Love: An Antebellum Argument over Slavery, Capitalism, and Personhood," in *Capitalism Takes Command: The Social Transformation of Nineteenth-Century America*, ed. Michael Zakim and Gary Kornblith (Chicago: University of

Chicago Press, 2012); Stephen Ashley, *The Breeding of American Slaves: True Stories of American Slave Breeding and Slave Babies* (CreateSpace, 2012); and Ned and Constance Sublette, *The American Slave Coast: A History of the Slave-Breeding Industry* (Chicago: Chicago Review Press, 2012).

61. "Business Letter from a Slave Trader of North Carolina," *Frederick Douglass' Paper* 31, March 1854. See also the "Last Will and Testament of Timothy Toughtless," printed in the *Edwardsville Spectator*, March 9, 1824.

62. Baptist, "'Cuffy,' 'Fancy Maids,' and 'One-Eyed Men,'" 1619–50; and Baptist, *The Half Has Never Been Told*, 215–59; Foster, "The Sexual Abuse of Black Men Under Slavery"; Brenda Stevenson, "What's Love Got to Do with It? Concubinage and Enslaved Women and Girls in the Antebellum South," *Journal of African American History* 98, no. 1, Special Issue: "Women, Slavery, and the Atlantic World" (Winter 2013): 99–125; Wendy Anne Warren, "The Cause of Her Grief: The Rape of a Slave in Early New England," *Journal of American History* 93, no. 4 (March 2007): 1031–49; Schermerhorn, *The Business of Slavery and the Rise of American Capitalism*, 140–53; Green, *Remember Me to Miss Louisa*; and K. J. Morgan, "Slave Women and Reproduction in Jamaica, c. 1776–1834," *History* 91 (302): 231–53.

63. Berry, *Swing the Sickle*, 77–84.

64. Lyle Saxon, Edward Dreyer, Robert Tallant, and the Louisiana Writers' Project, *Gumbo Ya-Ya: A Collection of Louisiana Folk Tales* (Boston: Houghton Mifflin, 1945), 226.

65. Johnson, *Soul By Soul*; Tadman, *Speculators and Slaves*; and Schermerhorn, *The Business of Slavery and the Rise of American Capitalism*.

66. Foster, "The Sexual Abuse of Black Men Under Slavery," 447.

67. Quoted in John Seh David, *The American Colonization Society and the Founding of the First African Republic* (Bloomington, IN: iUniverse, 2014), 48.

68. Pamela Bridgewater, "Un/Re/Dis Covering Slave Breeding in Thirteenth Amendment Jurisprudence," *Washington and Lee Journal of Civil Rights and Social Justice* 7 (April 2001): 11–43; Martha Hodes, *White Women, Black Men: Illicit Sex in the Nineteenth-Century South* (New Haven, CT: Yale University Press, 1997), 68–95; and Loren Schweninger, *Families in Crisis in the Old South: Divorce, Slavery, & the Law* (Chapel Hill: University of North Carolina Press, 2012), 17–31.

69. National Humanities Center, "On Slaveholders' Sexual Abuse of Slaves: Selections from 19th & 20th-Century Slave Narratives," *The Making of African American Identity*, vol. 1, *1500–1865* (Washington, DC: National Humanities Center, revised July 2009), 2–3.

70. Henry Bibb, *Narrative of the Life and Adventures of Henry Bibb, An American Slave, Written by Himself* (New York: Privately published, 1849), 38.

71. Davis, "Don't Let Nobody Bother Yo' Principle"; Thelma Jennings, "Us Colored Women Had to Go Through a Plenty: Sexual Exploitation of African-American Slave Women," *Journal of Women's History* 1, no. 3 (December 1990); and Stevenson, "Gender Convention, Ideals, and Identity Among Virginia Slave Women," 169–90.

72. Smallwood, *A Narrative of Thomas Smallwood*, 59.

73. Willie McCullough, *Slave Narratives, North Carolina Narratives*, vol. 11, part 2 (Washington, DC: LOC/WPA, 1941), 77.

74. Kramer, *The Slave-Auction*, 21–22.

75. Redpath, *The Roving Editor*, 92.

76. Douglas O. Linder, "Celia, A Slave, Trial (1855): An Account," 2011, http://law2.umkc
.edu/faculty/projects/ftrials/celia/celiaaccount.html. See also Melton A. McLaurin,
Celia, a Slave (Athens: University of Georgia Press, 1991), and the Celia Project, University of Michigan.

77. Weld and the American Anti-Slavery Society, *American Slavery as It Is*, 15.

78. Kramer, *The Slave-Auction*, 33–34. See also Emily Clark, *The Strange History of the American Quadroon: Free Women of Color in the Revolutionary Atlantic World* (Chapel Hill:
University of North Carolina Press, 2013).

79. Terri L. Snyder, *The Power to Die: Slavery and Suicide in British North America*
(Chicago: University of Chicago Press, 2015).

80. Redpath, *The Roving Editor*, 5–6.

81. Berry Slave Value Database.

82. Adams, *South-Side View of Slavery*, 66–68.

83. Article I, Section 2, Clause 3, US Constitution.

84. Tracy Edson to Clement M. Edson, Esq., March 13, 1836, Natchez Trace Collection
Supplement Mss 2.116/OD1223b, DBCAH. Values calculated using the *Measuring Worth*
website using the CPI (consumer price index) for 2014; however, the price wage for this
enslaved woman in 2014 dollars would be $228,872. See http://www.measuringworth
.com/uscompare/relativevalue.php, accessed October 31, 2015.

85. Cane Brake Plantation Records, DBCAH.

86. Frank Bell, *Slave Narratives, Texas Narratives*, vol. 16, pt. 1 (Washington, DC:
LOC/WPA, 1941), 61, emphases added.

87. Saxon et al., *Gumbo Ya-Ya*, 233.

88. Ibid., 244.

89. See Berry, "'Broad Is da Road Dat Leads to Death'"; and Willis Cofer, *Slave Narratives, Georgia Narratives*, vol. 4, pt. 1 (Washington, DC: LOC/WPA, 1941), 207.

90. Octavia George, *Slave Narratives, Oklahoma Narratives*, vol. 12 (Washington, DC:
LOC/WPA, 1941), 113.

91. Gross, *Double Character*, 138–39; and Sappol, *A Traffic of Dead Bodies*.

92. J. R. Bennett, "A Specimen of a Heart from a Stout, Healthy Negro Who Had
Received a Stab," *American Medical Monthly* 5 (1856): 1052, DBCAH.

93. *Second Annual Report of the Southern Mutual Life Insurance Company for the Year 1856*, 6
and 12.

94. War Department Collection of Confederate Records, RG 109, "Confederate Papers
Relating to Citizens or Business Firms," 29, NARA, M 346, Washington, DC.
The company advertised its need for dog skins in the Augusta, Georgia, *Daily Constitu-
tionalist* on July 10, 1862. Dog skins, used for carding cotton, were in great demand and
often purchased at fifty-five cents each. See Thomas Conn Bryan, *Confederate Georgia*
(Athens: University of Georgia Press, 1953), 104; and Allen D. Candler, *The Confederate
Records of the State of Georgia: Compiled and Published Under Authority of the Legislature*,
Vol. II (Atlanta: Chas P. Byrd, 1909), 363.

95. SMLIC Records.

96. "Narrative of Solomon Bayley," SHC, 42.
97. Ibid., 46.

CHAPTER 4

1. Gray, *The Confessions of Nat Turner*, 18.
2. John Copeland, "Dear Father, Mother, Brothers Henry, William, Freddy, and Sisters Sarah and Mary," from Charlestown Jail, VA, December 16, 1859, in *The Letters of John A. Copeland: A Hero of the Harpers Ferry Raid*, Oberlin College Digital Archives, http://www.oberlin.edu/external/EOG/Copeland/copeland_letter, accessed November 15, 2013.
3. Lucy Mae Turner, "The Family of Nat Turner, 1831 to 1954," *Negro History Bulletin* 18, no. 5 (February 1955): 127–46, quote on 128. For a description of her whipping, see Thomas Wentworth Higginson, "Nat Turner's Insurrection," *Atlantic Monthly* 8, no. 48 (August 1861): 3. Scholars debate the identity of Nat Turner's wife. Many believe she was an enslaved woman named Cherry; others believe she was "Fanny" or a woman named Mariah. Patrick Breen states, "Fanny was proposed by Lucy Mae Turner, who claimed to be Turner's granddaughter, but this has not been given credence by historians." See Breen, *This Land Shall Be Deluged in Blood: A New History of the Nat Turner Revolt* (New York: Oxford University Press, 2015), 194n9. However, slave-family studies from the 1980s to the present reveal evidence of multiple marriages, particularly after enslaved people were separated or sold. Given that enslaved people often had "serial marriages," I believe it is possible that Turner had more than one wife. This is not to suggest that he practiced polygamy, rather that when enslaved people changed owners, some formed new partnerships in order to survive the harsh realities of slavery. See JoAnn Manfra and Robert R. Dykstra, "Serial Marriage and the Origins of the Black Stepfamily: The Rowanty Evidence," *Journal of Southern History* 51, no. 3 (August 1985): 18–44. I choose to follow the descendant Lucy Mae Turner, knowing that the historical record on this fact is still being questioned. David Allmendinger followed similar genealogical leads as Drewry, suggesting that Cherry (Cherrie) Turner was the infamous Turner's wife, but both scholars had difficulty confirming this fact. See David F. Allmendinger, *Nat Turner and the Rising in Southampton County* (Baltimore: Johns Hopkins University Press, 2014), 261; and William Sidney Drewry, *The Southampton Insurrection* (Washington, DC: Neale Company, 1900).
4. Turner, "The Family of Nat Turner," 128.
5. See Johnson, *Soul By Soul*.
6. U. B. Phillips, "United States Slavery," in *Encyclopedia of the Social Sciences*, vols. XIII–XIV, ed. Edwin R. A. Seligman and Alvin Johnson (New York: MacMillan Co., 1934), 85.
7. Andrew Boone, *Slave Narratives, North Carolina Narratives* (Washington, DC: LOC/WPA, 1941), 133.
8. These figures are from a small subset of 201 individuals with these four skills. Roughly 10 percent (N = 1,709) of the enslaved people in this chapter had an identifiable skill, including cooks, nurses, carpenters, and drivers. See Berry Slave Value Database.

9. "Half-White Slave Who Defied Master and Overseer," in *The American Slave: A Composite Autobiography*, vol. 18, Fisk University Collection, ed. George P. Rawick (Westport, CT: Greenwood Publishing Company, 1972), 169.

10. Cane Brake Plantation Records, 1856–1858, DBCAH.

11. Ibid.

12. Charles Ball, *Slavery in the United States: A Narrative of the Life and Times of Charles Ball, a Black Man, Who Lived Forty Years in Maryland, South Carolina and Georgia, as a Slave Under Various Masters, and Was One Year in the Navy with Commodore Barney, During the Late War* (New York: John S. Taylor, 1837), v and viii., http://docsouth.unc.edu/neh/ballslavery/menu.html.

13. Philip J. Schwarz, *Gabriel's Conspiracy: A Documentary History* (Charlottesville: University of Virginia Press, 2012). See also Berry, "'Broad Is de Road dat Leads to Death.'"

14. *Laws of Virginia*, 91–112. See article x, vagenweb.org/hening/vol06–05.htm, accessed February 6, 2011.

15. Vincent Brown, *The Reaper's Garden: Death and Power in the World of Atlantic Slavery* (Cambridge, MA: Harvard University Press, 2010); D. Barry Gaspar, "'To Bring Their Offending Slaves to Justice': Compensation and Slave Resistance in Antigua 1669–1763," *Caribbean Quarterly* 30, nos. 3/4 (September/December 1984): 45–59; and Diana Patton, "Punishment, Crime, and the Bodies of Slaves in Eighteenth-Century Jamaica," *Journal of Social History* 34, no. 4 (2001): 923–54.

16. Suzanne Shultz, *Body Snatching: The Robbing of Graves for the Education of Physicians in Early Nineteenth-Century America* (Jefferson, NC: McFarland & Company, 1992), 8.

17. Todd L. Savitt, *Medicine and Slavery: The Diseases and Health Care of Blacks in Antebellum Virginia* (Urbana: University of Illinois Press, 1978), 293.

18. Rufus William Bailey, "An Address Delivered at the Annual Commencement of the Berkshire Medical Institution [Pittsfield, MA]," December 23, 1824, 23.

19. Ibid., 23; and Granville Sharp Pattison, ed., "Medical Schools," *Register and Library of Medical and Chirurgical Science: A Medical Newspaper* (Washington, DC), vol. 1, no. 3 (October 10, 1833): 25–30, SML.

20. Franny Nudelman, *John Brown's Body: Slavery, Violence, and the Culture of War* (Chapel Hill: University of North Carolina Press, 2004), especially chap. 2, "The Blood of Black Men: Rethinking Racial Science," 40–70.

21. Berry, "'Broad Is de Road Dat Leads to Death.'"

22. Here, I am making a clear distinction between enslaved monetary values at the moment of death and their monetary value(s) in the postmortem period. I am particularly indebted to Michael Sappol for his work *A Traffic of Dead Bodies*; and Nudelman, *John Brown's Body*, especially chap. 2, "The Blood of Black Men: Rethinking Racial Science," 40–70.

23. Drewry, *The Southampton Insurrection*, 101–2. Skinning was also a topic discussed by other medical doctors. See William James McKnight, *Jefferson County, Pennsylvania: Her Pioneers and Her People, 1800–1915* (Chicago: J. H. Beers & Company, 1917).

24. Drewry, *The Southampton Insurrection*, 102n2. On his skin being made into a change purse, see Lon Wagner, "Nat Turner's Skull Turns Up Far from Site of His Revolt," *Baltimore Sun*, June 15, 2003. I suspect that a doctor from James D. Massenburg's (also spelled "Massenberg") family had information about Turner's skeleton.

25. Original reference appeared in the *Petersburg Express*, July 17, 1860, source found in "Barbarism," *Vermont Phoenix* (Brattleboro), August 11, 1860. For Mallory's obituary, see the *New York Times*, July 21, 1860.

26. Kenneth Greenberg and Vincent Woodward are the exception in that they delve into the realm of possibilities relating to Turner's body. See Kenneth Greenberg, ed., *Nat Turner: A Slave Rebellion in History and Memory* (New York: Oxford University Press, 2003), especially chap. 1, "Name, Face, Body"; and Vincent Woodward, *The Delectable Negro: Human Consumption and Homoeroticism Within US Slave Culture* (New York: New York University Press, 2014), chap. 5, "Eating Nat Turner." Postmortem abuse also occurred in the aftermath of the Denmark Vesey, Charles Deslondes, and Sam Sharpe (Jamaica) uprisings and conspiracies. Recent scholarship by Walter Johnson and Alan Taylor address the widespread abuse that occurred after the War of 1812. See Walter Johnson, *River of Dark Dreams: Slavery and Empire in the Cotton Kingdom* (Cambridge, MA: Belknap Press/Harvard University Press, 2013); and Alan Taylor, *The Internal Enemy: Slavery and War in Virginia, 1772–1832* (New York: W. W. Norton, 2013). For the Caribbean literature, see Brown, *The Reaper's Garden*; Gaspar, "'To Bring Their Offending Slaves to Justice,'" 45–59; and Patton, "Punishment, Crime, and the Bodies of Slaves in Eighteenth-Century Jamaica."

27. See the scholarship of Ann Fabian, *The Skull Collectors: Race, Science, and America's Unburied Dead* (Chicago: University of Chicago Press, 2010); Richardson, *Death, Dissection and the Destitute*; Sappol, *A Traffic of Dead Bodies*; Shultz, *Body Snatching*; and Washington, *Medical Apartheid*.

28. See Fabian, *The Skull Collectors*; and Sappol, *A Traffic of Dead Bodies*, 93.

29. Wyndham B. Blanton, *Medicine in Virginia in the Nineteenth Century* (Richmond, VA: Garrett & Massie, 1933), 69–74; and Pattison, "Medical Schools."

30. James O. Breeden, "Body Snatchers and Anatomy Professors: Medical Education in Nineteenth-Century Virginia," *Virginia Magazine of History and Biography* 83, no. 3 (July 1975): 321–45, quote on 327.

31. New research by Catherine Neale suggests that Lewis Commodore and Anatomical Lewis are two different people. See Neale, "Slaves, Freedpeople, and the University of Virginia," honors thesis, University of Virginia, 1996; and Gayle M. Schulman, "Slaves at the University of Virginia," in *Slavery at the University of Virginia: A Catalogue of Current and Past Initiatives*, ed. Meghan Saunders Faulkner (Charlottesville: UVA IDEA Fund, 2013).

32. "Faculty of Jefferson Medical College to Dr. Robert Frame, March 29, 1839," Faculty Account Book, vol. 1, Acc. #00–12, UA-JMC 012, SML.

33. Samuel D. Cartwright, MD, "Reports from Mississippi: The Diseases and Particularities of the Negro Race," in *Southern Medical Reports*, vol. II, ed. Erasmus D. Fenner (New Orleans: D. Davies Sons & Company, 1851), 421–36, quotes on 427–28. Some might question Cartwright's conclusions because he had strong opinions about race that were not always true.

34. W. E. Horner, *Lessons in Practical Anatomy: For the Use of Dissectors*, 3rd ed. (Philadelphia: J. D. Auner, 1836, first published in 1823 by Edward Parker), CPP. Quoted material from "Dartmouth College Medical Notes, 2 September 1837," Pemberton Collection, Ayer Family Papers, Ms. N-684, MHS.

35. "Proclamation by Governor John Floyd, 17 September 1831," *Governor's Office, Letters Received, John Floyd, Record Group 3*, LVA, http://www.lva.virginia.gov/exhibits /deathliberty/natturner/proclamation25.htm, accessed June 14, 2014.

36. Alfred Maury, Francis Pulszky, J. Aitken Meigs, J. C. Nott, and George R. Gliddon, *Indigenous Races of the Earth, or, New Chapters of Ethnological Inquiry* (Philadelphia: J. B. Lippincott & Co., 1857).

37. Wendell Holmes Stephenson, *Isaac Franklin: Slave Trader and Planter of the Old South* (Gloucester, MA: Peter Smith, 1968). Anne Fausto-Sterling provides a compelling history of postmortem movement across the Atlantic in a study of Saartjie Baartman. See Fausto-Sterling, "Gender, Race, and Nation," 19–48.

38. Fabian, *The Skull Collectors*, 38–42.

39. Ibid., 106.

40. Ibid.

41. Samuel Morton and George Combee, *Crania Americana: Or, a Comparative View of the Skulls of Various Aboriginal Nations* (Philadelphia: J. Dobson, Marshall Simpkin, 1839).

42. Drewry, *The Southampton Insurrection*, 102n2. For work on the human skull, see the University of Pennsylvania collection of nineteenth-century physician Dr. Samuel George Morton and visit the Mutter Museum, also in Philadelphia.

43. P. Tidyman, "A Sketch of the Most Remarkable Diseases of the Negroes of the Southern States . . . ," *Pennsylvania Journal of the Medical and Physical Sciences* 12 (May and August 1826): 306–38, quote on 313.

44. Quoted in Weld and the American Anti-Slavery Society, *American Slavery as It Is*, 169, from the *Daily Free Trader*, February 12, 1838.

45. Greenberg, *Nat Turner*.

46. *The Liberator*, December 24, 1831.

47. Jacobs, *Incidents in the Life of a Slave Girl*, 98 and 99, available online at *Documenting the American South*, http://docsouth.unc.edu/fpn/jacobs/jacobs.html.

48. See Allmendinger, *Nat Turner and the Rising in Southampton County*, Appendix F; and Drewry, *The Southampton Insurrection*.

49. Allmendinger, *Nat Turner and the Rising in Southampton County*, 259.

50. Gray, *The Confessions of Nat Turner*, 18.

51. "Annual Announcement of Lectures: The Trustees and Professors of Jefferson Medical College" (Philadelphia, 1832), 5, SML.

52. John Harley Warner and James M. Edmonson, *Dissection: Photographs of a Rite of Passage in American Medicine, 1880–1930* (New York: Blast Books, 2009).

53. Turner, "The Family of Nat Turner," 127–46, quote on 130.

54. Robert Hayden, "The Ballad of Nat Turner," copyright 1966 by Robert Hayden, from *Collected Poems of Robert Hayden* (New York: Liveright, 1985), ed. Frederick Glaysher.

55. Rawick, *God Struck Me Dead*, 23.

56. Gray, *The Confessions of Nat Turner*, 7–10.

57. Jeremiah Cobb quoted in ibid., 22. References to Turner's skeleton and skin are found in Drewry, *The Southampton Insurrection*, 101–2. Contemporary accounts of the skull derived from a twenty-five-minute phone interview with former mayor Richard Hatcher of Gary,

Indiana, November 8, 2013. Hatcher has been collecting African American artifacts for a civil rights museum scheduled to open in Indiana; some reports suggest he has Turner's skull. At that time, Hatcher would "neither confirm nor deny" the rumor. Descendants of Turner have expressed their desire to bury it in Southampton near Turner's birthplace. For contemporary newspaper accounts, see Lon Wagner, "Nat Turner's Skull Found in Indiana," *Free Lance Star* (Fredericksburg, VA), May 6, 2003; and Wagner, "Nat Turner's Skull Turns Up Far from Site of His Revolt." In early October 2016, Hatcher met with descendants and delivered the skull for DNA testing. This book may be published before we know the results.

58. The price wage for Turner could be as high as $102,084, according to *Measuring Worth*. See also Stephen B. Oates, *The Fires of Jubilee: Nat Turner's Fierce Rebellion* (New York: Harper & Row, 1975), 125.

59. According to Allmendinger, Turner was "appraised at £35 (about $135) in 1811" at age eleven and "$450 in 1822" at age twenty-two. Allmendinger, *Nat Turner and the Rising in Southampton County*, 318.

60. Higginson, "Nat Turner's Insurrection," 173–87.

61. For discussions of this and the experience of women and children, see Vanessa Holden, *Surviving Southampton: Gender, Community, Resistance and Survival During the Southampton Rebellion of 1831* (Urbana: University of Illinois Press, forthcoming).

62. Higginson, "Nat Turner's Insurrection," 173–87. See online file at http://www .theatlantic.com/pastdocs/issues/1861aug/higginson.html. See the seven other petitions filed in Virginia accessible through the Digital Library of American Slavery, http://www .library.uncg.edu/slavery/results: PAR # 11677701, 11678305, 11678501, 11680204, 11680401, 11680508, and 11681127.

63. "Race, Slavery, and Free Blacks, Series I: Petitions to Southern Legislatures, 1777–1867," Nov. 22, 1831—Dec. 31, 1831 Accession # 001542–011–0037, PAR # 11383106.

64. "Race and Slavery Petitions Project at the University of North Carolina at Greensboro," PAR # 11383108; Records of the General Assembly, South Carolina, South Carolina Department of Archives and History, 1831, #62 Accession # 001542–011–0045, http://search.proquest.com/histvault?q=001542–011–0045, accessed August 19, 2014.

65. Weld and the American Anti-Slavery Society, *American Slavery as It Is*, 146.

66. "Laws of Muscogee, 1825 #3," Southeastern Native American Documents, 1730-1842, Galileo Digital Library of Georgia, http://dlg.galileo.usg.edu/CollectionsA-Z/zlna _search.html?Welcome (accessed April 10, 2014).

67. "To the Legislature of Virginia from William B. Jones, William H. Hardwick, James Bagby, Richard G. Morris, and John Reynolds," December 1831, Virginia Legislative Petitions, Richmond, VA, PAR # 11683124 LVA.

68. Jenifer L. Barclay, *The Mark of Slavery: The Stigma of Disability, Race, and Gender in Antebellum America* (Urbana: University of Illinois Press, forthcoming).

69. See, for examples, Gaspar, "To Bring Their Offending Slaves to Justice"; Patton, "Punishment, Crime, and the Bodies of Slaves in Eighteenth-Century Jamaica"; Brown, *The Reaper's Garden*; and Marisa J. Fuentes, *Dispossessed Lives: Enslaved Women, Violence, and the Archive* (Philadelphia: University of Pennsylvania Press, 2016).

70. Marvin L. Michael Kay and Lorin Lee Cary, "'The Planters Suffer Little or Nothing': North Carolina Compensations for Executed Slaves, 1748–1772," *Science & Society* 40, no. 3 (Fall 1976): 290n6.

71. Ibid., 292.

72. Ibid., 299.

73. Mary Kemp Davis, "What Happened in This Place? In Search of the Female Slave in the Nat Turner Slave Insurrection," in Greenberg, *Nat Turner*.

74. Jacobs, *Incidents in the Life of a Slave Girl*, 149. When Jacobs first escaped, Dr. Flint posted the following advertisement: "$300 REWARD! Ran away from the subscriber, an intelligent, bright, mulatto girl, named Linda, 21 years of age. Five feet four inches high. Dark eyes, and black hair inclined to curl; but it can be made straight. Has a decayed spot on a front tooth. She can read and write, and in all probability will try to get to the Free States. All persons are forbidden, under penalty of the law, to harbor or employ said slave. $150 will be given to whoever takes her in the state, and $300 if taken out of the state and delivered to me, or lodged in jail. DR. FLINT."

75. Jacobs was in hiding as early as age twenty-one and then went north in 1842 at twenty-nine. Her owner placed the ad when she "ran away," but he had no idea that she had remained in hiding on the plantation for seven years.

76. Derbes, "'Secret Horrors,'" 277–90; McNair, "Slave Women, Capital Crime and Criminal Justice in Georgia," 135–58; Wood, "Some Aspects of Female Resistance to Chattel Slavery in Low Country Georgia," 603–22; and Camp, *Closer to Freedom*. See also the work of Barbara Krauthamer, "Liberty's Diaspora: Enslaved Women's Liberation and Migration During the American Revolution," *Journal of the Early Republic* (forthcoming 2017); Krauthamer, "The Possibility of Pleasure: Runaway Slave Women and Sex in the Antebellum South," in *Slavery and Sexuality: Reclaiming Intimate Histories in the Americas*, ed. Daina Ramey Berry and Leslie Harris (Athens: University of Georgia Press, forthcoming), and Fuentes, *Dispossessed Lives*.

77. Kent Biffle, *A Month of Sundays* (Denton: University of North Texas Press, 1993), 104.

78. Elizabeth York Enstam, *Women and the Creation of Urban Life: Dallas, Texas, 1843–1920* (College Station: Texas A&M University Press, 1998), 30. See also Terry Baker, *Hangings and Lynchings in Dallas County, Texas: 1853 to 1920* (Fort Worth, TX: Eakin Press, 2016).

79. James M. Davidson, "'Resurrection Men' in Dallas: The Illegal Use of Black Bodies as Medical Cadavers (1900–1907)," *International Journal of Historical Archeology* 11, no. 3 (2007): 198.

80. Moses Roper, *Narrative of the Adventures and Escape of Moses Roper, from American Slavery* (Privately published, 1848), 16, available online at *Documenting the American South*, http://www.docsouth.unc.edu/neh/roper/roper.html.

81. Drew, *A North-Side View of Slavery*, 332.

82. SMLIC Records. Please visit my personal website, http://www.drdainarameyberry.com, for details. For discussions of insurance policies for other companies, see Karen Kotzuk Ryder, "'Permanent Property': Slave Life Insurance in the Antebellum Southern United States, 1820–1866," PhD diss., University of Delaware, 2012; and Sharon Ann Murphy, *Investing in Life: Insurance in Antebellum America* (Baltimore: Johns Hopkins University

Press, 2010). Also, it is worth mentioning the work of Bonnie Martin on slave mortgages. See Bonnie Martin, "Slavery's Invisible Engine: Mortgaging Human Property," *Journal of Southern History* 76, no. 4 (November 2010): 817–66.

83. *Report of the Executive Committee of the Georgia Relief & Hospital Association to the Board of Superintendents, with the Proceedings of the Board, Convened at Augusta, Georgia, October 29, 1862* (Augusta: Steam Press of Chronicle & Sentinel, 1862); and SMLIC Records.

84. SMLIC Records.

85. State Laws of Maryland, Session Laws 1860, Chapter 390, Archives of Maryland; and the *Baltimore Underwriter and Internal Revenue Record* 1, no. 2 (August 15, 1865): 2, col. 3.

86. Benjamin Quarles, *Allies for Freedom: Blacks and John Brown* (New York: Oxford University Press, 1974), 120–21.

87. John. L. Preston, "The Execution of John Brown: Eyewitness Account," *Lexington Gazette*, December 15, 1859, http://www.wmi.edu/archives.aspx?id=8183, accessed September 15, 2013.

88. Ibid.

89. Quarles, *Allies for Freedom*, 131.

90. Frederick Douglass, *The Life and Times of Frederick Douglass* (1881; repr., New York: Pathway Press, 1941), 350–54.

91. John Copeland, "My Dear Brother," December 10, 1859, in *The Letters of John A. Copeland: A Hero of the Harpers Ferry Raid*, Oberlin College Digital Archives, http://www.oberlin.edu/external/EOG/Copeland/copeland_letters.htm, accessed October 15, 2013. In Turner's *Confessions*, he makes several references to the "heavens," indicating that both men believed in an afterlife. Turner referenced the "heavens" as a place where he saw figures and learned about events to come.

92. Copeland, "Dear Father, Mother, Brothers Henry, William, Freddy, and Sisters Sarah and Mary."

93. Nudelman, *John Brown's Body*, especially chap. 2, "The Blood of Black Men: Rethinking Racial Science," 40–70; and Steven Lubet, "Execution in Virginia, 1859: The Trials of Green and Copeland," Northwestern Public Law Research Paper No. 12–12 (May 2012): 19, SSRN: http://ssrn.com/abstract=2065470.

94. I found mixed reports here; one said the bodies were placed in poplar coffins and brought back to the jail.

95. James Monroe, "A Journey to Virginia in December, 1859," *Oberlin Thursday Lectures, Addresses, and Lectures* (1898), John Brown Virtual Exhibit, Oberlin College Archives, http://www.oberlin.edu/archive/exhibits/john_brown_new/lecture.html, accessed April 25, 2016.

96. Ibid.

97. Ibid. See also the essay by Lubet, "Execution in Virginia, 1859."

98. Monroe, "A Journey to Virginia."

99. This monument states, "A cenotaph erected to honor the 'colored citizens of Oberlin' who died during or because of their participation in John Brown's raid on Harper's Ferry. J. A. Copeland died 12/16/1859 age 25 years, S. Green died same at age 23 years old, and I. S. Harry died aged 24." See Lubet, "Execution in Virginia, 1859"; and Steven Lubet, *Fugitive Justice: Runaways, Rescuers, and Slavery on Trial* (Cambridge, MA: Belknap Press of Harvard University Press, 2010).

100. "Dear Husband," from Brentville, August 16, 1859, in *Governor's Message and Reports of the Public Officers of the State, of the Boards of Directors, and of the Visitors, Superintendents, and Their Agents of Public Instruction or Interests of Virginia* (Richmond, 1859): 116–17, Special Collections, LVA, Richmond. Online in the 2009 *African American Trailblazers in Virginia History*, http://www.lva.virginia.gov/public/trailblazers/res/Harriet_Newby_Letters.pdf, accessed June 26, 2014.

101. Quote from Annie Brown, daughter of the late John Brown, in James Taylor, Nathaniel F. Downing Sr., George C. Rutherford, and James A. Tolbert Sr., *The Life and Death of Dangerfield Newby: One of the Black Raiders That Came with John Brown* (Ranson, WV: Jefferson County Black History Preservation Society, 2005), 8.

102. Osborne Anderson, *A Voice from Harper's Ferry: A Narrative of Events at Harper's Ferry; with Incidents Prior and Subsequent to Its Capture by Captain Brown and His Men* (Boston: Privately published, 1861), 40.

103. After his birth were Lucy, Emily, Almira, Gabriel, Mary, James, Ann, William, Edward, and John. See Taylor et al., *The Life and Death of Dangerfield Newby*, 1.

104. Anderson, *A Voice from Harper's Ferry*, 40.

105. L. B. Taylor Jr., "The Demise of Dangerfield Newby," in *Civil War Ghosts of Virginia* (Williamsburg: L. B. Taylor and Progress Printing Co., 1995), 41–42; also see Taylor et al., *The Life and Death of Dangerfield Newby*, 14.

106. Lorenz Graham, "Dangerfield Newby," in *Dictionary of American Negro Biography*, ed. Rayford Whittingham Logan and Michael R. Winston (New York: W. W. Norton and Co., 1982), 473; Taylor, *Civil War Ghosts of Virginia*, 6; and Richard J. Hinton, *John Brown and His Men; With Some Account of the Roads They Travelled to Reach Harper's Ferry* (New York: Funk & Wagnalls, 1894), 290.

107. Taylor, *The Life and Death of Dangerfield Newby*, 17.

108. Thomas Featherstonhaugh, "The Final Burial of the Followers of John Brown," *New England Magazine*, April 1901; copy of John Brown Pamphlets, vol. 3, Boyd B. Stutler Collection, West Virginia State Archives, online via http://www.wvculture/history/jbexhibit/, accessed August 27, 2014. See also Taylor, *The Life and Death of Dangerfield Newby*, 18.

109. Lou V. Chapin, "The Last Days of Old John Brown," *Overland Monthly* 33 (April 1899): 328. This document is part of the Brown Family Collection, 1838–1943, Mss HM 53560–53575, box 1, folder 11, Huntington Library, Pasadena, CA.

110. The buttons are part of the Walter Pantovic Artifact Collection, Avery Research Center, College of Charleston, http://lcdl.library.cofc.edu/lcdl/catalog/lcdl:54714, accessed August 27, 2014. For descriptions of the interment, see Featherstonhaugh, "The Final Burial of the Followers of John Brown"; and Taylor, *The Life and Death of Dangerfield Newby*.

111. "Dear Husband," from Brentville, April 22, 1859, in *Governor's Message and Reports of the Public Officers*, 116–17, Special Collections, LVA. Also available online in the 2009 *African American Trailblazers in Virginia History*.

112. In 1931, a memorial for Heyward Shepherd (another African American killed during the Brown raid) was erected by the Daughters and Sons of the Confederacy. However, Shepherd was a free black man who was killed by Brown and his followers. See

Mary Johnson, "An 'Ever Present Bone of Contention': The Heyward Shepherd Memorial," *West Virginia History* 56 (1997): 1–26.

113. Featherstonhaugh, "The Final Burial of the Followers of John Brown," and "John Brown's Companions," *Los Angeles Herald*, September 17, 1899.

114. I used the income value of a commodity. See *Measuring Worth*, http://www.measuringworth.com/uscompare/relativevalue.php, accessed January 4, 2015.

115. Jacqueline Trescott, "Descendants of Va. Family Donate Nat Turner's Bible to Museum," *Washington Post*, February 16, 2012.

116. Henry Highland Garnet, "An Address to the Slaves of the United States of America, Buffalo, N.Y., 1843 (Rejected by the National Convention, 1843)," Digital Commons, http://digitalcommons.unl.edu/cgi/viewcontent.cgi?article=1007&context=etas, accessed April 25, 2016.

117. Hilary McD. Beckles, *Britain's Black Debt: Reparations for Caribbean Slavery and Native Genocide* (Kingston, Jamaica: University of the West Indies Press, 2013).

CHAPTER 5

1. Delaney, *From the Darkness Cometh the Light or Struggles for Freedom*, 54.

2. Redpath, *The Roving Editor*, 279.

3. "Slave Auction at Richmond: Sale of Negroes by Auction," *Anti-Slavery Standard* 1 (May 1835): 57.

4. Frederick Law Olmsted, quoted in original source from *The Cotton Planter* and reprinted in *A Journey in the Back Country* (New York: Mason Brothers, 1860), 58.

5. Richard Steckel, "Mortality and Life Expectancy," in Berry, *Enslaved Women in America*, 212–14.

6. Here I am evoking the work of Nell Painter and Orlando Patterson, hoping to offer additional perspectives on the ways enslaved people coped with their captivity. I appreciate their work and that of Vincent Brown and Mia Bay. See Nell Painter, "Soul Murder and Slavery: Toward a Fully Loaded Cost Accounting," in Nell Painter, *Southern History Across the Color Line* (Chapel Hill: University of North Carolina Press, 2002), 15–39; Orlando Patterson, *Slavery and Social Death: A Comparative Study* (Cambridge, MA: Harvard University Press, 1982); Vincent Brown, *The Reaper's Garden: Death and Power in the World of Atlantic Slavery* (Cambridge, MA: Harvard University Press, 2008); and Mia Bay, *The White Image in the Black Mind: African-American Ideas about White People, 1830–1925* (New York: Oxford University Press, 2010).

7. Blassingame, *Slave Testimony*, 440–41.

8. Steckel, "Mortality and Life Expectancy," 212; and Richard Steckel, "Biological Measures of the Standard of Living," *Journal of Economic Perspectives* 22 (Winter 2008): 129–52.

9. Stacey K. Close, *Elderly Slaves of the Plantation South* (New York: Garland, 1997).

10. Genovese, *Roll, Jordan, Roll*, 510–11.

11. Kramer, *The Slave-Auction*, 30.

12. Moses Grandy, *Narrative of the Life of Moses Grandy* (London: C. Gilpin, 1843), 51–52.

13. Blassingame, *Slave Testimony*, 9–10.

14. Close, *Elderly Slaves of the Plantation South*, xiv.

15. Margaret Hall Hicks, "Early Life in Texas: Washington-on-the-Brazos," unpublished manuscript, 40, courtesy of Agnes Matula.

16. Fett, *Working Cures*, 221n63; and Venie Deas-Moore, "Home Remedies, Herb Doctors and Grannie Midwives," *World and I* (January 1987): 474–85.

17. Redpath, *The Roving Editor*, 116.

18. Ibid., 92.

19. Rita Hargrave, "Health and Healthcare of African American Older Adults," *Ethnogeriatrics*, Stanford School of Medicine, https://geriatrics.stanford.edu/ethnomed/african _american.html, accessed November 23, 2015. See also Richard Steckel, "A Peculiar Population: The Nutrition, Health, and Mortality from Childhood to Maturity," *Journal of Economic History* 46 (September 1986): 721–41; and *Historical Statistics of the United States: Millennial Edition Online*, Cambridge University Press, http://hsus.cambridge.org.

20. All quoted material in this paragraph comes from C. G. Parsons, *A Tour Among the Planters: An Inside View of Slavery* (1855; repr., Savannah, GA: Beehive Press, 1974), 234–36, emphasis in the original.

21. Ibid., 85–89.

22. Berry, "'In Pressing Need of Cash'"; and Russell, "Articles Sell Best Singly," 1161–1209.

23. This was also true of Eva who "COST NOTHING," according to a broadside indicating a sale by Alonzo White (SCHS); and Redpath, *The Roving Editor*, 8.

24. "An Uncommonly Gang of SIXTY-FIVE NEGROES Accustomed to the Culture of Cotton and Provisions," January 23, 1860, Hutson Lee Papers, SCHS.

25. Kramer, *The Slave-Auction*, quoted material on 20, 23, and 32.

26. Figures derived from the 1857 list give a total population of 151 enslaved people, of which 36 (23.8 percent) were age forty or older. Cane Brake Plantation Records, 1856–1858, DBCAH.

27. Ibid.

28. Kramer, *The Slave-Auction*, 35–40.

29. A closer look at the family letters does not suggest such benevolence. See the Henry Waller Papers, Huntington Library, Pasadena, CA, and the Carson Papers at the McClung Historical Collection at the East Tennessee History Center, Knoxville, TN.

30. Anderson, "Dr. James Green Carson."

31. "Plans Home for Ex-Slaves, 1913," Slavery Scrapbook Collection, 1909–35, box 3L398, DBCAH.

32. A. H. Churchill, "Promoting Ex-Slave Home," *Daily Sentinel*, June 13, 1916; and "Endorses Ex-Slave Home," *Daily Sentinel*, June 14, 1916, Slavery Scrapbook Collection, 1909–35, DBCAH.

33. Daina Ramey Berry and Jermaine Thibodeaux, "'To Be Swift in Accepting Our Legal Equality': Creating Black Texans and Reproducing Heteropatriarchy at the 1883 Colored Men's Convention," paper presented at the Colored Conventions Conference, Delaware Historical Society, 2015; and Alwyn Barr, "Early Organizing in the Search for Equality: African American Conventions in Late Nineteenth Century Texas," in *Seeking Inalienable Rights: Texans and Their Quest for Justice*, ed. Debra A. Reid (College Station: Texas A&M University Press, 2009). See also, "Colored Conventions: Bringing Nineteenth-Century Black Organizing to Digital Life," http://coloredconventions.org,

accessed March 5, 2016.

34. Redpath, *The Roving Editor*, 147–48.

35. SMLIC Records.

36. This value reflects the real price with the CPI percentage increase from 1860 to 2014. The labor value of Charlotte would be equivalent to $147,000. *Measuring Worth*, http://www.measuringworth.com/uscompare/relativevalue.php, "income value" conversion.

37. For the complete story of Isaac, see Redpath, *The Roving Editor*, 269–81. Details about the conspiracy can be found at *The Slave Rebellion Web Site*, http://slaverebellion.org/index.php?page=an-insurrection-plotted-by-slaves-in-camden-south-carolina#_ftn25, accessed March 17, 2015.

38. Redpath, *The Roving Editor*, 273.

39. Ibid., 275.

40. Ibid., 276.

41. Matthew 22:36–40, New International Version.

42. Redpath, *The Roving Editor*, 277.

43. Ibid., 279.

44. Ibid., 280–81.

45. Ibid., 281.

CHAPTER 6

1. Berry, "'Broad Is da Road Dat Leads to Death'"; SMLIC Records.

2. "My dear serpent-killer," Fran Bowen to Jeffries Wyman, C12.2, November 25, 1845, CLM. I wish to thank Sowandé Mustakeem for providing a transcription of this letter.

3. "Jim's Revelations: Threatened by the Students, Be Prepared to Resign," *Philadelphia Press*, December 8, 1882.

4. Washington, *Medical Apartheid*, 86–100, quoted material on 86–88.

5. Figure quoted is the CPI for the year 2014. See Samuel H. Williamson, "Seven Ways to Compute the Relative Value of a U.S. Dollar Amount, 1774 to Present," *Measuring Worth*, 2014, www.measuringworth.com/uscompare, accessed September 5, 2014.

6. See Phineas T. Barnum, *The Life of P. T. Barnum: The World-Renowned Showman* . . . (New York: Redfield, 1855; repr.; Urbana: University of Illinois Press, 2000); Benjamin Reiss, *The Showman and the Slave: Death and Memory in Barnum's America* (Cambridge, MA: Harvard University Press, 2001); "P. T. Barnum, Joice Heth and Antebellum Spectacles of Race," *American Quarterly* 51, no. 1 (March 1999): 78–107; and Sappol, *A Traffic of Dead Bodies*, 92–93.

7. Quoted in Reiss, *The Showman and the Slave*, 129.

8. "Post-Mortem Examination of Slave, July 9, 1853," in the Black History Collection, box 3P52, folder #6, DBCAH. The author wishes to thank Ava Purkiss for the transcription of this document.

9. Reports from the New York Medico-Chirurgical Society (1857), NLM 16, 121–22. For other dissections of black men, see "Notes on the Dissection of a Negro," *Journal of Anatomy and Physiology* 13, no. 3 (1879): 382–86.

10. Jenifer L. Barclay, "'The Greatest Degree of Perfection': Disability and the Construction of Race in Southern Slave Law," in "Locating African American Literature," ed. Rhondda

Thomas and Angela Naimou, *South Carolina Review* 46, no. 2 (Spring 2014): 27–43.

11. Barney Stone, *Slave Narratives, Indiana Narratives* Supplement Series 1, vol. 5 (Washington, DC: LOC/WPA, 1941), 186-87.

12. For a history of anatomy, see Sappol, *A Traffic of Dead Bodies*, chaps. 2 and 3, 44–97; and for contemporary conversations, see John C. McLachlan and Debra Patten, "Anatomy Teaching: Ghosts of the Past, Present and Future," *Medical Education* 40 (2006): 243–53.

13. Sappol, *A Traffic of Dead Bodies*, 103.

14. Shultz, quoting Sozinsky, in Shultz, *Body Snatching*, 14–15.

15. Daniel Drake, *Pioneer Physician of the Midwest* (Philadelphia: University of Pennsylvania Press, 1961), 71–72.

16. Blanton, *Medicine in Virginia in the Nineteenth Century*, 69.

17. Sappol, the primary author who identified this trade, is joined with a handful of other scholars who address this topic. See Sappol, *A Traffic of Dead Bodies*.

18. Some of the records used here do not identify the enslaved or free status of the deceased person, but they often identify race.

19. Tadman, *Speculators and Slaves*, esp. chap. 3, 47–82.

20. It is equally important to consider "agricultural calendars on both sides of the Atlantic." See Stephen D. Behrendt, "Seasonality in the Trans-Atlantic Slave Trade," *Slave Voyages*, http://www.slavevoyages.org/tast/assessment/essays-seasonality-01.faces, accessed November 10, 2014.

21. These references are for eighteenth- to nineteenth-century mortuary politics, to borrow from Vincent Brown. See Brown, *The Reaper's Garden*; Nudelman, *John Brown's Body*; and Martha V. Pike and Janice Gray Armstrong, *A Time to Mourn: Expressions of Grief in Nineteenth Century America* (Stony Brook, NY: Museums at Stony Brook, 1980).

22. Shultz, *Body Snatching*, 30.

23. Craig Steven Wilder, *Ebony & Ivy: Race, Slavery, and the Troubled History of America's Universities* (New York: Bloomsbury Press, 2013).

24. Shultz, *Body Snatching*, 14.

25. Breeden, "Body Snatchers and Anatomy Professors," 321–45; Edward C. Halperin, "The Poor, the Black, and the Marginalized as the Source of Cadavers in United States Anatomical Education," *Clinical Anatomy* 20 (2007): 489–95; and David C. Humphrey, "Dissection and Discrimination: The Social Origins of Cadavers in America, 1760–1915," *Bulletin of the New York Academy of Medicine* 49, no. 9 (September 1973): 819–27.

26. Kinney, "'A Dictate of Both Interest and Mercy'?" 1–47; Halperin, "The Poor, the Black, and the Marginalized;" Stephen C. Kenny, "The Development of Medical Museums in the Antebellum American South: Slave Bodies in Networks of Anatomical Exchange," *Bulletin of the History of Medicine* 87 (Spring 2013): 32–62.

27. Wilder, *Ebony & Ivy*; and Brian Altonen, "Timeline of Medical Schools," http://brianaltonenmph.com/6-history-of-medicine-and-pharmacy/hudson-valley-medical-history/the-post-war-years/the-early-medical-profession-in-new-york/part-6-a-period-of-change/a-timeline-of-medical-schools/, accessed August 7, 2014.

28. However, there is rich evidence of physicians discrediting the work of nontraditionally trained medicinal healers, in particular, African American women. Fett, *Working Cures*; and Savitt, *Medicine and Slavery*.

29. Shultz, *Body Snatching*, 22–23.

30. "In the Ghostly Old Times: Gruesome Troubles of a Medical Doctor Then and Now," American Press Information Bureau, October 16, 1906, newspaper clipping in the William Shippen Jr. Faculty Folder, UPENN.

31. Sappol identifies others in *A Traffic of Dead Bodies*, 100; Nystrom, *The Bioarchaeology of Dissection and Autopsy in the United States*; and Kristina Kilgrove, "How Grave Robbers and Medical Students Helped Dehumanize 19th Century Blacks and the Poor," *Forbes*, July 13, 2015.

32. William Shippen, ". . . To the Public," *Philadelphia Chronicle*, November 8, 1770, CPP, pamphlet no. 46.

33. Shultz, *Body Snatching*, 30.

34. Massachusetts Anatomy Act of 1831, CPP; and "Passing the Torch: Hersey Professorship in Anatomy," *Harvard Medical School Perspectives*, 1989, 2.

35. Jeffries Wyman Papers, CLM.

36. "Passing the Torch," 2.

37. "My dear serpent-killer," Fran Bowen to Jeffries Wyman.

38. Thomas Francis Harrington, *The Harvard Medical School: A History, Narrative, and Documentary*, vol. 2 (New York: Lewis Publishing Company, 1905), 651.

39. Sappol, *A Traffic of Dead Bodies*. See also Helen MacDonald, *Human Remains: Dissection and Its Histories* (New Haven, CT: Yale University Press, 2005); and Richardson, *Death, Dissection, and the Destitute*.

40. Breeden, "Body Snatchers and Anatomy Professors," 335–36.

41. Drake, *Pioneer Physician of the Midwest*, 73–74.

42. Daniel Drake, MD, *Pioneer Life in Kentucky*, introduction by Emmet Fields Horne (New York: Henry Schuman, 1948), xvi and xvii.

43. Ibid., xxiv.

44. *Dr. Daniel Drake's Letters on Slavery to Dr. John C. Warren, of Boston*, reprinted from the *National Intelligencer* (Washington, DC), April 3, 5, and 7, 1851; "Letter Two" (New York: Schuman's, 1940), 46.

45. Sappol, *A Traffic of Dead Bodies*, 53–63.

46. Charles Russell Barden, "Anatomy in America," in *Bulletin of The University of Wisconsin: Science Series* 3, no. 4 (September 1905): 85–208, quote on 143.

47. *Annual Announcement of Lectures, Jefferson Medical College* (Philadelphia: Clark & Roser, 1832), quotes on 406, SML.

48. *Annual Announcement of Lectures*, Session 1836, vol. 7; and *Catalogue of the Students and Graduates for the Session 1835*, vol. 6 (Philadelphia: William F. Geddes, 1836), 4–9, SML.

49. Letter addressed to P. C. Barton, MD, Dean of Faculty, Jefferson Medical College, Philadelphia, October 22, 1828, UA-JMC 011, Bound Correspondence, 1826–1938, Col. 1, Acc. # 00–011, SML.

50. *Annual Announcement of Lectures*, Session 1836, vol. 7; and *Catalogue of the Students and Graduates for the Session 1835*, vol. 6. See also Fausto-Sterling, "Gender, Race, and Nation."

51. "A Lecture Delivered in Jefferson Medical College: Has the Parotid Gland Ever Been Extricated?" (Philadelphia: Students of Jefferson Medical College, 1833), 2–16, quotes on 5–7, SML.

52. Pattison, "Medical Schools," 25–26.

53. Sappol, *A Traffic of Dead Bodies*, 109.

54. "Catalogue of the Officers & Students of Jefferson College, Canonsburg, Pa.: March 1828" (1828), *Jefferson Medical College Catalogs*, Paper 2, emphasis added. http://jdc.jefferson.edu /jmc_catalogs/2.

55. Faculty Account Book, 1826–1839, vol. 1, Acc. # 00–012, SML.

56. "Twelve Letters of Dr. Jeffries Wyman," *Journal of the History of Medicine* (October 1965): 314.

57. Alexander Jones, MD, *An Oration Delivered Before the Central Medical Society of Georgia at Its Annual Meeting in Milledgeville, 2nd December 1828* (Augusta: W. Lawson's Job Office, 1829), 13–15 (emphasis in original).

58. Samuel Henry Dickson, MD, *Introductory Lecture Delivered at the Commencement of the Fourth Session of the Medical College of South Carolina, November 1827* (Charleston: W. Riley, 1828), 5–6 and 24.

59. Drake, *Pioneer Physician of the Midwest*, 71.

60. Weld and the American Anti-Slavery Society, *American Slavery as It Is*, 170.

61. *Daily Picayune*, May 29, 1839.

62. Paul F. Eve, *Address Delivered in the Masonic Hall as the Commencement of the First Course of Lectures of the Medical Institute of the State of Georgia* (Augusta: B. Brantly, 1832), 1–8.

63. Circular and Catalogue of Savannah Medical College, *Announcement of Lectures 1857–8 with an Address By George A. Gordon, Esq.* (Savannah: George S. Nichols, 1857), quoted material on 10, 11, 15, 20–22, and 29. For the medical student exodus, see John Duffy, "A Note on Ante-Bellum Southern Nationalism and Medical Practice," *Journal of Southern History* 34 (May 1968): 266–76, esp. 272–73.

64. Lane Allen, "Grandison Harris, Sr.: Slave, Resurrectionist and Judge," *Bulletin of the Georgia Academy of Science* 34, no. 4 (September 1976): 192–99, quotes on 192 and 193.

65. Tommy L. Bogger, *Free Blacks in Norfolk, Virginia, 1790–1860: The Darker Side of Freedom* (Charlottesville: Biological Society of UVA, 1997), 129–30.

66. Allen, "Grandison Harris," 193.

67. "Record Book #1 of the Faculty of the Medical College of Georgia, October 17, 1833– November 18, 1852," Augusta, January 6, 1852, 151, GML. Values computed as CPI adjusted for 2014 dollars. See Berry Slave Value Database; and derived from Samuel H. Williamson, "Seven Ways to Compute the Relative Value of a U.S. Dollar Amount, 1774 to Present," *Measuring Worth*, 2015.

68. Tayna Telfair Sharpe, "Grandison Harris: The Medical College of Georgia's Resurrection Man," in *Bones in the Basement: Postmortem Racism in Nineteenth-Century Medical Training*, ed. Robert L. Blakely and Judith M. Harrington (Washington, DC: Smithsonian Institution Press, 1997), 212–13.

69. Staff, "Grave-Robbing Slave Had a Vital Role for Medical College of Georgia," *Augusta Chronicle*, August 1995. Article found on Ancestry.com, September 13, 2000. See also Sharpe, "Grandison Harris."

70. Allen, "Grandison Harris, Sr.," 192–99.

71. "Account Book #2 of the Dean of the Faculty of the Medical College of Georgia," GML, April 22, 1853, and May 14, 1853.

72. "Account Book #2 of the Dean of the Faculty of the Medical College of Georgia," GML, May 14, 1853; November 29, 1853; December 17, 1853; January 2, 1854; March/April 1854; July 14, 1854; November 15, 1854; December 4, 1854; February 6, 1855; March 16, 1855; March 27, 1855; May 5, 14, 23, 1855; October 29, 1855; November 16, 17, 1855; January 6, 1856; February 22, 1856; November 12, 22, 1856; December 15, 31, 1856; and February 6, 1857.

73. Augusta, February 15, 1858, "Record Book #2 of the Faculty of the Medical College of Georgia, December 14, 1852–April 14th, 1879," GML. Values computed in Berry Slave Value Database and derived from the CPI adjusted for 2014. See Samuel H. Williamson, "Seven Ways to Compute the Relative Value of a U.S. Dollar Amount, 1774 to Present," *Measuring Worth*, 2015, www.measuringworth.com/uscompare/, accessed February 9, 2015.

74. Warner and Edmonson, *Dissection*, 21, 65, and 134.

75. "General News," in *New Haven Evening Register* XLI (December 13, 1881).

76. "Record Book of the Medical Faculty of the Medical College of Georgia," book 11, October 9, 1909–January 27, 1912, pp. 849, 890, and 1083, GML.

77. Stephanie Hunter, "Resurrection Man Dug Way into History," *Augusta Chronicle*, June 21, 1996; and Blakely and Harrington, *Bones in the Basement*.

78. Tracie Powell, "Exhumed Bodies Laid to Rest," *Augusta Chronicle*, November 8, 1998. For a recent article on Harris's legacy, see Bess Lovejoy, "Meet Grandison Harris, the Grave Robber Enslaved (and then Employed) by the Georgia Medical College," Smithsonian.com, May 6, 2014.

79. "My Dear Sir," letter addressed to "Dr. Parker Cleveland, MD, Professor Chemistry, etc.," Brunswick, ME, September 25, 1830, Nathan Ryano Smith Collection, HS-HSL. All quotes in this paragraph are from the same source. Dr. Jeffries Wyman also worked with Louis Agassiz, the Swiss-born biologist and professor at Harvard who produced daguerreotypes of half-naked formerly enslaved people.

80. Nancy Kercheval, "Baltimore's Real-Life Body Snatcher," *Daily Record Online*, October 24, 2002.

81. "Dear Sir" letter, March 31, 1831, Nathan Ryano Smith Collection, HS-HSL. All quotes in this paragraph are from the same source.

82. Thomas Jefferson Medical College Faculty Account Books, 1836, SML.

83. H. I. Thomas to John Staige Davis, August 31, 1849; September 5, 1849; November 5, 1849; November 30, 1849; and November 27, 1849, John Staige Davis Papers, UVA.

84. Breeden, "Body Snatchers and Anatomy Professors," quotes on 326–27. We know that poor whites and free blacks were also used in the dissecting room. See Edward C. Halperin, "The Poor, the Black, and the Marginalized"; David Humphrey, "Dissection and Discrimination: The Social Origins of Cadavers in America, 1760–1915," *Bulletin of New York Academy of Medicine* 49, no. 9 (September 1973): 819–27; and Todd Savitt, "Blacks as Medical Specimens," in Savitt, *Medicine and Slavery*, 281–307.

85. Lewis Minor to John Staige Davis, September 18, 1850; September 30, 1850; October 10, 1850; November 4, 1850; November 15, 1850; November 27, 1850; November 30, 1859; and December 14, 1850, John Staige Davis Papers, UVA.

86. George E. Gifford Jr., ed., "Twelve Letters from Jeffries Wyman, M.D. Hampden-Sydney Medical College, Richmond, VA, 1843–1848," *Journal of the History of Medicine* (October 1965): 309–33, quoted material on 314–15, emphasis in original.

87. Ibid., 310–33.

88. Breeden, "Body Snatchers," 327.

89. List of prices quoted in ibid., 333; and in Tommy L. Bogger, *Free Blacks in Norfolk, Virginia, 1790–1860: The Darker Side of Freedom* (Charlottesville: Carter G. Woodson Institute Series in Black Studies, 1997), 130. For original source, see John Staige Davis Papers, UVA.

90. Breeden, "Body Snatchers."

91. "Old Chris—The Anatomical Purveyor," unpublished typescript, courtesy of TMCC.

92. "A Study in Real Life: Chris Baker and His 'Subjects' at the Medical College," *Richmond Dispatch*, October 29, 1893.

93. Ibid.

94. *Richmond Daily Dispatch*, December 12, 1882; and Rich Griset, "Scholar Documents Purported Tale of a 19th Century Body Snatcher," *Diverse Issues in Higher Education* (October 22, 2010). For details about Baker's alleged role in the Pollard murder, see Suzanne Lebsock, *A Murder in Virginia: Southern Justice on Trial* (New York: W. W. Norton and Co.), 287–90.

95. John W. Brodnax, "To Old Chris," in Richard B. Easley, ed., *The X-Ray*, Vol. 13 (Richmond: Medical College of Virginia, 1926), 72.

96. Miscellaneous documents in Chris Baker folder, TMCC.

97. Lucretia Mott, "A Sermon to the Medical Students" (Philadelphia: Anti-Slavery Society, 1849), 10, 11, and 16, CPP.

98. "In the Ghostly Old Times," UPENN.

99. Sappol, *A Traffic of Dead Bodies*, 45.

100. Shultz, *Body Snatching*, 78–80, quote on 79.

101. *Medical Record* (New York), December 23, 1882, 724.

102. "Jim's Revelations: Threatened by the Students Be Prepared to Resign," in *Philadelphia Press*, December 8, 1882.

103. Halperin, "The Poor, the Black, and the Marginalized," 489–95; and David C. Humphrey, "Dissection and Discrimination: The Social Origins of Cadavers in America, 1760–1915," *Bulletin of New York Academy of Medicine* 49 (September 1973): 819–27.

104. "Body-Snatching," *Sunday Times*, December 10, 1882, in CPP scrapbook.

105. "Light Out of Darkness," *Inquirer* (Philadelphia), December 12, 1882, in CPP scrapbook.

106. "The Horrible Graveyard Disclosure and the Excitement It Has Occasioned—Politics and Personalities," *Sunday Mercury* (Philadelphia), December 10, 1882, in CPP scrapbook.

107. "General News," *New Haven Evening Register*, December 13, 1881.

108. Lebsock, *A Murder in Virginia*.

109. "Meeting Minutes, Georgia State Medical Board, 1826–1887," Georgia Anatomical Board Papers, HS-MSS013, Box 12, Folder 9, GML.

110. All quoted material in this paragraph comes from "The Business of Bodies: Grave-Robbing Scandal Brought Slave Anatomical Board to Supply Needed Cadavers for Medical Study," *We the People: Pennsylvania in Review*, August 11, 1937, periodical found in CPP.

111. Ibid., 10–12.

112. Dr. William Forbes, *History of the Anatomy-Act of Pennsylvania* (Philadelphia: Philadelphia Medical Publishing Company, 1898).

113. Breeden, "Body Snatchers and Anatomy Professors," 324.

114. Others, like Dr. John Collins Warren (1778–1856), preferred a postmortem autopsy and for the bones of the deceased to be preserved for educational purposes. See J. B. S. (John Barnard Swett) Jackson, 1806–79, "Autopsy of Dr. John Collins Warren (1778–1856)," *Center for the History of Medicine: On View*, Francis A. Countway Library of Medicine, Harvard University, http://collections.countway.harvard.edu/onview /items/show/12775, accessed February 10, 2015.

115. Samuel D. Gross, MD, *Autobiography of Samuel D. Gross, MD, with Reminiscences of His Times and Contemporaries in Two Volumes*, vol. 1 (Philadelphia: W. B. Saunders, 1893), 29–30.

116. However, when Gross died, in 1885, he was one of the first persons in the United States to have his body cremated. Gross, *Autobiography*, quote on 110. See the collection of Gross obituaries in the Samuel D. Gross Papers, MS-4 boxes 2 and 3, SML.

117. "History of Cremation," Cremation Association of North America, http://www .cremationassociation.org/?HistoryOfCremation, accessed January 16, 2015. See also "Another Body to Be Cremated: The Remains of Samuel D. Gross to Be Reduced to Ashes," *New York Times*, May 8, 1884.

118. "Another Body to Be Cremated."

119. "Albert Monroe Wilson (1841–1904)," *Penn Biographies*, University of Pennsylvania Archives & Records Center, http://www.archives.upenn.edu/people/1800s/wilson _albert_pomp.html, accessed June 19, 2012. See also *University of Pennsylvania Bulletin* (1909): 210; and the University of Pennsylvania Alumni Record, 1904. Wilson appears in the class photos of 1865 and 1868, UPENN.

120. Annie Cheney, *Body Brokers: Inside America's Underground Trade in Human Remains* (New York: Broadway Books, 2006), especially the "Human Price List," xv. See also Scott Carney, *The Red Market: On the Trail of the World's Organ Brokers, Bone Thieves, Blood Farmers, and Child Traffickers* (New York: HarperCollins, 2010); and Mary Roach, *Stiff: The Curious Lives of Human Cadavers* (New York: W. W. Norton and Co., 2004).

121. Anatomical Donation Program, Mercer University, Macon, GA, https://medicine .mercer.edu/basic-macon/adp/, accessed February 7, 2015.

122. Barnum, *The Life of P. T. Barnum*, 176.

EPILOGUE

1. Douglass, *The Life and Times of Frederick Douglass*, 350–54.

2. Saidiya Hartman, *Lose Your Mother: A Journey Along the Atlantic Slave Route* (New York: Farrar, Straus, and Giroux, 2007), 6.

3. Keckley, *Behind the Scenes*, 24.

4. Turner, "The Family of Nat Turner, 1831 to 1954," 128.

5. For full text of the resolution, see "Bill Tracking Session 2014," LVA, http://lis.virginia .gov/cgi-bin/leg604.exe>141+ful+SJ84, accessed October 11, 2014; Rich Griset, "Black Market: Lost in the Annals of History, a Professor Unearths the Medical College of

Virginia's Original Body Snatcher," *Richmond Style Weekly*, August 18, 2010; and the documentary film *When the Well Runs Dry* (2015, dir. Steve Lerner and Reuben Aaronson).

6. Quoted material in this paragraph comes from Richardson, *Death, Dissection and the Destitute*, 72. For more on the contemporary red market see Carney, *The Red Market*, and Cheney, *Body Brokers*.

7. Isaiah 6:6.

8. "The Slave Mingo's Poem," in Kramer, *The Slave-Auction*, 47–48.

NOTE ON SOURCES

1. Karl Jacoby, "Slaves by Nature? Domestic Animals and Human Slaves," *Slavery & Abolition* 15 (April 1994): 89–99, esp. 89. Mia Bay found this to be the case as well, but she includes African American rejection of such "connections." See Bay, *The White Image in the Black Mind*, 129–45.

2. See Brown, *The Reaper's Garden*; Douglas R. Egerton, "A Peculiar Mark of Infamy: Dismemberment, Burial, and Rebelliousness in Slave Societies," in *Mortal Remains: Death in Early America*, ed. Nancy Isenberg and Andrew Burstein (Philadelphia: University of Pennsylvania Press, 2002), 149–62; Gaspar, "'To Bring Their Offending Slaves to Justice,'" 45–59; and Patton, "Punishment, Crime, and the Bodies of Slaves in Eighteenth-Century Jamaica."

3. Johnson, *Soul by Soul*.

4. Baptist, *The Half Has Never Been Told*.

5. I converted all figures to US dollars, controlled for inflation, and compiled the data based on the 1860 dollar. I used the David-Solar-based_Cc2_Inded1860100 found in Susan B. Carter, Scott Sigmund Gartner, Michael R. Haines, Alan L. Olmstead, Richard Sutch, and Gavin Wright, eds., *Historical Statistics of the United States: Millennial Edition Online*, Cambridge University Press, http://hsus.cambridge.org/HSUSWeb/HSUSEntryServlet.

6. All the figures in this combined database have been converted to 1860 dollars and controlled for inflation. Robert W. Fogel and Stanley L. Engerman, *Slave Sales and Appraisals, 1775-1865*, ICPSR07421-v3 (Rochester, NY: University of Rochester [producer], 1976), Ann Arbor, MI: Inter-university Consortium for Political and Social Research (producer and distributor), 2006-10-11, http://doi.org/10.3886/ICPSR07421.v3; Robert W. Fogel and Stanley L. Engerman, *New Orleans Slave Sale Sample, 1804-1862*, ICPSR07423-v2 (Rochester, NY: University of Rochester), Ann Arbor, MI: Inter-university Consortium for Political and Social Research (producer and distributor), 2008-08-04, http://doi.org/10.3886/ICPSR07423.v2; and Robert A. Margo, *Union Army Slave Appraisal Records from Mississippi, 1863-1865* (Cambridge, MA: Robert A. Margo, Harvard University [producer], 1979), Ann Arbor, MI: Inter-university Consortium for Political and Social Research [distributor], 1991, http://doi.org/10.3886/ICPSR09427.v1; and Berry data. The original set contained 81,182 enslaved individuals' values, prior to omitting outliers and those listed with missing information; this book relies on 64,193 enslaved people's commodified values. My data is also available at ICPSR.

7. Wilma A. Dunaway, "Slavery and Emancipation in the Mountain South: Evidence, Sources, and Methods," Virginia Tech Online Archives, Table 8.5. See also Stephanie McCurry, *Masters of Small Worlds: Yeoman Households, Gender Relations, and the Political*

Culture of the Antebellum South Carolina Low Country (New York: Oxford University Press, 1997).

8. See Berry, "'Broad Is de Road Dat Leads to Death'"; Richard Bell, *We Shall Be No More: Suicide and Self-Government in the Newly United States* (Cambridge, MA: Harvard University Press, 2012); Snyder, *The Power to Die*; and Terri L. Snyder, "Suicide, Slavery, and Memory in North America," *Journal of American History* 97 (June 2010): 39–62.

9. Maryland Insurance Administration, *Slavery Era Insurance Policy Report* (April 2012), http://www.mdinsurance.state.md.us/sa/docs/documents/consumer/slaveryerareport, accessed August 13, 2014.

10. For the Walmart case, see Lewis et al. v. Wal-Mart Stores et al., case no. 02-944EA, in the US District Court for the Northern District of Oklahoma. See newspaper reporting on the case in L. M. Sixel, "Profiting from Death? Lawsuit Filed in Wal-Mart Life Insurance Case," *Houston Chronicle*, April 15, 2002. For similar cases from companies such as Camelot Music, Nestlé, Procter & Gamble, and Pitney Bowes, see Ellen E. Schultz and Theo Francis, "Companies Profit on Workers' Deaths Through 'Dead Peasants' Insurance," *Wall Street Journal*, April 19, 2002.

11. The recent film *Belle* (2013; dir. Amma Asante; DJ Films) was also about an insurance policy.

12. Josiah C. Nott, "Statistics of Southern Slave Population: With Special Reference to Life Insurance," *De Bow's Review* 4, no. 3 (November 1847): 275–89; Ryder, "'Permanent Property'"; Todd L. Savitt, "Slave Life Insurance in Virginia and North Carolina," *Journal of Southern History* 43 (November 1977): 583–600; Eugene D. Genovese, "The Medical and Insurance Costs of Slaveholding in the Cotton Belt," *Journal of Negro History* XLV (July 1960): 146–55; Sharon Anne Murphy, "Securing Human Property: Slavery, Life Insurance, and Industrialization in the Upper South," *Journal of the Early Republic* 25 (Winter 2005): 615–52.

Index

abroad marriages, 123–24

"An Act Directing the Trial of Slaves Committing Capital Crime," 98

"An Act to Incorporate the Southern Slaveholders Insurance Company of Maryland," 118

Adams, Lydia, 26, 219n57

Adams, Nehemiah, 33–34

Adeline (enslaved woman), 10–11

adolescents/young enslaved adults: appraisals/insurance valuations, burials, 89–90; 58, 85–89; commodification of, 65–66, 83–85; gynecological health, 72; health risks and mortality, 62, 74; murder of, 86; preparations of for sales, 68; resales of, 63; sale prices, 58, 83–85; sexual maturity, implications, 60–63, 78–83, 85; spiritual awakening, 61–62, 90

advertisements: auction catalogs/announcements, 45, 136–37; for breeders, 19–21; commodification data from, 114, 209; livestock terms in, 12, 68; for medical schools/lectures, 102, 158, 164, 212; revelations of health issues in, 24–25, 139; seeking cadavers, 167; seeking runaways, 114, 234n74; for skulls, 106; for women with children, 45, 48

Affleck, Thomas, 42

afterlife: diverse beliefs related to, 94; and soul value, 62, 110, 120–21, 194; Turner's and Copeland's beliefs, 110–11, 235n91. *See also* elderly/superannuated enslaved; soul value

agility. *See* strength, assessments of

Airlie Plantation, East Carroll Parish, Louisiana, 140, 209

Alabama, "Master and Slave" statute, 47

Alfred (enslaved child), 56

Allrick (enslaved elder), 137

anatomical dissection/research: and autopsies, 148–51, 185; bone cleaning/articulation, 104, 160, 179; brain size studies, 106; burials following, 126, 193; and curiosity about disease, 167, 169; curiosity about female bodies, 167; efforts to disrupt, 159, 182–83; history/timeline for, 99, 202–4; legalization of, 184–85, 188; mutilation during, 125; outdoor dissections, 177; preparation and storage of bodies, 155–56, 163–65; and race-based science, 94, 104, 106–7, 190; role in medical education, 164–65; types of valuations, 6–7. *See also* cadaver trade; death/mortality; grave robbers/resurrectionists; medical education

anatomy legislation, 99, 153, 160, 164, 183–88, 192. *See also* cadaver trade

Anderson, Jeremiah, 125–26

Anderson, Osborne, 124

Andrew (enslaved youth), 88

Andrews, Ethan Allen, 33, 49

Ann (enslaved woman), 88

Anna Eliza (enslaved youth), 85

Annette (enslaved elder), 97

appraisal value: adolescents/youth, 58, 83–86; and child-bearing potential,

120; final words (attr.), 91; honoring of
after death, 127; imagined epitaph for,
109; postmortem value, 111; price wage,
233n58; rebellion and execution, 93;
rewards offered for capture, 111; skull,
traffic in, 105–7, 197, 232–33n57; soul
value, 10; visions, belief in an afterlife,
110–11, 235n91. *See also* Southampton,
VA, rebellion
"Twiggs" (enslaved child), 88–89

unborn enslaved offspring, valuations of, 27
University of Maryland Medical School,
Baltimore, 173
University of North Carolina School of
Medicine, Chapel Hill, 177
University of Pennsylvania, medical educa-
tion at, 106, 158
University of Virginia (UVA), Charlottes-
ville, Medical Department: anatomy
education at, 102–3; Commodore's role,
103; purchase of cadavers, 53, 121, 161,
174–75
"unsoundness," challenges of defining, 71–72
US Constitution, three-fifths clause, 84
US Department of Agriculture (USDA),
meat grades, 68
Utsey, Shawn, 195

Vaughan, John C., 143–44
Veney, Bethany, 78
Virginia anatomy legislation, 186; compen-
sation of enslaved for human property
losses, 98; legislation following South-
ampton rebellion, 109; *Partus Sequitur
Ventrem*, 11
Virginia Commonwealth University
(VCU), Richmond, 8–9, 102, 195

wages, price wages/labor values, 67, 145,
170–71, 228n84, 233n58, 239n36
Walker, Edward, 61–62

Waller, Benjamin S., 51–52, 140
Walmart insurance practices, 211
Warren, John Collins, 159–60, 162, 245n114
Washington, George, 148–49
Washington, Harriet A., 8
Washington, Jesse, 102
Watkins, Sylvia, 80
Watson, William, 163
Weld, Theodore Dwight, 112
"While the infant and the mother, loud
shriek for each other. . ." (song), 30–31
White, Mingo, 37
White, Thomas, 175
Whitehead, Richard H., 177
Williams, Malissa, 102
Williams, Mollie, 12
Winchester Medical School, Virginia, 102,
121, 126
Wisdom, Andrew C., 114–15
women, enslaved: African-born vs. domestic, 31–32; and buyer preferences,
18; categories of, 217n28; death during
childbirth, 90; gynecological health, 72;
as healers, 51; insurance appraisals for,
142–43; labor specialization among, 18,
217n28; mortality, 31; in prison, compensation of owners, 48; pricing, price
fluctuations, 14–15, 17–18; resistance
shown by/reprisals against, 17, 114, 116;
reproductive health issues, 74; termina-
tions of pregnancy, 77–78; use of in exchanges, 20; valuations, factors affecting,
24–25, 76–77, 95–96; wages, 228n84.
See also breeders/breeding wenches;
family, separation from; motherhood,
mothers; sexual coercion and abuse
Wooldridge, Alexander Penn, 140–41
Wyman, Jeffries, 160, 165, 176

Young, Joshua, 126

Zorn, Mr. (Moravian missionary), 73–74

About the Author

Daina Ramey Berry is an associate professor of history and of African and African diaspora studies, as well as the Oliver H. Radkey Regents Fellow in History, at the University of Texas at Austin. She is the author of *Swing the Sickle for the Harvest Is Ripe: Gender and Slavery in Antebellum Georgia*. She is also an award-winning editor of *Enslaved Women in America: An Encyclopedia* and of *Slavery and Freedom in Savannah*. Berry served as one of the technical advisors for the remake of the miniseries *Roots* (A&E Network, History Channel, 2016) and has been a regular guest on the Learning Channel's *Who Do You Think You Are?*, helping to trace the ancestry of Spike Lee, Alfre Woodard, Aisha Tyler, and Smokey Robinson. Her scholarship has been supported by the National Endowment for the Humanities, the American Council of Learned Societies, the American Association of University Women, the Ford Foundation, and the College of Physicians of Philadelphia. Berry is also a Distinguished Lecturer for the Organization of American Historians, serves on the editorial boards of two historical journals, and is the coeditor of the Gender and Slavery book series with the University of Georgia Press.